PHILIP DIAMOND'S
COVENT GARDEN F

Philip Diamond was born in Romania and came to Britain as a child just before World War II. After doing National Service, he tried various careers but not until he cast a line from Southend Pier and caught his first fish did he feel he had found something he really wanted to do—sell prime-quality fish. First he opened a wet-fish stall in Jubilee Market, Covent Garden and then Covent Garden Fishmongers, which now operates from Chiswick.

He lectures regularly at the Leith School of Food and Wine, and has appeared on television in the BBC programmes *Bazaar*, *Food and Drink* and *A Taste of Health*. He serves on the Committee of the London Branch of the National Federation of Fishmongers and is often quoted in the press when fish is in the news.

He lives with his wife, Maureen, in north London.

Jackie Hunt has been fascinated by food and its preparation all her life. She has travelled extensively throughout Europe, Africa, Asia and the US, acquiring an appreciation of and familiarity with the cuisines of many cultures. She worked with the Thai restaurateur, Vatcharin Bhumichitr on his book, *The Taste of Thailand*. She lives with her husband, literary consultant Andrew Best, in south London.

Covent Garden
Fishmongers

'Here's food for the belly, and clothes for the back, but I sell food for the
    mind! (shouts the newsvendor)
Here's smelt, O!
Here ye are, fine Finney haddick!
Hot soup! nice peas-soup! a-all hot! hot!
Ahoy! ahoy here! live plaice! all alive O!
Now or never! whelk! whelk! whelk!
Who'll buy brill O! brill O!
Capes! water-proof capes! sure to keep the wet out! a shilling a piece!
Eels O! eels O! alive! alive!
Fine flounders, a shilling a lot! Who'll buy this prime lot of flounders?
Shrimps! shrimps! fine shrimps!
Wink! wink! wink!
Hi! hi! hi! here you are, just eight eels left, only eight!
O ho! O ho! this way—this way—this way! Fish alive! alive! alive O!'

'Billingsgate', Henry Mayhew, *London Labour
and London Poor*, 1851

PHILIP DIAMOND'S
COVENT GARDEN FISH BOOK

WITH
JACKIE HUNT

KYLE CATHIE LTD

This book is dedicated to
RAY CAYLESS (1911–1992), Fishmonger
A generous and gentle man

ACKNOWLEDGEMENTS

Every book published owes a debt to innumerable people who have given encouragement and assistance in a variety of ways. This book is no exception. If some names seem to be omitted this is our error and is not meant in any way to offend. Our gratitude and thanks then to Andrew Best, our literary agent and counsellor; Charlie Caisey of K. C. Fisheries; Kyle Cathie, most patient editor and publisher; Darren Cannon and Steve Clements, J. Bennett (Billingsgate) Ltd; Carolyn Cavele, Food (and other) Matters, whose constant support and help is and has been so much appreciated; Arthur Cook, Bridlington Trawlers; Martin Lane of Loch Fyne Oysters Limited, Elton; Chris Leftwich, Chief Inspector to The Worshipful Company of Fishmongers, who has given expert advice; the McIlhenny Co., makers of TABASCO Pepper Sauce; Ray Sandys, of Sandys, Whitton; Colin Smales, Hull; John Shelton of J. Bennett (Billingsgate) Ltd who has been generous in support; Garry Diamond, my elder son and partner and my second-greatest critic; Maureen Diamond, my greatest critic, my wife and friend; my many colleagues; my customers and friends for their always valued support, some of whom have contributed to this book; David Holbrook and the crew of the *Margaret H* for their patience with a landlubber and their generous hospitality; and a special tribute to all those who spend their working lives at sea, and sometimes lose them, to give us this precious food source. Finally to all those who have given permission for their material to be used.

Philip Diamond & Jackie Hunt

First published 1992 in Great Britain by
Kyle Cathie Limited
3 Vincent Square London SW1P 2LX

ISBN 1 85626 063 1

Philip Diamond and Jackie Hunt are hereby identified as the joint authors of this work in accordance with Section 77 of the Copyright, Designs and Patents Act 1988.

A Cataloguing in Publication record for this title is available from the British Library

Typeset by Rowland Phototypesetting Limited, Bury St Edmunds, Suffolk.
Printed by Butler and Tanner Limited, Frome and London

CONTENTS

The Authors and Publishers would like to thank the
following for financial help with the cost of the colour
illustrations:

J. Bennett (Billingsgate) Ltd., London

McIlhenny Co., Avery Island, LA, USA

John Koch Ltd., London

Oak Lodge Salmon Ltd., London

INTRODUCTION

'Of all nacyons and countres, England is best served of Fysshe, not onely of al maner of see-fysshe, but also of fresshe-water fysshe, and of all maner of sortes of salte-fyshe.'

Andrew Boorde, 1542

As a fishmonger myself, I was interested to read that an article appeared in one of the major newspapers complaining about the lack of service to be had from the nation's fishmongers. Specifically, it spoke of a particular fishmonger who did not skin, fillet and bone according to requirement and request. It also mentioned the lack of training generally among fish-counter staff in most supermarkets, and the awful possibility that soon the only fish available to us would be pre-prepared, pre-packaged, of doubtful freshness and over-priced.

As well the article drew attention to the lack of knowledge about fish and its preparation on the part of many cooks and shoppers, and their consequent fear of asking for exactly what they want.

I have every sympathy with the author of this article and whole-heartedly agree with his comments on the sad lack of information and confidence shown by people who would like to eat more fish, but don't know what to ask for or how to deal with it. Fish is not expensive compared with most meat products, but I am constantly amazed at the number of people who come into my shop who don't know any names other than cod or haddock. Good fish though they are, there are so many other species to choose from, all with special qualities. An unfamiliar species is often regarded with some suspicion, perhaps because the customer doesn't know how to prepare it, hasn't heard of it before or doesn't know how it will taste. Let me reassure everyone here and now: there are, in my opinion, no fish on the market in Britain and in Europe (or elsewhere, come to that) that don't taste good.

I accept that it is the responsibility of fishmongers to help educate their customers in buying fish and preparing it for the table. So I have decided to try to do my part in educating the fish-eating public, and perhaps to try to convert those for whom fish is an occasional exception to their regular eating habits. This book is designed to help the customer and the cook to learn what kinds of fish are available and to realise that it is a food that can be approached without trepidation in its selection, preparation, cooking and eating. Above all, I hope to show how you can enlist the support of your fishmonger and use his skills and knowledge to your own benefit. The following are my mottoes:

- Fish is good for you.
- Fish is not necessarily expensive (some fish are far cheaper by weight than any meat).
- Fish is easy to prepare.
- Fish is quick to cook.
- Fish tastes good.

Like most other businesses, the retail fish trade is undergoing a period of change with shop closures commonplace in many parts of the country. Those independent retailers who survive the next few years will be a new breed: the fish entrepreneurs.

Selling fish in a high street shop is a high risk activity: the product is perishable and fishmongers must have the highest stock turnover ratio in the retail trade (two to three days). A recent report said that hygiene, helpfulness and quality were the three most important considerations of the regular fish shop customer. And I believe the retailer should give what the customer wants, and at the same time offer the public a wider range of fish.

When I started in this business in 1976 I made a conscious decision to buy for quality rather than price. I have stuck to that criterion and think it is sad when others do not. And some major retailers do not! I have visited a major emporium in London several times and have seen fish for sale that I wouldn't keep on my slab. Young people are health conscious and are aware of the value of fish, but they can easily be put off by a single bad experience. The older generation may be reluctant to try new species, but I believe that a good fishmonger can educate customers, whatever their age.

I try hard to develop a good relationship with my customers so that they trust me and my product and, even more importantly, are not shy to ask for my advice. However, I don't always win, especially when the person I'm serving thinks he knows more than I do because a distant relation was a fisherman. Many buyers are unsure of what to do with some of the new imported species available (and so, I suspect, are many of my fellow fishmongers). I personally cook each new species at home before stocking it in the shop and experiment with simple methods—grilling, baking, frying, steaming—to find out which method gives the best result. Only then can I pass this information to my customers.

I came into the retail fish business by accident. I had a passion for seafishing with rod and line and if I was lucky enough to catch a fish I really enjoyed cooking and eating it to experience the extraordinary flavours the sea has to offer.

Within the 73% of the earth that is covered by water there are some 30,000 different species of fish from which only 350–400 are commercially exploited. With today's technology many of these can be brought to your table either fresh or frozen. However, it has been said that the British, a people surrounded by water, eat only about 1kg/2lb of fish per household per year. This is extraordinary. The fishermen of this country land so much quality fish and in such variety. It is the mainland Europeans who have profited from our narrow-mindedness; they really appreciate fish and buy our prime fish and shellfish gladly. Container lorries line up at our ports and buy the best that British trawlers bring in, pay cash, and drive it out of the country and into the Belgian, Dutch, French, Italian and Spanish processing plants, which sell it back to us at double the price. What is left after the best has been taken out is sent to our markets where the average fishmonger has to buy. However, retailers are beginning to believe that a better buy might be had by purchasing stock direct from the ports.

Why do we eat so little fish? Why does the average British consumer not demand the best that money can buy? I suspect it is because fish has too often provided a cheap alternative to meat. This attitude is starting to change as more people go abroad and enjoy exciting 'taste experiences' and want to repeat them at home. People like Keith Floyd have done wonders, too, through television presentations and books to promote the eating of fish with gusto and enthusiasm.

Nutritionists tell us that fish is valuable in a balanced diet and that it is an easy way to ensure that we have some of the essential vitamins, A and D in particular. 'Oily' fish—herring, mackerel, tuna, sardine—are particularly good sources of these vitamins. It is said that eating an oily fish twice a week may actually lower cholesterol levels in the blood and therefore help to prevent heart disease; it is also a rich source of protein, vitamins and minerals, and is extremely easy to digest. I suppose you could say: 'A herring a day keeps the doctor at bay.'

I have another theory: fish is the last food that man goes out to hunt in its own environment. It has not as yet been subjected to the total interference of intensive farming methods with hormone growth producers, antibiotics, herbicides and pesticides. It is as near a perfect food as you are likely to find.

PHILIP DIAMOND

AT SEA

Fishing is a young man's business, I was told, and after five days of fishing the northern sector of the North Sea, I believe it. David Holbrook, skipper of Bridlington's *Margaret H* trawler, comes from a fishing background. His father, Harvey Holbrook, handed the boat over to David when he was just 20 years old. Harvey Holbrook is skipper of a larger steel trawler and for many years has been top skipper of the area. Top skipper means that he lands fish worth about £500,000 per annum. David, who occasionally beats him on his weekly catch, brings in some £300,000 a year. Between them, David and his father cover the whole of the North Sea.

Margaret H has a crew of four. David Holbrook, 24, skipper; David Cockrel, 24, deckhand and cook; Alistair Spendlow, 27, deckhand and fishroom man; Gordon Simpson, 58, deckhand. Gordon is the oldest deckhand in Bridlington, and I guess he wouldn't know what else to do with his life. Everybody was very good to me and made allowances for my being on board and getting in their way, letting me watch them work and answering my endless questions, all with good humour and patience.

Margaret H is named after David's mother and is one of thirty boats fishing out of Bridlington; only six years ago there was double that number. The boats go out to sea for periods of between seven and fourteen days. My trip was in early November. The weather wasn't too bad, though I certainly wasn't able to sunbathe on deck. I guess at the back of my mind I was hoping for the experience of a force 10–12 gale, but it wasn't to be. Still, we had high seas and fog. Weighing 16 stone I was able to withstand my frame being buffeted around whilst the crew went about their duties as if they were walking on a football pitch. On the Scottish west coast they have to deal with open Atlantic waters, but for me the North Sea fog was sufficiently eerie and frightening. Even though the ship's radar acts as a second pair of eyes, I like to see for myself where I'm going and what's around me. At times, in the middle of the night when everyone was busy, I was allowed to sit in the captain's chair in the wheelhouse keeping an eye on the radar. Once, with fog swirling around us, I saw a spot appear which seemed to get larger and closer very quickly: another boat, I was told, about five miles ahead. With my lack of knowledge and imagination I thought we were on a collision course with an oil tanker.

4

The week prior to my trip the catches were large and there was thus a lot of concentrated hard work, but while I was on the boat the catches were only moderate and I sensed a certain amount of boredom from the inactivity between the trawls. I wondered how these lads coped with the long periods away from home and family, the conditions within which they worked, and the uncertainty of their chosen profession. I did ask, but I wonder if I got the truth. I believe it is in their blood. Some children who live in fishing ports play truant from school just to hang around the boats to do odd jobs, waiting until they are 16 when they can go to sea. Then there is the money. If the boat has a good skipper the money can be very high. Earnings from the catch will be roughly divided between the boat and the crew after running deductions, such as diesel, repairs, etc. What they earn depends on how much they have caught and how good the market is when they come back into port. Better prices are had during the winter months when fish is scarcer. One week they may earn a great deal; the next there may be a glut of fish which depresses the price (I wonder why this hardly ever shows up in the wholesale markets), and they may earn hardly anything at all. Yet there is no trade union and all are happy with the situation the way it is and has been for many years.

Margaret H goes to sea all year round except for a short period in summer when she is taken out of the water for a major overhaul and clean up. If a crew member wants time off he must find a replacement for the time that he will be away; otherwise he can't take leave.

She (all vessels are female) is a 20 metre or 60ft wooden keel boat which carries an amazing range of equipment: radar, self-steering, sonar fish-finder, computer, with television cameras in all compartments so that the skipper can see what is going on. The computer is programmed by David Holbrook and displays all his favourite fishing grounds. *Margaret H* recently went through a £130,000 refurbishment with grants from the EEC and the Sea Fish Industry Authority. Surprisingly, grants are available only for refitting boats, but not for building new ones, which in fact would cost only a little more.

The net is a 30 metre or 90ft concord trawl, which is shaped like an old-fashioned nightcap: 20 metres or 70ft across at the mouth, tapering down its length to the 'cod end', which is more or less a constant diameter and of a smaller mesh size. The mouth of the net is kept open by enormous trawl doors. The length of line from the boat to the net is three times the depth of the water, a lot of line. The roof of the net (headline) is kept up by floats and the whole lot is dragged along the sea bed at 3 knots or 3.2mph. The reason for this is that fish can comfortably swim for twenty minutes at this

5

speed before tiring; as the bottom of the net disturbs the fish, they rise and swim along at the mouth of the net. After about twenty minutes they start to drop back into the net and finally into the cod end, with the smaller fish escaping through the mesh. It's a mixed bag and it seems that these bottom-feeding fish—cod, haddock, plaice, sole, ling, coley, etc.—all swim at the same speed.

An average trawl takes between four and five hours and once we reached our fishing areas four trawls were completed in each twenty-four hour period. Without additional sophisticated and expensive equipment there is no way of telling how large or small a catch might be. While the trawl was going on and after the last lot of fish had been put away, young David Cockrel did some cooking under some pretty ghastly conditions. He threw together some excellent fry-ups and stews; other times we just went to the refrigerator or sea-lockers and helped ourselves to pork pies, crisps or cakes. On small boats you grab something when you feel like it, and don't worry too much about substantial meals.

The galley and eating area with its refrigerator and Calor gas stove, cupboard and store lockers, was also the recreational area. If you had time you could watch television or a video, but the one tape on board must have been seen hundreds of times, and spare time was usually spent in bunks asleep.

Sleep is all important. The bunks are situated below the waterline and on top of the engine room. To get into your bunk is an amazing manoeuvre; it is like a long, four-sided box with a small entry on one side, and it's either feet first or head first, double up, get the other half of your body into the bunk, and then stretch out. I guess this design stops you falling out during bad weather. But the worst thing was the drone of the engine and the sloshing of the waves on the outside of the hull. But when you are tired to the very bone you sleep anyway.

Why is fishing a young man's game? The answer is only too clear: it is ten days' work with only two hours' sleep per day if there are good hauls. Putting the catch into the preparation room, putting out the nets for the next catch, and, entirely by hand, gutting, washing, separating and sizing the species, icing and stacking the boxes, can take up to four hours, depending on the size of the catch. Then you start all over again. Then there is the bending down and lifting all the heavy gear; sometimes the trawl doors that hold the mouth of the net open get stuck and have to be hauled bodily back on board. The kit boxes of fish, each weigh about 70kg or 150lb, and *Margaret H* can handle more than 600 kit boxes, which have to be pulled, pushed and stacked. This all takes enormous strength and you have to be very fast. The name of the game, I was told, is speed: the faster you are, the better you are; the faster you are, the more rest you can get. If you are not catching fish, it's boring; if you are catching fish, then it's exhausting.

All this is done on the North Sea where at one moment the sea is like a millpond and an hour later your body is aching from the jarring that comes with high seas. *Margaret H* goes out in all weathers and stays out in force 10–12 winds. David Holbrook has total responsibility for the safety of his crew and boat, and the livelihood of his crew. Everything depends on him. Only 24, when he's very tired he looks like a man twice his age with the burdens of the world on his shoulders. It's that type of boat and it's that type of men who go out into a hostile environment to bring back a harvest of seafood. Amazing men, amazing place.

Whilst the North Sea is mainly fished for cod and haddock, the catch is usually mixed—gurnard, pollock, ling, skate, sole and whiting come in too. Quality fish like halibut and turbot are particularly sought after by the Danish fleet who have been found to use an indestructible monofilament net with a particularly fine mesh which becomes an invisible curtain when hung in the water. Fortunately, this type of net is now illegal, for even though they are cut adrift by natural situations or by British trawlers ploughing through them, they continue to kill dolphins, seals and fish in large numbers which simply rot.

Other fleets competing for good catches in the North Sea are Belgian, Dutch, French and Norwegian. I saw only two other boats on my five-day trip, and they were from the depleted Scottish fleet. These days, of course, the North Sea contains other vessels besides fishing boats. As well as the permanently sited oil rigs there are the drill rigs that move from field to field, drilling and capping off, then moving on. Trawlers are not allowed closer than 500 metres to these rigs and they are scrupulous in observing this edict. However, repairs to British oil rigs are not always carried out in so scrupulous a manner, and often nets are seriously damaged by debris left on the sea bed. Whilst I was on board *Margaret H* a gigantic boulder was brought up, and then it was all hands to the crochet hooks to repair the nets which had been torn to pieces, all this done in high seas.

Contrary to expectation I did not see any obvious pollution or any fish that seemed to be victims of pollution. Without exception, all the fish caught were perfectly healthy. However, there is evidence of declining numbers because of over-fishing and really large fish of any variety are now rarely seen. Unfortunately also brought up in the nets are fish too small or of no market value. These are cast overboard, but the majority are already dead.

Maintaining records of catches is one of the skipper's most boring tasks. The Ministry of Agriculture, Farming and Fisheries (MAFF) needs these records to keep check on quotas, and David Holbrook spends a lot of time trying to keep the paperwork up to date. Controlling over-fishing is a major headache. One opinion I have heard expressed is that control can be achieved only by reducing the fleet further; increasing the minimum mesh size to 110mm (which is what the *Margaret H* uses) and increasing the minimum landing size to 45mm (the European Commission has recently agreed to an increase in mesh size, and there are now also restrictions on the use of drift nets often used by the tuna fishing fleets, but there is a move to ban their use altogether); and cutting down the fishing effort and spending fewer days at sea. But the men who fish the North Sea have to make a living; unlike farmers they do not get subsidies for not producing. Members of Parliament, I was told, are interested only in producing food from the land.

David Holbrook told me that when he fishes the Norwegian sector he has to put on a 125mm net that allows a lot of small fish to escape, but he can still make a good living because the fish there are larger. He said that if he fished with this net in the British sector, 75% of the catch would escape and what was left wouldn't even pay for his diesel.

Four years ago, David Holbrook's favourite ground was the 'Compass' in the North Sea. In those days he could rely on January and February for the large cod to come in, and when spring arrived the haddock came too. Now he says there is almost nothing there because the nets are too small and because of over-fishing.

After five days it was good to be back at Bridlington and on land again. It took three hours for my landlegs to return. The fish was landed in boxes onto the quay where a refrigerated trailer was waiting to take the catch to Hull market to be sold to processor, dealer and fishmonger. Hull market specialises in cod and haddock; Grimsby sells a mixed bag—dabs, skates, dogfish, whiting and pollock—and Lowestoft has mainly flat fish like plaice, soles and dabs. Some of the local names for various fish stretch the imagination. Cod, according to size, can be codling, nits, chattypots, scrag or greens. Norway cod can be redcoats, soldiers or squaddies; haddock is grounder, chat or medium. Small witch soles are called postage stamps or bastard dabs.

I was intrigued by the superstitions of the fishing community. Wives do not do any washing on the day their husbands go to sea, and some don't sweep during the time their men are at sea as they would be washing them away or sweeping them out of the house. In the old days, a wife wouldn't wind worsted by candlelight while her husband was at sea in case the ship's steering was confused. Whistling at sea is unlucky, that's whistling up the wind; and, of course, the boat is never male. It was believed that it was unlucky to meet a woman on the way to the boats, but I'm sure that can no longer be true! I've since learned that there are many regional variations: Cornish fishermen believed that churchmen bring bad luck; and in the north and east there were various animals which should never be named, pigs (in Scotland these brought particularly bad luck if met on the way to the boats), cats, rabbits and hares among them. Another banned word is 'lawyer', but I'm pretty sure that it's not only fishermen who feel that way. I don't know whether the custom is still observed, but apparently the fishermen of the Isle of Man would carry a dead wren with them when at sea for protection from drowning.

Meeting the men, sharing their lives for a few days and watching them work, confirmed my belief that fish should not be regarded as a cheap food. The harvest of the seas is hard won. It is estimated that one fisherman is lost at sea every eight days.

We in the United Kingdom should be prepared, as are our friends in France and Belgium, to pay an appropriate price for such a valuable food provided for us by this special breed of men. It is a lonely life away from family and friends; the discomforts are many, and the work is hard and often exhausting. It is not for me: to be fast asleep and be awoken because the trawl has to be pulled in, to struggle into your waterproof, rush up slippery ladders into a cold night, haul in the nets, then start gutting the catch in icy sea water, packing the fish, repairing the nets. No, it's definitely not for me.

THE BASICS

CHOOSING AND BUYING

'One of the really essential ingredients in fish cookery is the one that so often is missing, namely a good fishmonger.'

Delia Smith, Complete Cookery Course

Seafood is more swiftly perishable than meat and poultry and you should take great care to make sure of its freshness. There are a number of points to remember.

1. If you live inland, Monday is not a good day to buy fish. Wholesale markets are closed on Sundays and Mondays, so most retail shops find it difficult to get fresh supplies. As always, there are exceptions to the rule because sometimes your fishmonger can get deliveries straight from the coast, so don't be afraid to ask him.

2. Use sight and smell. Look at your retailer and his premises. Is he reasonably tidy, with clean fingernails, fresh overall or apron? (It would be unreasonable to expect a fishmonger who was also preparing the fish to remain spotless.) Are the premises clean? No broken tiles, no rust on the fridges and other equipment? Is there plenty of ice around? And is the fish well presented? His attitude to all this will undoubtedly be reflected in the quality of the fish he sells. But don't stop there. Use your nose. What does the place smell like? Fresh fish has a wonderful clean smell of the sea; and fresh salmon smells of freshly sliced cucumber. So, the appearance and smell of your retailer's premises come first.

3. Next, look at the fish. It is easier to judge freshness in whole fish, and patterns of spoilage vary in species. So use your eyes. Not too many fishmongers will take kindly to you prodding their display. When your fishmonger picks up a whole fish you will be able to see if it is stiff and firm: if it's limp and head nearly touches tail, forget it! The eyes should be full and bright with black pupils and transparent corneas. They should not be sunken and opaque as if they are in need of a cornea transplant. The skin should be shiny with a coat of clear natural slime, not dry and gritty. The brilliance of the colour of the skin also indicates the freshness. You may have the nerve to ask to see the inside of the gills. That will be because you know that when fresh the gills are suffused with oxygenated blood and should be red to rosy pink; they undergo colour changes as the blood decomposes: from red—dark red—brown—purple—to green. At this point the principal smell is of stale cabbage.

13

4. Fillets and pieces of fish should be translucent rather than milky-white, firm and springy to the touch with no discolouration around the edges. The flesh should be intact and not beginning to break up.

5. Shellfish deteriorates even more quickly than fish. It is best to buy it live and cook it at home, but if buying cooked shellfish look for the following:

Crabs and lobsters. Shells should be intact; if cracked, the flavour and texture of the meat may have been damaged during cooking. They should feel heavy for their size. Cooked crabs and lobsters that feel light may have recently moulted and will therefore be in poor condition. Poor quality shellfish may contain water so test them by shaking them close to your ear—you may hear water sloshing. Stale and old cooked shellfish have a strong smell of ammonia.

6. *Live shellfish*—crab, lobster—should have their claws intact and should react pretty smartly when lifted or prodded. A tired lobster is a dying lobster.

7. *Bivalves*—clams, mussels, scallops and oysters—are always bought live and, to determine freshness, you should see that they are all tightly closed with uncracked shells. They should not be gaping, and if tapped should give a dull thud (they're full); if slightly opened, give a tap and watch them close (they're still alive). Scallops are the exception to this rule; they can be sold gaping open. 'Wild' (in season) mussels have become very popular over the past years. I prefer to buy from Scotland or Norfolk as these mussels seem slightly more 'meaty'. I buy large sacks which empty into shallow trays so that my customers can see what they are buying, and can also see that when I give the mussels a shake just before I measure them (I sell them by the pint) the shells either quickly close or I discard them. Out of season, farmed mussels are always available. Increasingly, you see them bagged up in plastic mesh nets or in plastic bags. I prefer cotton net or the plastic mesh as you can see what you are getting and the fish themselves are well ventilated (I know the plastic bags have holes punched in them, but I personally don't think that's enough).

Cockles are a species of clam and when bought live the same criteria apply.

8. *Gastropods—Single shellfish*—whelks and winkles—are usually sold cooked, but if live the foot should be covered by a little dark 'trapdoor' and if touched the foot should go back into the shell. My assistant, Eddie, uses the shop on Sundays to sell shellfish. One day he had a number of complaints from customers that they couldn't get the winkles out of their shells. Well, I wasn't totally surprised: they were still alive, so naturally

retreated as far back as possible into their shells when they were prodded with a pin. First, boil your winkle . . .

When buying cooked single shellfish still in their shells, you can be guided only by your nose. The same applies to all shellfish meat out of shell and ready to eat (cockles, crab, mussels, whelks)—use your nose. If it doesn't smell fresh, don't buy it.

9. *Smoked fish*. Look for a bright, glossy surface, firm texture, and a pleasant smoky smell. Soggy fish means that the raw fish was either of poor quality or frozen. And the older it gets, the stickier it gets. Put an old, stale Finnan haddock in the dark and the bones will glow, with phosphorus. It's quite eerie.

I am often asked about the merits of frozen versus fresh fish. I believe there is nothing as good as a fresh fish, though some freeze quite well. And there is a marked difference in quality between a fish that has been frozen in a commercial freezer and a fresh fish frozen in a domestic freezer. The commercial freezing is at a much lower temperature and it seems to affect the quality of the flesh. Defrost a piece of cod or halibut, or any other firm-fleshed fish that has been subject to commercial freezing for twelve hours or more, and you will find the deterioration is immediately apparent. The flesh has lost its firmness and starts to fall apart and, of course, the fresh colour and odour has entirely gone. I once defrosted a piece of halibut and left it in the refrigerator for a day; it was just like a sponge sitting in a pool of water. I do occasionally buy frozen fish, but I tell my customers what it is. I sometimes have to store fish in my own freezer, but it doesn't reach the low temperatures of the commercial freezers and therefore comes out in reasonably good condition.

It is also pleasing to note that wet fish stalls in some branches of large supermarkets are also indicating those fish which have been frozen.

YOU AND YOUR FISHMONGER

'In a fishmonger's shop more is done, after the purchase is made, to save the customer trouble than is done in any other food shop.'

Madame Prunier's Fish Cookery Book

If, as we hope, you are going to make fish a large proportion of your diet, and when you have identified the most convenient fishmonger for you (having made sure that he or she meets all the standards mentioned on pp.13), *make friends*. I have been lucky enough to have made an enormous number of friends among my customers and they ask questions, which they know will be answered, about the fish I have in the shop and how to deal with them, and they come back and tell me how they have enjoyed it, or not! To establish and maintain a good relationship with your fishmonger, and to make sure you get the very best service, there are some simple points of etiquette to observe.

The fish on the slab did not get there by itself and in most cases it is unlikely to have been delivered. Your fishmonger has probably been up since 4 a.m. to select from the market the freshest and best he can for your table, and he wants to please. To help him do so:

- *Ask* for his advice on cooking and preparation, if you are unsure yourself. He will be glad to help; but don't ask for advice if you don't intend to listen.
- If you don't see what you want on the slab, *ask* for it. Sometimes it may be kept in the refrigerator, particularly in the summer months.
- *Ask* for quantity and portion size according to your pocket and need, and please remember that fish does not come in square shapes so all portions cannot be of equal size and shape.
- *Remember* that all fish sold whole are weighed before cleaning and preparing.
- *Remember* that all flat fish come with one dark and one white side, so try to avoid asking for all white sides (incidentally, with only one or two exceptions, such as the Greenland (mock) halibut which is dark on both sides, the dark side is usually the thicker and better).
- *Don't* wait until the fish has been wrapped and in the bag before you ask for it to be handled in any particular way.
- *Help* your fishmonger by being precise about your requirements. Ask

16

for your fish to be: left whole, gutted and scaled only, gutted and filleted, head left on, cut into steaks/cutlets, pocketed for stuffing, etc.

- *Don't* ask for fish trimmings for stock when you have bought your fish elsewhere.
- *Don't* leave your shopping until the last minute. There are few things more irritating to a fishmonger than to be asked for a sprat for the cat just as he is locking the door.
- *Do* come back and tell him how much you enjoyed what you bought, or if you were disappointed.

We fishmongers might have differences of opinion over some things, but on one we are all agreed: we want our customers to be satisfied. If I bring home a whole fish I haven't had time to clean in the shop, my wife Maureen complains bitterly about the mess—scales stuck to the walls and local cats raiding our bins looking for the heads. She feels, rightly, that fish should be fully prepared in the appropriate place. Usually I prepare fish for my customers, as do most fishmongers at no extra cost. I believe it is part of our job, as I believe that a customer can justifiably ask, and expect a knowledgeable answer to, the following questions:

- How much will I need for x people?
- What is the best way to cook it? Poached? Steamed? Grilled? Fried? (Deep/shallow?) Use it for soup/stew?
- Can you suggest any other fish in this price range I might try?
- Can you suggest some other fish I might use with it in a soup/stew?
- There is a fish (name) that has been recommended; do you normally stock it?
- No? Would you please get some for me?
- It's out of season/not available just now? Then could you suggest a substitute?

And then I should like to hear:

- Thank you very much. I'll be in again tomorrow.

17

A NOTE ON NUTRITION

'There is no country so plentifully supplied with so many varieties of fish as Great Britain, and there is no doubt that if it were more generously used it would be conducive to better health.'

The Good Wife's Cook Book (date unknown)

No book on fish should omit some mention of its importance in our diet, so the following information is included for those readers who like to know what they are putting in their mouths.

Professor Michael Crawford and David Marsh in *The Driving Force* (1989) state that: '. . . the foods man ate throughout 99.8 per cent of his history and those which he eats today are different in many ways. There is only one exception and that is seafoods . . . This . . . makes one wonder if people who still rely on fish and seafoods have retained any advantage? In so far as the commonest degenerative disease of Western populations, namely heart disease, is concerned, the answer to that question would be yes.'

Fish muscle or flesh contains between 15 and 20% protein and, depending on the species, a much higher variation of fat—between 0.5 and 20%. Recent research has shown that cold water fish fats are mostly *un*saturated while fish from warmer waters contain a much lower degree of unsaturation.

There are 11 essential vitamins:

A	Retinol	C	Ascorbic acid
B1	Thiamin	D	(mostly produced by the action
B2	Riboflavin		of sun on the skin)
B3	Niacin	E	
B5	Pantothenic acid	Folic acid	
B6	Pyridoxine		
B12			

Fish flesh is a valuable source of protein and white fish has a vitamin content similar to that of lean meat. Vitamins A and D are found in fatty fish and in the livers of various species; cod and halibut oils have been most popularly used as vitamin supplements. Fish is also a source of major minerals—calcium, chlorine, iron, magnesium, phosphorus, potassium, sodium, sulphur—and trace elements—cobalt, copper, chromium, fluorine, iodine, manganese, selenium, zinc.

In white fish—though this might vary with species—they occur (mg per 100g edible): calcium (22), copper, fluorine, iodine, iron (0.5), magnesium (23), phosphorus (171), potassium (300), sodium (120), zinc (0.4).

Vitamin A or Retinol. Necessary for vision in dim light and for the maintenance of healthy skin and tissues that excrete mucus. Fish is a major source, particularly fish liver oils. The following small table gives comparative amounts in common foods:

micrograms*/100g (edible)

Cheddar cheese	363
Eggs	190
Lamb liver	19,900
Old carrots	2,000
Cod liver oil	18,000
Halibut liver oil	900,000

Vitamin B3 or Niacin. Deficiency results in pellagra, dark and scaly skin. The main sources in our diet are meats, potatoes, breads and fortified cereals, but niacin is also importantly available in fish.

micrograms/100g (edible)

Cheddar cheese	6.2
Chicken	9.6
Beef (stewing steak)	8.5
Eggs	3.7
White bread	2.3
White fish	6.0

Vitamin B6 or Pyridoxine. This vitamin is needed for the formation of haemoglobin and is involved in the metabolism of amino acids. Deficiency is rare, but pregnant women may benefit from slightly increased intakes.

Fairly widespread, the main sources are meat, eggs, whole cereals and fish.

micrograms/100g (edible)

Beef (stewing steak)	0.27
Chicken	0.29
Wholemeal bread	0.12
White fish	0.29

---

* A microgram is one millionth of a gram.

Vitamin B12. Needed by blood cells; deficiency can lead to pernicious anaemia. It is only available in animal products and some micro-organisms such as yeast. Liver is the richest source, but fish contains useful amounts.

micrograms/100g (edible)

Cheddar cheese	1.5
Eggs	1.7
Beef, lamb, pork	2.0
Lamb's liver	54.0
White fish	2.0

Vitamin D. Much of our requirement of vitamin D is obtained from sunlight, but children and pregnant/lactating women should ensure that they have sufficient. Oily fish is a particularly good source, as the following table shows:

micrograms/100g (edible)

Cheddar cheese	0.3
Eggs	1.6
Beef	0
Liver	0.8
Herring and kipper	22.4
Salmon (canned)	12.5
Margarine	7.9
Cod liver oil	212.5

Anyone whose childhood was spent during the Second World War will remember the daily dosage of cod or halibut liver oil (sometimes helped down with treacle). There are considerable differences in the amounts of vitamin D to be found in fish liver oils as the following table shows:

Fish liver oil	*Vit. D (micrograms per g)*
Cod	1.25–5
Halibut	25–100
Sea bass	100–125
Sword fish	100–250
Yellow fin tuna	325–1125
Striped tuna	5500–6250

Omega 3 is the collective name for two fatty acids which have a lowering effect on blood fats, thus decreasing the chances of blood vessels clogging up with cholesterol. They can also help make the blood flow more easily, thus reducing the likelihood of a heart attack. Omega 3 may also help reduce inflammation from rheumatoid arthritis and psoriasis. Omega 3 is found almost exclusively in oily fish.

Fish	*Omega 3*
(per 100g)	*fatty acids (g)*
Mackerel	2.5
Herring (Atlantic)	1.6
Mullet	1.1
Halibut (Greenland)	0.9
Tuna	0.5
Cod (Atlantic)	0.3
Haddock	0.2
Sole	0.1

Fish is not just good for you, it is necessary for you. As P. G. Wodehouse's Bertie Wooster said of his immortal manservant: 'There are no limits to Jeeves' brain power. He virtually lives on fish.'

EQUIPMENT

If you are going to prepare fish yourself you must have at least one good razor sharp knife. Ideally you would have a long-bladed, flexible knife for filleting, a long and strong-bladed knife for cutting off heads and through the backbone, and a small knife for small jobs.

It is possible to spend an enormous amount of money on kitchen equipment designed especially for cooking fish: various sizes of fish kettles for poaching whole fish; a turbotier for flat fish; stock pans, sauciers and all manner of frying pans. But if you have to choose only one item, I recommend a wok. You can poach, steam, sauté, deep fry, shallow fry and stir fry, and make sauces in this versatile pan. Woks are even available with a non-stick coating. A sauté pan, deeper sided than a frying pan, is another useful and versatile piece of equipment (it too can be found with a non-stick coating).

The normally equipped kitchen should provide most of your needs: a colander or two (preferably stainless steel); one or more long-handled sieves to strain stocks and sauces; fish slices of various sizes; scissors to trim off fins and snip away unwanted bits; slotted or perforated spoons; a wooden mallet or rolling pin to flatten fillets, tenderise an octopus or crack a crab claw; a wire skimmer (found in Chinese stores and available in various sizes) to scoop up fried food from hot oil or pieces of fish from a poaching liquid or removing unwanted bits from anything; kebab skewers; food tongs for turning fish under or over a grill; long-handled fish grids for cooking fish over a barbecue and enabling their easy removal; pastry brush or brushes (the broader the better) for keeping fish oiled or moist while grilling and for painting on savoury oils or pastes; palette knife for spreading pastes or butters; a zester for citrus fruit skins needed for sauces; baking, casserole, pie and all other kinds of cooking dishes used in a kitchen's working week; and a plentiful supply of kitchen paper. Also useful is a pair of tweezers to remove pin-bones from smoked salmon and other bony fish; a pair of pliers can be used for the same purpose on large fish. And rubber gloves in case you need them.

Not essential but nice to have: fish scaler (though you can use the back of a strong knife); crab crackers and lobster pickers; a paella pan; a home smoker.

Most people will suggest an oyster knife. I have successfully improvised with a pair of scissors and a strong-bladed knife, the scissors to clip a piece from the front of the joined shells, and the knife to insert into the little crack created and complete the opening of the oyster and cut the muscle. After a season of using this technique (which I found better than the traditional oyster knife) there came on the market a gadget which combined the functions of the scissors and the knife. It has a small pair of clippers attached to a blade, and was invaluable when I was recently cajoled into helping out at an Irish oyster stand at the International Food Exhibition and had to open about 500 oysters a day for four days. It saved my hands from being ripped to pieces.

PREPARATION TECHNIQUES

'A man who cannot tell a crayfish from a lobster, or a herring—that admirable fish which comprises all the different flavours and essences of the sea—from a mackerel or a whiting . . . may be compared to a man who cannot distinguish . . . a Beethoven symphony from a military march.'

Guy de Maupassant

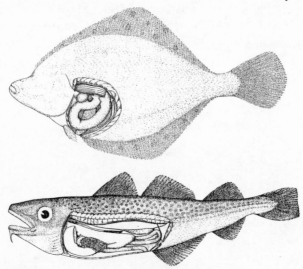

It is important to know that all the following aspects of preparing a fish *can and will be done for you by your fishmonger—if you ask*. Nevertheless I think it is important to know how to do some of these things yourself—you never know, you may find yourself on a desert island, with or without eight records, with or without the Bible and Shakespeare, but certainly with this book!

Scaling and gutting can be a messy business, so do it next to the kitchen sink where there is running water to hand. It's also best to do it either on an easily cleaned surface (perhaps a large cutting board kept specially for the purpose) or on sheets of newspaper that can catch and wrap the debris and be easily disposed of.

Have all the equipment ready. You don't want to have to grope in the kitchen drawer for something with fingers full of fish scales.

- Rubber gloves, if needed.
- Kitchen scissors to trim fins and other odd bits.
- Nail scissors to snip out the gut of small fish.
- Scaler or scaling brush, or use the blunt side of a strong knife.

24

- Selection of knives: small and sharp for slitting the belly; strong and sharp to remove head; flexible and sharp for filleting.
- Pair of tweezers to remove small bones or clean small fish through the gills (or pliers, if you're dealing with a monster).
- Kitchen paper to dry the cleaned and washed fish.

The order of preparation is:

- Cut off or trim fins (particularly important on those fish with spiky fins, such as rascasse, which can give you a nasty prick if you don't remove them before getting on with the rest of the job).
- Scale.
- Remove head, if necessary.
- Clean.
- As necessary: fillet, bone, skin, pocket for stuffing, cut into cutlets or steaks.*

TRIMMING

All round and flat fish should have fins removed or trimmed if you are going to serve the fish whole, and the tail can also be trimmed to fit the dish. However, one way to tell whether a fish is cooked through is to pull on a dorsal or pectoral fin to see if it comes away easily, in which case it's done; so you can just trim one or other of these fins. Keep the trimmings to make a stock or sauce. You will see from the diagram where the fins are.

SCALING

Except for the Dover sole (which in any case is skinned), flat fish do not need to be scaled. But nearly all round seafish *do* need to be scaled, as well as some freshwater fish.

Cover all surrounding surfaces in newspaper and use a perforated guard on the sink drain, or use a colander, to ensure that loose scales are caught and don't block the drain. Hold the fish by the tail as firmly as you can and, working towards the head, scrape or brush off the scales until they are all removed. Some people prefer to scale fish while it is held in a bowl of water. Wash the fish under cold running water and pat dry before the next step.

* Cutlet: a slice across the middle of the fish where the abdominal cavity has been emptied.
 Steak: a slice across the middle or towards the end of the fish which is a complete cross-section.
 Middle cut: a large section of the fish (usually the thickest and choicest part) which will necessarily include the backbone. You can ask your fishmonger to remove the backbone, thereby cutting the piece into two equal parts (sometimes done with a middle cut of salmon in order to make gravlax where the 'curing' mixture is sandwiched between the two halves).

CLEANING/GUTTING

If, on gutting a fish such as herring, mullet or salmon, you find a roe, you may like to reserve it to eat by itself (herring, salmon); to make *taramasalata* (grey mullet); to garnish (salmon caviare); or to add to a sauce to add substance and flavour.

Round fish Remove the head if you wish. Cut if off just behind and with the gills. Then just follow the next two steps.

1. Through the belly: with a sharp knife or scissors, starting from the vent, slit the belly to the head. Don't cut too deep otherwise you might cut into the gall bladder which will taint the flesh. Remove the gut—with your fingers or the knife—wrap well and dispose of the lot (remember the smell on a hot day and the number of local cats ready to raid your dustbin). Use the scissors to cut away any remaining entrails. Scrape away the blood sac running along the spine. Remove the gills as they can impart a bitter flavour to the cooked fish. Wash well under cold running water and use your thumb to rub away any remaining traces of the blood sac. Wipe dry with kitchen paper.

2. Through the gills: a particularly useful procedure if you want to use a stuffing. The technique takes a little practice, but it's worth it. Ease back the gill cover and gently insert and hook your little finger round the throat and, still very gently so as not to break the throat away from the innards, start to pull out the entrails which will still be attached to the gills. On larger fish, you might find it necessary to make a small incision at the vent to release the gut at that end. Then with finger and thumb, and knife, remove everything in one go from the head. Use a spoon to give the inside a final scrape, wash thoroughly and dry. Make a small opening on the belly side of the anal fin; this will allow you to wash the fish through.

Flat fish These are usually gutted at sea, but if you do have to gut one, it is extremely easy. The belly is a small pocket immediately below the head, and head and gut can be removed with just two cuts with a stout, sharp knife. If you want to keep the head on, use the same procedure as step 1 above, making a small cut just behind the gills and removing the gut.

FILLETING

Always keep in mind the bone structure of whatever fish you are about to tackle. These diagrams should be of some help:
Use discarded head, bones and trimmings for stock.

Round fish Smaller fish are quite easy to fillet; larger fish need calm and care, so take your time and carefully fold back the cut flesh so you can see what you are doing.

Cut off the head then lay the scaled fish on a board, on one side, tail towards you, back of the fish towards the knife. Holding the fish steady with the palm of your non-cutting hand, and using the flexible sharp knife, slice along the back from head to tail, cutting in until you feel the spine.

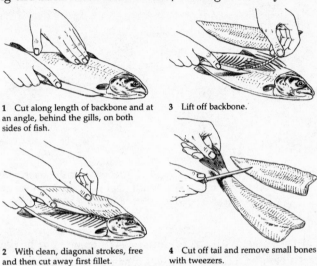

1 Cut along length of backbone and at an angle, behind the gills, on both sides of fish.

3 Lift off backbone.

2 With clean, diagonal strokes, free and then cut away first fillet.

4 Cut off tail and remove small bones with tweezers.

Lift the edge of the fillet to see what you are doing, and start to slice the flesh away from the ribs and tail until you can lift off the whole fillet. Turn the fish over, head towards you, and remove the other fillet.

Butterfly fillets Very useful for all those small oily fish like herring, mackerel, pilchards, trout and sardines.

Cut off head and tail or just the head. Slit the belly the full length of the fish and clean, wash and pat dry. Open up the fish and lay it skin side up. Depending on the size, use your thumb or heel of your hand, and press firmly down along the backbone. Turn the fish over—you will find that nearly all the bones have been loosened from the flesh. Lift the backbone away—the fine rib-bones will come with it—starting from the head end, snip the backbone free at the tail end if you have left the tail on, and use tweezers to remove any hair bones that are left.

Leaving head and tail on (pocketing) will give you a boned-out fish ready for stuffing. The procedure is exactly the same, except you have to snip the backbone free at both ends before pressing along the backbone. (This procedure is fine to do at home, but a fishmonger would use a knife to avoid crushing or bruising the flesh.)

Flat fish Small flat fish are best left whole. Filleting them is wasteful and the fillets are hardly worth the bother. Decent-sized fish—first, cut off the head then decide whether you want whole fillets—the two complete sides of the fish—or half-fillets, in which case you will have four pieces. Oddly enough, cutting four fillets is the easier, so we shall start with that procedure.

 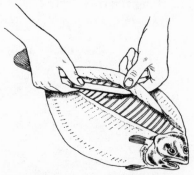

1   Cut off fins, and make incisions down length of backbone, and just below head.

2   Slide knife under each fillet and cut until fillet is freed. Remove and repeat with remaining three fillets.

At home, always start with the underside (white side). The dark side is usually much thicker and therefore gives a firmer base to work on. Again, lay the fish, tail towards you. Insert the point of your good sharp blade in the centre of the back—at the top of the backbone. Cut down along the backbone to the tail. Insert the blade, cutting edge towards you, at the point you first started, keeping it parallel with the strong rib bones. Slice the flesh away with downward semi-circular movements, first on the left-hand side (if you are right-handed), folding it back as you go so you can see what you are doing. Then repeat the procedure with the right-hand side (you may find it easier to turn the fish to face you). When you have removed these two fillets, turn the fish over and repeat the procedure on the underside.

To get two whole fillets: first remove the head, following its outline with your knife. Place the fish tail *away* from you, white side up, so you can see the line of the backbone more clearly. Use a damp cloth to help hold the fish firmly with your non-cutting hand. Insert the tip of your knife at the top of the backbone and feel for the upper side of the rib bones. Slide the flat blade, cutting edge towards either the left or the right-hand outer fin (whichever is more comfortable), under the flesh but on top of the ribs, until the tip of the knife reaches the tail. Using long, slicing movements,

28

cut the flesh away, from backbone to outer edge, keeping the blade as close as possible to the ribs. Cut the fillet clean away from the outer fins. Fold the flesh back to reveal the ribs of the cut side and the backbone. Cut the flesh away from the backbone and using the same slicing motions, cut the other half of the fillet away from the ribs and then separate the whole fillet at the outer edge.

Turn the fish over and repeat the process on the other side.

Flat fish fillets should be very lightly scored two or three times on the skin side to ensure they do not lose their shape on cooking.

SKINNING

Dover soles These fish are usually skinned before cooking, depending on preference, either both sides or dark side only. It's a very quick process. First, trim the fins, then lay the fish on your working surface, dark side up, tail towards you. With a sharp knife, slit the skin just where the tail begins and lift up enough skin in order to get a firm grip. Take hold of this flap with one hand, hold the fish down with the other (you can use a cloth or kitchen paper to help prevent slipping), and with one long strong movement from tail to head, pull off the skin. It will stop at the mouth, so ease the loose skin over and, holding the head, repeat the process on the other side from head to tail; or cut it off at the mouth, and just scale the white side. Wash and pat dry. Use the skin for stock.

With the exception of Dover sole, the dark skin only is removed from flat fish.

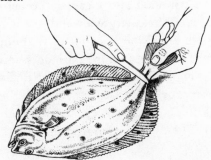

1 Cut through the skin above the tail.

2 Pull the skin up and back towards the head (a little salt on your fingers will ensure a good grip).

It is not strictly necessary to skin most of the other flat fish as the skin is very thin and can be easily scraped off after cooking, though my fellow-fishmonger, Charlie Caisey, always skins his lemon sole because it is easy and he feels it looks more presentable.

Whole round fish are done only *after* cooking, if at all. Poached salmon or sea trout are only skinned after cooking and prior to decorating with sliced cucumber or other embellishments.

Fillets, round or flat To skin or not to skin? It all depends on how you intend to cook the fish, and on preference. Fillets of sole, for example, that you intend to stuff and roll should be skinned (Dover sole would have been skinned before filleting). Don't forget to roll them *skin-side* in—it helps to keep their shape. Otherwise, small fillets are hardly worth the trouble and, because they are so fiddly, you would probably be unhappy with the result. Even large fillets are usually best left with skin to enhance flavour and enrich the cooking liquid.

They are easy to skin, however, if you want to. Use a sharp knife and a cloth or some kitchen paper to help you get a grip. Lay the fillet skin side down on your working surface. At the extreme tail end of the fillet make a small nick in the fish and work the blade of your knife between flesh and skin until there is enough skin free for you to grip. Your hands will work away from each other, one pulling the skin in one direction and the other working the knife in the opposite direction keeping the blade almost flat between flesh and skin and using short sawing motions, and keeping the skin as taut as possible. Take care not to cut into the skin, but don't worry if you do—you will just have to make another start. Put the skin in the stockpot.

BONING FOR STUFFING

Round fish There are two methods:

1. Through the belly. Once you have trimmed and cleaned the fish, continue the belly opening to the tail. Open the cavity wide and, using a sharp knife or scissors, cut off each rib from the backbone. Without piercing the skin, gently run the blade of a sharp knife along the length and each side of the backbone to make sure every rib is free. Turn the fish on its back—if it's not there already—and use your scissors to cut through the backbone at the head, pull it out carefully, cutting it free at the tail end. Now you have only the ribs to deal with. These can be removed either with a knife, tweezers or with pliers.

2. Through the back. This method allows more stuffing in the finished fish and makes serving easier. After trimming the fins and scaling where appropriate, you can either first clean through the gills (see p.26 above) or take out the entrails with the boning. Lay the whole fish on its side with the tail towards you. Insert your filleting knife just at the back of the head and, as if you were going to fillet the fish, start to slice the flesh from the

bones being careful not to cut through the stomach and stopping short of the tail. Turn the fish over and repeat the procedure. With a pair of scissors cut through the spine at the tail and at the head and gently lift out the bones and entrails all in one go. Wash and pat dry, and the fish is ready for stuffing.

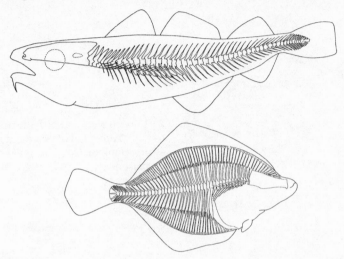

Flat fish Boning a flat fish for stuffing is sometimes called 'pocketing'. After gutting the fish, lay it dark skin up on your working surface and start just as you would to make four fillets, *except* you do not make the final cut to the outside edges to release the fillets. When the fillets are loosened from the backbone and ribs (but still attached by the outer bones), with scissors or strong knife, cut through the backbone at the head and tail, then lift the fish and break the backbone by bending it in two or three places. The broken pieces of backbone and rib can be easily removed with, if necessary, the aid of a knife and/or tweezers. Rinse and pat dry.

EELS

Very small eels should simply be beheaded and cleaned by slitting down the belly. You can then cut them in pieces and do with them as you will.

Larger eels are dealt with quite easily, more by peeling than by skinning. If you wish, rub the fish with coarse salt or bran to deal with the surface slime. With a small sharp knife, slit the skin all round the head, below the gills. Ease the skin away from the flesh until you have enough to grip with a cloth or some kitchen paper. Then—this is the peeling part— hold firmly onto the head and pull the skin down towards the tail. You have skinned your eel.

31

There is no need to skin a conger eel as the skin is very soft and you can cut through it easily. A fishmonger will present it to you already cut into steaks, with the skin *on*.

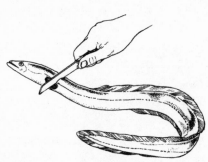

1 Make cut in skin behind neck fins.

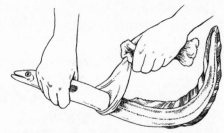

2 Loosen skin and pull off from head to tail. (You could attach head to a strong hook or nail, and pull skin *downwards*.)

SHELLFISH

I prepare shellfish for my customers, but some prefer to do it themselves.

Many people do not like the idea of killing live shellfish, particularly crab or lobster, by plunging them into boiling water, though they enjoy eating the finished product. Nor do they relish the usual alternative of killing with an awl or knife. Another option is to leave the creature in a bowl of fresh water, which will drown it, or to put it in a pan of cold water and bring it slowly to the boil. The fish becomes drowsy as the water warms. At least one well-known food writer whose works can be bought in a national supermarket chain avoids the issue altogether and refers only to ready-cooked crab or lobster.

All shellfish are best cooked in either fresh seawater—clearly, not always possible—or in water of a similar salinity. I add about 250g/8oz salt to 4 litres/1 gallon of water. Most food writers, I believe, recommend far too long a cooking time for live shellfish. As soon as they are cooked through (see the times recommended below) they can be plunged into icy cold water to stop the cooking process. Smaller fish, like langoustines, are cooked: they will rise to the surface when they are cooked through.

Crab A crab plunged live into boiling water will shed its legs and claws. No harm is done if you are going to use the flesh, but it is not so good if you want to sell whole cooked crab. So we use an equally humane method to kill crabs *before* cooking: turn the crab on to its back and with a pointed knife, awl or screwdriver, pierce the crab with a swift firm upward thrust through the mouth to meet the inside of the upper shell right behind the eyes.

Cooking time depends on size. For 500g–1kg/1–2lb allow 15 minutes; 1–1.5kg/2–3lb allow 20 minutes. The water should be at a gentle boil throughout.

To open the crab and prepare its meat for the table is not difficult. When the cooked crab is cool, first twist off the two large claws and the legs. Hold the body upside-down in your two hands with its head away from you. Place your thumbs at the join of the upper and lower sections, press up and away from you and the two sections should come apart. Remove the gills (dead man's fingers) and the mouth and stomach, and throw them away. All the meat left, white and brown, is edible. Spoon and scrape it out, mix or separate as you wish. Crack the main claws with a wooden mallet, a rolling pin or the handle of a good stout knife. Give the claw a sharp tap on each side with the heel of a heavy knife, then a gentle tap in the middle, and you should have a clean break. Hitting it on a hard surface will shatter the claw and you will have to pick out the bits of shell. Remove all the white meat. If you can't get the delicious meat out of the legs (I love to chew the juice and meat from them), crush and put them in the stockpot. Similarly, if you don't want to use the main shell to present the meat, drop that in the stockpot too.

Lobster This creature can be killed by plunging it head first into boiling water. Death is instantaneous. But do make sure you have a pan large enough to hold it. One or two minutes' boiling will turn the shell red and the lobster can be removed from the pan for further preparation for cooking. To completely cook the fish: bring the water back to boiling point, then turn the heat down and simmer for 15 minutes (½–1kg/ 1–2lb); no more than 25 minutes for 1–2kg/2–4lb and above.

The alternative method of killing a lobster is to swiftly cut it in half. Use a strong pointed knife, and stretch the lobster out (back up), look for the cross-shaped mark at base of head shell, plunge the point of the knife into this mark, cut quickly up the middle to the head, pushing the knife right through to the belly. Turn the knife and immediately cut down the middle of tail, just to the side of the centre line or you will split the intestine. You

33

should be prepared for reflex jerks of both halves. You can then cook it in whichever way you wish.

To prepare a lobster for the table, remove the claws and legs, and use one of the following methods:

1. If you want to use the half shell, turn it on its stomach, extend the tail and insert your knife between the body and tail and cut down right through, first along the line naturally indicated on the body, then, turning the fish around, do the same to the tail. Remove and discard from both halves of the fish the stomach, which looks like a little grit sack, from just behind the eyes, and the black vein-like intestine which runs from the body down the length of the tail. Remove the tail meat from the shell and cut away the thin papery covering from the underside of the flesh. Detach and reserve the pink berry-like roe (coral) if any, which is sometimes found in the female (hen) lobster, and the green-grey liver (tomalley). Then lift and discard the gills.

2. Or remove the entire tail of a whole boiled lobster. Pull the body and tail apart. Lay the tail on its back, pare away the papery tail covering. The tail meat can then easily be removed in one piece. The body can be slit in two and edible meats removed.

To extract the meat from the claws, break each into its three sections, crack them with a wooden mallet, rolling pin or the handle of a large stout knife. The meat of the large claw joint can be most easily removed in one piece if you pull the pincer section back as far as it will go. Remove all the meat with any utensil to hand, skewer, lobster pick or small knife.

Use the claw shells for stock if you are not going to eat them. Likewise crush the legs and put them into the stockpot, and if you are not going to use the shell, crush it and add that too.

Crawfish are also killed by dropping them into boiling water.

Prawns and shrimp On inland markets you will rarely see live prawns and shrimp. You will however find uncooked tiger prawns and the like (whole or tails). Preparation depends on whether you want to cook the raw prawn with the shell on or off. With the shell on, simply rinse, then, depending on type and size, remove the heads only (remembering they will make a superb stock); remove heads and shell but retain the tails; or shell them completely, remembering to remove if necessary the black intestinal tract (or 'vein') with the point of a knife. Cooked pink or brown shrimp, if you are lucky enough to find them, can be eaten whole if they are very small, or just beheaded. Most of us in the trade believe that the brown shrimp is the best-flavoured shellfish, as well as being among the cheapest.

Oysters You might need to rinse and brush them lightly to get rid of any mud. To open them, use an oyster knife or the special tool described on p.23. To avoid cutting your hands, hold the oyster in several layers of cloth. Top and bottom of an oyster are quite easy to distinguish, particularly on the Pacific oyster: the top shell (the lid) is fairly flat and the under shell is cup-shaped. So remember to keep them top side up or you will lose the lovely liquor inside. Force the blade through the hinge, sliding the blade along and releasing the lid of the oyster from the muscle, then run your blade under the fish to make sure it is fully loosened from the bottom shell. Pick off any bits of broken shell. Keep the opened oysters on ice and eat within four hours.

Clams Rinse, if necessary. If you want to eat them raw, either prise them open with an oyster knife or lay in a hot oven for a few minutes to open them. Keep them cool.

Mussels As well as making sure the fish are still alive (see p.187) you should check mussels for mud. Sometimes an apparently closed live fish is simply a pair of shells full of mud. Take the mussel between your thumb and forefinger and try to rub the shells together. If they stay firmly together you can be sure there is a live mussel in there. Scrub and debeard as necessary.

Cuttlefish Treat as squid in removing head and innards, then cut down the centre of the body in order to remove the large central bone (beloved of keepers of canaries and other caged birds).

Octopus Very small fish are usually left whole and just cleaned. You have probably had a dish of octopus in a spiced sauce while on the Mediterranean coast. Much of the octopus available has already been cleaned and tenderised but you may have to deal with it yourself. Cut off and reserve the tentacles, removing the central beaky mouth. Cut out and discard the head, turn the body sac inside out and remove and discard all the entrails. Turn it right side out and try to remove any mottled skin from the body and from the tentacles (this is easier on small fish), but if it proves difficult, wait until the beast is cooked. Octopus can be tough. Some people throw it about in the kitchen sink to tenderise it or batter it with a rolling pin or some similar implement. Alternatively, you can cook it in a little oil in a very slow oven for 2–3 hours or so until tender. Then cook it as you wish.

Squid Whole squid may look rather daunting, but they are quite simple to clean. Pull the tentacled head from the body and it will come away with the innards. Cut off the tentacles just below the eyes and set aside. Discard the head and attached innards. Inside the body sac is a long transparent piece

35

of cartilage, the backbone, known as a 'pen' or 'quill', which can easily be pulled out. Now pull or scrape off the mottled membrane-like skin, at the same time squeezing out any matter that might remain inside, such as the creamy roe. Wash the sac under water leaving it milky white. The fins may be left on the sac or trimmed and used in stock.

WAYS TO COOK (METHODS)

'Fish is exciting to buy because it is so beautiful to look at. I find it almost impossible to pass the fish counter without buying something, even if I have not planned to eat fish that day. Fish is quick and interesting to cook, adapting itself to all sorts of wonderful sauces.'

Josceline Dimbleby, The Cook's Companion

The best ways to cook or prepare fish are the simplest whether you grill, fry, poach, steam or bake. Firm-fleshed white fish, shelled crustacea or shellfish and sliced squid can be 'cooked' by marinating for two or more hours in an acid dressing based on lemon or lime juice or wine vinegar (*ceviche*).

Grilled, fried, poached or steamed fish are usually served *with* a sauce, while baked fish is often cooked *in* a sauce.

Baking This method requires the fish to be placed in the oven to cook, usually in a pre-prepared sauce or surrounded by flavourings, uncovered or covered or wrapped in paper or foil (*en papillote*). In *The Practical Fishmonger and Fruiterer* (1914) there is some dismay that this method of cooking in a paper bag, which had come into practice some years previously, had since become unpopular, apparently because of the price of the paper. Baking is also the method most successfully adapted to the microwave.

Boiling An out-of-fashion method of cooking fish and perhaps better named 'simmering'. Fillets or pieces of fish can be simmered in water and/ or milk or wine with selected flavourings. Cutlets or steaks with bone will give the best result.

Braising Part-stew, part-bake, a casserole in which one or more species are mixed, with herbs and/or vegetables, stock, wine or water, tightly covered and cooked either in the oven or on top of the stove.

Frying Deep frying is the total immersion of the fish in hot oil and is the method used in the local fish and chip shop where fillets are either battered or covered with egg and breadcrumbs before frying. The Italian *fritto misto* is a deep-fried dish made up of a mixture of prawns, mussels, roundels of squid, and pieces of firm white fish like monkfish, cod or halibut and sometimes salmon, all having been dipped in a light batter before deep frying. The batter or other coating is necessary in order to protect the flesh from becoming overcooked and hard. Other coatings might be a fine- or medium-ground oatmeal, cornmeal, matzah meal (finely crushed unleavened crackers) or sometimes just flour.

A coating should also be used before shallow frying. A traditional Scottish dish is whole herring or trout dipped in oatmeal before frying in a shallow skillet, preferably in bacon fat.

To present any simple fried fish: clean, scale and trim a whole fish (red mullet, snapper or sea bream), rinse and thoroughly dry, inside and out. Season the cavity with salt and pepper. Finely slice two or three onions (red, if you have them), separate the layers and spread them over a serving dish, sprinkle some finely chopped parsley over the onions, and follow with the juice of half a lemon. Dredge the fish with seasoned flour, shake off the excess and shallow or deep fry in hot oil for 4–5 minutes on each side. Drain on kitchen paper, then lay the cooked fish on the prepared dish and serve with a sauce of your choice.

Grilling/barbecuing Grilling is often done in the grill part of an oven and thus *under* the heat source; barbecuing is always *over* the heat source. There are now available kitchen hobs with a barbecue-type grill attachment, and there are also very useful ridged pans, square or round, that can be used on top of a conventional hob. Barbecues have become increasingly popular in this country during the summer months and many people now enjoy grilling outdoors their fresh sardines or mackerel, bream, snapper, steaks of shark, swordfish, or tuna; and there are now on the market barbecue grills that can be used indoors as well. If you are lucky enough to live near an appropriate open space, an open wood fire makes an event of very simple fare.

Use small to medium-sized whole fish (flat or round) or fillets, steaks/cutlets. Whole fish (with or without head), particularly the round, should be scored on each side to ensure the flesh is cooked through to the bone. All cuts should be protected from losing moisture by a thorough brushing with butter or oil first, or the addition of a vinaigrette or other fat-based dressing, and you can marinate the fish before cooking as well. Grill grids should be well-oiled before cooking to prevent sticking. Whole oily fish (such as mackerel, herring or sardine) hardly need anything more than the merest brush with oil before grilling to prevent the skin from burning.

After cooking, the fish can be served with any sauce or accompaniment of your choice.

Microwave Many people use a microwave successfully (Sophie Grigson is a particularly keen advocate), but times of cooking will depend on the type and model of microwave cooker. There is no doubt that it can save time, but so far as cooking fish is concerned, there is not quite as much saving. And you cannot fry fish in a microwave. However, there are many recipes available which would allow you to use your microwave for the first steps before finishing with a sauce. For those who regularly use the microwave, Barbara Kafka's *Microwave Gourmet* has an excellent chapter on fish and seafood which she opens with the statement: 'One of the microwave oven's star turns is cooking seafood . . . the fish stays moist and cooks through absolutely evenly.'

Poaching Whole fish, fillets, steaks or cutlets can be poached. The poaching liquid can be a pre-made full stock, which will strengthen and deepen flavour, or a *court-bouillon*, a light mixture of water/wine and selected herbs and flavourings simmered together to amalgamate the flavours, or water/milk. The fish is then submerged in the warm liquid (not hot, particularly true for a whole fish where the skin will immediately shrink and then split), covered, and simmered for the requisite amount of time which will vary according to the type and size of fish. It is a good way to treat whole fish or delicate fish.

When poaching a salmon or sea trout to serve cold, I bring the water just up to the boil, then remove the pan from the heat and the fish will continue to cook. When the water is hand-cool, I remove the fish and test by pulling a dorsal fin to ensure it comes out easily. It can be left in the cooled liquid, though the flesh is quite absorbent and the fish might be a bit difficult to remove in one piece unless you use a fish kettle which has a removable trivet. You can easily improvise by wrapping the fish in muslin or another cloth with enough material at either end to enable you to lift out the fish.

Roasting Not a method usually associated with fish, but it can work extremely well with monkfish. A whole tail, trimmed, can be treated just like a chicken or a leg of lamb: brush with oil, insert slivers of garlic/rosemary/lemon zest, put in the oven and roast for about thirty minutes.

Similarly, a whole fish can be roasted in a hot oven. Choose a large fish, at least 1kg/2lb when cleaned, such as a sea bass, sea bream, snapper or grey mullet, make sure it is thoroughly dried after rinsing and score each side four or five times. Put some flavouring in the cavity, such as bayleaf, dill or fennel leaf, tarragon or thyme, paint thoroughly with olive oil and roast on a rack over a baking dish in a hot preheated oven. I also roast what I call a 'baron' of cod—a 1-1.5kg (2-3lb) middle cut of a large fish.

Because fish easily loses moisture when cooked and salt will draw moisture out, it is important not to add much salt until it is served. Baste with olive oil from time to time. Cooking time will depend on the thickness of the flesh (not just the weight), but would be roughly between 20 and 35 minutes (15 minutes per 2.5-cm/1-inch at the thickest part). If you have an oven that operates a fan and grill simultaneously, you will probably be able to ensure that the skin becomes crisp.

Steaming A simple and nutritious way to cook as no flavour is lost to a cooking medium (liquid or oil). Small whole fish, fillets, steaks or cutlets can be cooked in a steamer over simmering water or stock. The vessel can be the steaming section of a large saucepan (these are increasingly available) or Chinese bamboo steamers (particularly useful since they can be stacked to steam two or more dishes at the same time, and can be used in conjunction with a wok). If neither of these is available, the food to be steamed can be put on a plate on top of an inverted bowl in a large pan of water, making sure that the water does not touch the bottom of the plate, or between two oiled or buttered dinner plates over a pan of simmering water.

Stir frying Most people are familiar with this technique. Using a wok or similar pan (large, deep, with sloping sides), you need only a small amount of cooking oil. The oil is heated, the items are added cut in small pieces to allow fast cooking and stirred or tossed while frying with other flavourings, such as soy, added during the cooking process. Only *firm-*fleshed fish should be used for stir frying otherwise it will break up with the constant movement. Tuna, eel, huss, monkfish and almost any shellfish or squid are suitable for cooking by this method.

Sushi and sashimi The Japanese serve raw fish as *sushi* and *sashimi*. The fish has to be *very* fresh and preferably firm-fleshed; it is sliced thin to very thin and served with the delicious *wasabi* (green horseradish paste) and finely sliced ginger preserved in rice wine or vinegar (see p.222). *Sushi* is pieces of fish surrounded by cooked vinegared rice, wrapped in seaweed and sliced into bite-size roundels—very attractive on the plate. All kinds of firm white fish can be used as well as tuna, mackerel and shellfish, and it is quite easy to prepare at home. The fish is more easily sliced if chilled beforehand.

MEASURES

To try to maintain exact equivalents of weights and volumes would terrorise the average cook and be near impossible. I don't think that anyone need get too excited about exact measurements when cooking from this book. Proportion is much more important, so it is much wiser and easier to stay with the same units of measure and don't mix them: use *either* imperial (British) *or* metric. Everyone comes to some sort of compromise and makes approximations. These are what we have used:

Weight

1oz	=	30g
4oz (¼lb)	=	125g
8oz (½lb)	=	250g
12oz (¾lb)	=	375g
1lb	=	500g
1½lb	=	750g
2lb	=	1 kilo

Liquid measure

Equally inexact and approximated:

1 teaspoon	=	5ml
1 tablespoon	=	15ml
1fl.oz	=	30ml
4fl.oz	=	120ml
¼ pint	=	150ml
8fl.oz	=	250ml
½ pint (10fl.oz)	=	275ml
1 pint (20fl.oz)	=	550ml
1½ pints (30fl.oz)	=	800ml
2 pints (40fl.oz)	=	1 litre

Some dry measures are also given in teaspoons and tablespoons/ml.

Temperatures

We are becoming used to Centigrade as well as Fahrenheit and most new electric ovens only give Centigrade measures. Equivalents are:

F	C	Gas mark
250	130	½
275	140	1
300	150	2
325	165	3
350	180	4
375	190	5
400	200	6
425	215	7
450	230	8
475	240	9

We all know our own ovens best. It is assumed that all ovens are calibrated to exactly the same standard, but I do sometimes wonder. The new fan-assisted ovens should eliminate 'hot spots'. The recipes given can stand a tolerance of a few degrees as they are mostly given at temperatures between 190–200°C (375–400°F).

41

FLAVOURINGS AND
INGREDIENTS

'The great European hunger for the exotic spices was largely responsible for the development of Italy, Portugal, Spain, Holland and England into major sea powers during the Renaissance, for the discovery of the New World, and for advances in astronomy, timekeeping, and the science of magnetism.'

Harold McGee, On Food and Cooking, (1984)

Long gone are the days when fish on Friday was met with moans, groans and a wish for Sunday. Recently the United Kingdom has absorbed communities from all over the world, and they have brought with them their unique cuisines for us to enjoy. I doubt there is a city or large town in the country where you can't find an Italian, Greek, Bangladeshi/Indian/Pakistani, Chinese, Japanese, Indonesian, Malaysian, Thai or Vietnamese restaurant now, and these are being joined by African, Caribbean and Mexican specialists. And not only are there now many specialist stores where we can find the right ingredients for all these different kinds of food and flavours, but supermarkets are also responding to the demand by stocking all manner of fruit, vegetables, spices and flavourings. Fresh ginger, lemon grass, chillies and coriander are to be seen next to the celery, carrots and onions; soy sauce and *hoi sin* with the ketchup and brown sauce; cardamom and cumin sit with the nutmeg and cinnamon.

The Romans were dab hands with seasonings and their tastes were recorded by Apicius. They concocted a highly-prized fish pickle or sauce which mixed the gills, intestines and blood of the mackerel with salt, vinegar, parsley, wine and sweet herbs. This was allowed to sit in the sun until it became thick and was bottled after two or three months.

> Take this costly gift, the proud sauce
> That's made from the first blood
> Of a still breathing mackerel.
> Martial, 13.102
> (*The Roman Cookery of Apicius*,
> translated by John Edwards)

Apicius himself used the livers of red mullet—very extravagant at the time.

As well as introducing us to different flavours, immigrant communities, especially from China, India, and South-East Asia, have introduced to us species of fish from their regions. Today increased travel has played its part too. Since the Second World War British tourists have become far more ambitious in their holiday planning. A day-trip to Boulogne (still worth doing for a meal at some of the excellent fish and seafood restaurants) is no longer the great adventure it once was. The Mediterranean coast, the African coasts, the Seychelles, India, South-East Asia and the Caribbean have all been tried and tasted. And the taste has lingered.

I have tried to include recipes that reflect the amazing variety that is available to us and to give an introduction to the various flavourings that can be used with fish.

FLAVOURINGS

Anchovy Bottled essence or paste is a useful part of the store cupboard and a dash or more can transform a simple sauce. Preserved fillets can be mashed into a butter or spread.

Basil Fresh basil (easily grown on a sunny windowsill) combines well with tomato in any sauce, and is essential for the Italian pesto which can make a very tasty accompaniment to fish. Dried is also readily available.

Bayleaf Fresh if you can get it, but dried leaves are perfectly good. Essential to stocks and poaching liquids.

Bean sauce Black or yellow soy beans are used in these bottled sauces. Available from specialist stores and many supermarkets. Bass in black bean sauce is a favourite dish in Chinese restaurants.

Capers The unopened buds of a Mediterranean shrub pickled in vinegar, which gives them a sharp flavour, or salt. I doubt that there is a fish restaurant in the country that doesn't offer at some time skate *au beurre noir*.

Cardamom Either whole pods or ground. A wonderfully fragrant and aromatic spice which is very good in white or tomato-based sauces. It can be used in combination with other spices in a flavoured butter or spiced dressing to brush on fish.

Cayenne A chilli powder.

Chervil A delicate-leaved and subtly-flavoured herb which is very popular with chefs and often used instead of parsley as a garnish for fish or in fish soups. You can also find it dried.

Chilli Fresh, they come in various shapes and sizes. The yellow, green or red 'scotch bonnet' type are popular in West Indian communities and can be extremely strong. Of the more frequently found elongated chilli peppers, the general rule is the smaller the hotter, green or red. Take care when using them. Remove the seeds if you prefer as they contain a great deal of the hot oil, wash your hands immediately after handling them as a careless wipe of the eye can result in a deal of discomfort. You can find them dried, simply crushed or in powder form (also called cayenne).

Chives One of the most popular garden herbs of the onion family, they can add flavour and colour to any dish. Usually chopped or slivered and added at the last minute.

Cinnamon Not often used with fish, but can add a little something extra to a tomato or other sauce to serve with a well-flavoured fish.

Coriander leaf Increasingly available in supermarkets and greengrocers as well as specialist stores. Distinctive, slightly peppery flavour. Can be used as a garnish or as an integral part of a dish. Hardly any seafood dish from South-East Asia would be served without it.

Coriander seed Whole seeds are used in stocks; the ground powder in sauces. A very useful spice.

Cumin The seed is usually ground, and is particularly good if you grind your own (lightly dry fry first). One of the spices used in commercial curry powder, but it can add its distinctive flavour to a sauce on its own.

Curry powder A mixture of ground spices, usually: clove, cinnamon, coriander, cumin, chilli, fenugreek, ginger and turmeric. Proportions and strength depend on the brand. Don't keep the pre-mixed pastes or powders too long. You could also make small quantities to your own taste.

Dill leaf A classic accompaniment to fish, either snipped into a sauce or a sprig as a garnish. It is the major flavouring in the popular cured salmon, gravlax (or gravad lax). As with all herbs, fresh is best, but it can be found dried.

Dill seed Can be added to stocks and poaching liquids.

Fennel bulb An increasingly popular vegetable, traditionally used with fish.

Fennel leaf Has an aniseed flavour and the fronds can be either snipped into a sauce or butter, or used as a garnish.

Fennel seed Like dill, add to stocks or poaching liquids.

Fish sauce An oriental bottled 'sauce', though more a salty liquid made from various species of dried fish, it is very popular in South-East Asia, particularly Thailand and Vietnam where it sometimes replaces soy. Becoming more widely available now.

Five-spice powder A Chinese mixture made up of anise pepper, star anise, cassia or cinnamon, cloves and fennel.

Garlic Use only fresh, either sliced, chopped, crushed or minced.

Ginger The fresh root can now be found in most supermarkets and greengrocers. Don't buy too much at a time as it will dry out. The average amount used is a piece between 1–2.5cm/½–1in, skinned, chopped, crushed or slivered. The juice can be extracted by crushing in a garlic press.

***Hoi sin* sauce** A sweetish sauce based on fermented soy bean. It can be added to a stir fry or used as a dip (combined with soy), barbecue sauce or as a marinade for strong-flavoured fish.

Horseradish Occasionally you can find fresh horseradish which should be grated and used immediately. It takes your breath away, but is wonderful, particularly with smoked fish. Otherwise, it is available grated and bottled, or in a cream sauce. In Central Europe it is mixed with beetroot (*chrane*) and eaten with fried fish or *gelfilte* fish. The Japanese green horseradish powder, *wasabi*, has a marvellous clean sharp flavour and is an essential part of *sushi* and *sashimi*.

Juniper The main flavouring of gin. A few dried berries are particularly good when added to the poaching liquid of Finnan haddock.

Lemon The most used garnish for any fish dish as chunks, slices and juice.

Lemon grass Another South-East Asian ingredient that is becoming very popular. The stalk should be finely chopped and added to poaching liquids and sauces. It is rather hard and chewy and not worth trying to eat once it has imparted its lemony flavour to the dish. Very good with shellfish dishes. Also available dried.

Lime An alternative to lemon, but not quite so sharp. Particularly good used for *ceviche*.

Lime leaves Usually only seen in specialist Oriental stores, fresh and dried. The fresh are dark-green and glossy. They are from the citrus lime and are used specially in China, India and South-East Asia. They add a citric freshness to steamed fish and to light soups.

Lovage Sometimes called sea parsley, it looks a little like angelica. You would have to grow your own (it's an attractive plant and looks good in the herb garden). Chop it into a white sauce and don't add pepper, and it will look as good as it tastes with poached or steamed fish.

Mint Not often thought of as accompanying fish, but it can make a very refreshing change in a hollandaise or a béchamel sauce.

Mirin A Japanese rice wine, low in alcohol. Sweetish, and combines well with soy sauce and a little sugar to make a sauce to accompany *sushi/sashimi* or perhaps fish kebabs, and can be included in a light soup stock.

Mustard, prepared So many types to choose from that can make subtle differences with varying degrees of coarseness and flavourings. As a dry powder it can be mixed with water or vinegar to make up the sharp 'English' mustard or be added to flour to season it, or used in sauces.

Mustard seed Black or yellow, use in spicy sauces (dry fry gently first).

Orange Use the juice as part of a marinade or sauce. Very good in combination with soy.

Oregano One of the *herbes de Provence*. Flavour vinegar with a fresh sprig. It is part of a bouquet garni for stocks and poaching liquids.

Oyster sauce Bottled. Frequently used in Chinese and South-East Asian dishes. Made with, among other things, oyster juice.

Paprika The sweet red capsicum (pepper) dried and ground. Don't buy too much at a time as the flavour fades. Add to flour with salt to season it to dip fillets before frying or sprinkle on before grilling.

Parsley Curly or flat, it has a wonderful flavour on its own or in combination with other herbs. Hardly a plate of fish is served without a sprig of parsley, and parsley sauce is probably the most well-known sauce in Britain to serve with fish.

Pepper There was a time when most British households only knew pepper as a pale brownish-grey powder. Ground white pepper is still widely used, but now often freshly ground. Less aromatic than black pepper, it is very good with fish. Ground black peppercorns are most frequently available on restaurant tables. And now we have pink and green, dried or in brine. They all make valuable additions to sauces, stocks and poaching liquids. In a major supermarket, I recently found fresh small branches of peppercorns, a real treat.

Rosemary A sprig of fresh rosemary is wonderful used on a grill or barbecue and will benefit any fish.

Saffron Very expensive, but you need only very little. Mainly used to give a rich orange-yellow colour. Buy the tiny cellophane packets of the thread (stigma of the autumn-flowering crocus). A traditional ingredient of bouillabaisse, also of paella.

Salt Only mentioned here to allow us to recommend the use of sea salt, fine or coarse. It does make a difference.

Shallots Smaller than onions and with a 'finer' flavour. In nearly all the recipes in this book they are preferred, but a small onion can be substituted.

Sorrel Makes a classic sauce to accompany poached or steamed fish. Cooked in a little butter, it virtually melts. The spinach-like leaves have a sharp, lemony flavour and you don't need masses of it. Easily grown in the garden, you can also buy it fresh from the supermarket or greengrocer. Like most fresh herbs, it can be frozen.

Soy Probably the most well-known of the Oriental flavourings. The thicker dark sauce is rather less salty than the light, and it adds colour as well as flavour. Used in many fish recipes from South-East Asia.

Spring onions/scallions Particularly good mixed with ginger and placed on a fish with some soy sauce before steaming.

Tabasco The most popular and well-known pepper sauce that enhances flavour and adds piquancy to so many dishes. Used most frequently with shellfish but a dash or two with any fish or fish soup can work wonders. Use sparingly.

Tarama The basis of *taramasalata*. A paste made of the roe of the grey mullet and salt, you can find it in some Greek stores. A recipe can be found on p.106.

Tarragon Another classic accompaniment to fish. Add a little chopped fresh or dried to the butter or oil before you fry; put a couple of fresh sprigs into a bottle of white wine vinegar to flavour it; use it in a sauce; or as a garnish.

Thyme Another essential ingredient in bouquet garni for use in stocks and poaching liquids.

Tomato Unless you grow your own tomatoes, or can buy the fresh Italian (Roma) plum tomatoes or organically grown tomatoes, cook with the canned, with or without the juice depending on how you will use them. The rest are pretty tasteless and hardly worth the price.

Tomatoes, sun-dried An Italian speciality discovered by food-writers in recent years and sold in oil in jars, but much cheaper if bought in the dried form, rinsed, cooked for about 15 minutes in water and wine vinegar, drained and patted dry, then covered with quality olive oil. They make a well-flavoured sauce to accompany fish or a paste to brush on before grilling or barbecuing.

Turmeric An ingredient of most Indian curry powders. Adds a unique aroma and its wonderful yellow colour. Occasionally found fresh. Buy it if you find it and add it to your favourite fish curry. But a word of warning: use rubber gloves and an apron when handling it as the colour, though very attractive, is very difficult to remove, even from the hands.

Vermouth A fortified white wine that is versatile and can transform a sauce. Tastes vary, but we favour the French Noilly Prat (especially for Phil's mussels).

BUTTERS AND OILS

In *Italian Food*, Elizabeth David quotes from *Moving Along* by G. Orioli, in which an Apulian chef gives some advice on frying fish: 'The chef then went into the question of how to fry fish; it was a more difficult accomplishment than it seemed to be. Fried fish must be crisp—not wet and flabby as they often were. Only barbarians used fat or butter. Olive oil, and nothing else, should be used.'

In *French Provincial Cooking*, she recommends simmering all fats including olive oil for about half an hour before using for deep frying, saying that this practice also reduces the possibility of frothing and boiling over. We certainly agree that olive oil is best for frying fish, but it can also be quite expensive, particularly the first pressing 'virgin' oils (which I think are better used in other ways). But there are now various qualities of olive oil available, including a 'light' olive oil.

Incidentally, as well as eating more fish, recent studies have indicated that increasing the use of extra virgin or virgin olive oil—as in the Mediterranean diet—has a positive effect on your health, another reason to cook your fish in olive oil.

Other vegetable oils are: corn, grapeseed, mustard, peanut, safflower and sunflower; hazel and walnut oils are very expensive and highly flavoured, and best used for salads, though those familiar with south-west France might think differently; sesame oil which gives a very distinct flavour is often used with another oil in the rough proportion 1:4. For those who like to know such things, safflower, sunflower and corn oil—in that order—have the highest percentage of polyunsaturates; olive oil is largely a monosaturate. Coconut oil and palm oil (used a lot in West African dishes) are almost entirely saturated and make any dish, even fish, heavy and rich.

If you are going to use butter in cooking, use unsalted. Clarifying it is simple: melt it in a small pan, strain it through a sieve lined with muslin to remove the white solids. This increases its burning point. Indian ghee is a clarified butter. A mixture of butter and oil, approximately equal amounts, is a good shallow-frying medium.

CREAMS AND YOGHURTS

Single or double cream, *crème fraîche* or yoghurt—the difference lies mainly in the fat content and the degree of natural sweetness. They can all be added to sauces and to marinades. The table below gives approximate amounts of fat:

	Total fat per 100g (3.5oz)
Fromage frais	0.1
Fromage frais with added cream	8.0
Greek strained yoghurt	10.0
Crème fraîche (soured cream)	20.0
Single cream	20.0
Double cream	47.5

SAUCE THICKENERS
The following are alternatives to wheat flour, the plain flour you have in your cupboard and which you probably usually use to make sauces. They are particularly useful if you have to cater for a gluten-free diet.

Arrowroot A light alternative to wheat flour to thicken a sauce. Gives a more translucent look. Very easily digestible and you may be familiar with it as a 'pudding' to settle an upset tummy.
Cornflour Frequently used in Chinese cooking to thicken sauces. It also results in a relatively clear sauce.
Potato flour Particularly good for thickening soups.
Rice flour Used mainly by Chinese and South-East Asians to thicken sauces and soups.

If you want to experiment, try tapioca or water chestnut flour found in Chinese stores.

VINEGARS
In the shop we carry a line of French vinegars which comes in all varieties and flavours—dill, garlic, *herbes de Provence*, tarragon, seaweed. They are mainly based on a white wine vinegar, but one or two have a red wine base. Then there is balsamic vinegar, champagne vinegar, chilli vinegar, cider vinegar, raspberry vinegar, rice vinegar and sherry vinegar as well as the malt vinegar you will find on seafood stalls in so many British coastal resorts. Each has its distinctive flavour and use depends on the dish you are preparing and personal taste.

BUTTERS, BATTERS, MARINADES, SAUCES AND STOCKS

BUTTERS

A dab of a seasoned or flavoured butter can transform a piece of simple poached fish by complementing its natural flavour and enriching the total dish. George Lassalle, food writer and a great proponent of fish in his *The Adventurous Fish Cook*, supports this simple method of presenting a dish, as do many other food writers.

Another way to use a flavoured butter is as a base for a white sauce (bechamel) or velouté (sauce made with stock).

Use unsalted butter, add salt (sea salt preferably) if you like (but remember that if you freeze the butter both the salt and the flavouring will become more intense); a little freshly ground black (aromatic) or white pepper, or cayenne; and perhaps a squeeze of lemon or lime juice. Obviously two or more of the following could be combined to make a butter to suit your own taste, for example: parsley/chives/coriander; mustard/dill.

The most commonly known butter is *maître d'hotel*, a mixture of parsley, lemon juice, salt and pepper, sometimes with a little mustard. Other classic combinations are: Worcester sauce, wine vinegar or lemon juice (1–2 teaspoons each), pinch each of dry mustard, salt and cayenne, 1 egg yolk (devilled butter); 1 teaspoon each fresh tarragon, chervil, chives, parsley, a few leaves of spinach, 1–2 finely chopped shallots (blanched then refreshed by plunging into cold water) with a little salt if necessary, blended into green or ravigote butter.

A food processor is effective and fast if the amounts are not too small, but you can also get a good mix by using softened butter and a fork. The handchopped herbs make a coarser texture.

Amounts of flavouring substances for 125g/¼lb butter are, roughly and according to taste (all herbs assumed to be fresh):

    3 tablespoons herbs (finely chopped)
    2 teaspoons spices
    2 tablespoons minced vegetables (fennel, mushrooms, capers,
        chives, gherkins, sweet peppers)
    2–3 tablespoons anchovies (canned or essence)
    2–3 small red or green fresh chillies
    1–2 medium cloves garlic, crushed

Experiment and use whatever you might have available, and increase or decrease amounts according to taste. Remember that the butter can absorb only a certain amount of acid such as lemon juice or vinegar before the two substances start to separate.

Other herbs, spices and flavourings to choose from or to use in combination are:

Anchovy (essence, paste, or tinned fillets)
Basil
Capers
Cayenne
Crab
Dill
Chervil
Curry
Cod's roe (smoked)
Coriander (leaf)
Coriander/cardamom/cumin (ground)
Fennel (leaf)
Garlic
Green peppercorn (or pink)
Horseradish (good with leaf dill or fennel)
Lime
Lobster
Mustard (dry or prepared)
Noilly Prat
Orange and lemon, grated zest
Orange and herb (e.g. sage, rosemary, chives, parsley, fennel, tarragon)
Paprika
Parsley
Peppers (sweet red, skinned)
Pernod or Ricard (use with some finely chopped herbs)
Shallots
Shrimp (2 tablespoons fresh or 1 tablespoon dried, and be sure to add lemon juice and a little cayenne)
Smoked salmon pieces
Sorrel
Tabasco sauce
Tarragon
Thyme
Tomato (sun-dried)
Vermouth (use with some finely chopped herb)
Vinegar, wine
Watercress
Worcester sauce

Smoked cod's roe butter (*no* salt, but add ground pepper and a good squeeze of lemon juice) makes this rather expensive commodity go a little further. It is particularly delicious on a lightly poached, grilled or steamed fillet of white fish (brill, cod, coley, haddock, halibut, plaice, sole, turbot, whiting). The same goes for smoked salmon. You can use scraps, and can buy packets of smoked salmon pieces at a considerable saving.

All flavoured butters are good with white fish. Oily fish (herring, mackerel, sardine) has quite a lot of fat in itself, but the stronger flavour means you can use a stronger butter, with mustard, horseradish or Tabasco, for example, together with a herb of your choice and as much lemon or lime juice as the butter can absorb without separating. Adding flavoured butter is a simple way to moisten a fish that tends to be dry.

BATTERS

Except for fish and chip shops and chic Japanese restaurants, battered fish seems to have gone out of style. This is probably because of the amount of fat that can be absorbed in a batter if it is not properly made, if the cooking oil isn't hot enough when the battered food is immersed, and if it hasn't been properly drained. There is nothing worse than trying to eat a grease-sodden piece of fried fish, but it is a method of cooking that we shouldn't ignore and, well-done, it can be absolutely delicious: a light golden-brown covering that crunches in the mouth makes a wonderful contrast to the delicate flavour within.

Like all things, it takes a little practice, so don't be downhearted if you don't get a perfect result first time. Try again. We have given two batter recipes here, but you may have your own favourite formula.

The consistency of good batter should be that of pouring cream, and a batter will improve if left to stand at room temperature for at least an hour.

JANE GRIGSON'S EGG WHITE BATTER

120g/4oz plain flour	150ml/¼ pint lukewarm
Pinch of salt	water or beer
1 tablespoon olive oil	White of 1 large egg

In a bowl mix the flour, salt, oil and water or beer and beat well together. Cover and let stand. Just before you use the batter, beat the egg white stiff and fold it into the batter.

Elizabeth David increases the amount of olive oil, but it is much the same mixture.

TEMPURA BATTER

Most food writers recommend beating tempura batter until smooth, but in fact the batter should be undermixed and a number of little lumps of dry flour are perfectly acceptable, even desirable. And the water used should be *icy cold*.

120g/4oz plain flour	180ml/6fl.oz icy cold water
1 large egg yolk	

Into a mixing bowl sift the flour. Beat the egg yolk and water together, pour into the flour and mix quickly.

Some cooks recommend that the pieces of fish or prawns be dipped first into flour (excess shaken off) before being dipped into the batter.

MARINADES

Marinades can be as simple or as complex as you like, and as spiced as you can take. The minimum amount of time to have the fish absorb any flavour and to moisten, is about half an hour and can be as much as twelve hours or overnight. The simplest mixtures can also be used simply to rub into the slashed flesh of a whole fish before cooking. The following mixtures will, we hope, stimulate a few ideas of your own; and you will find others in some of the recipes given.

1. 4 tablespoons oil
   Juice of ½ lemon
   Salt and pepper to taste

2. 4 tablespoons dry or medium sherry
   Ginger juice (2.5cm/1in piece of ginger peeled, coarsely chopped and
      squeezed through a garlic press to extract juice)
   1 teaspoon sea salt

3. Juice and grated rind of 2 oranges
   4 tablespoons oil
   1 tablespoon chopped parsley
   Salt and pepper to taste

4. 2 tablespoons oil
   2 tablespoons vermouth
   Juice of ½ lime
   1 tablespoon chopped chives
   1 tablespoon chopped parsley

5. Juice and grated rind of 1 orange
   Juice and grated rind of 1 lemon
   2 tablespoons dark soy sauce
   2 tablespoons oil
   1 clove garlic, finely chopped

6. 2 tablespoons oil
   2 tablespoons light soy sauce
   1 tablespoon lemon or lime juice
   ½ teaspoon ground cumin
   1 teaspoon chopped chives

7. 4 tablespoons oil
   3 tablespoons white wine vinegar
   1 teaspoon prepared mild mustard
   1 teaspoon sugar
   1 tablespoon chopped tarragon

8. 4 tablespoons oil
   120ml/4fl.oz yoghurt or *crème fraîche* (soured cream)
   4 green/red chillies, chopped
   Juice of 1 lemon
   Small piece ginger, finely chopped/crushed
   ½ teaspoon ground coriander
   ½ teaspoon ground turmeric
   Coarsely chopped coriander leaves

Chef Antony Worrall Thompson in the *Sunday Express* magazine once published an excellent recipe for marinated red mullet. For 6 people: 1 cleaned and scaled mullet each, slashed two or three times on each side. He mixed the juice of 4 limes and the zest of 1 lime, 1 chopped chilli, 1 chopped clove garlic, 1 chopped red onion, and 1 teaspoon caster sugar and marinated the fish for 4–5 hours, turning them from time to time. No further cooking was required, but you could try putting them under a hot grill for 2 or 3 minutes on each side if you prefer.

SAUCES

Some people believe that sauces are used to *mask* the flavour of an unsatisfactory piece of fish or meat. Nothing could be further from the truth: sauces *enhance* or *complement* whatever you are serving. They should never overwhelm though they might have a quite distinct flavour.

The simplest sauce is one which uses the flavours of the cooked fish and incorporates them into a liquid medium to pour over the fish. If you have baked a fish in a sauce or *en papillote*, the flavours are already incorporated in the sauce; if you poach a fish you can use the poaching liquid to make a quick velouté, with some additional enhancing herbs and perhaps whisk in cream or yoghurt or an egg yolk; if you have fried a fish, you can deglaze the pan with some stock, wine, cream or yoghurt, or any combination that seems appropriate, and add herbs or other flavourings if you like. You can make a quick sauce by reducing some good fish stock, whisking in pieces of chilled butter, sharpening it with lemon juice or adding a little wine, vermouth or Pernod. Drop in some chopped fresh herbs if you like too. Or

54

you can thicken some good reduced stock by stirring in some *beurre manié*—flour (or cornflour or other starch) kneaded with a knob of butter. You could also add a blend of starch and oil, then season as you like.

The following list is by no means comprehensive. You will find other sauces included in the recipes.

There are two recipes from Keith Floyd's *Floyd on Fish* that we like. His hollandaise sauce takes the mystery out of the recipe and, with the aid of a food processor, makes it easy to achieve by the most inexperienced cook. His mother's parsley sauce, he tells us most endearingly, is 'the best in the world'.

FLOYD'S HOLLANDAISE

500g/1lb unsalted butter	Freshly finely ground black
4 eggs	or white pepper
Juice of 1 lemon	

First, melt the butter in a pan with a pouring lip. Crack the eggs into the bowl of your food processor, add the lemon juice and pepper. Whizz for a couple of seconds. With the machine still running, pour the melted butter slowly into the eggs until the sauce thickens. And voilà! Keep the sauce warm over a pan of hot water.

Floyd also recommends (as do we) varying the sauce by adding chopped mint or blanched sorrel, or any other fresh herb, such as dill or tarragon.

Butter sauces use a similar process without the eggs: a liquid base— stock, for example—with some acid added in the form of citric juice or vinegar, and over medium heat the butter is beaten into it to thicken.

If you don't want to use butter, use yoghurt or *crème fraîche* to thicken. Either way, additional flavourings can be added in the form of fresh herbs, anchovy essence or whatever takes your fancy.

55

FLOYD'S MUM'S PARSLEY SAUCE

50g/2oz butter	300ml/½ pint warm milk
3 tablespoons plain flour	Salt and pepper to taste
300ml/½ pint light fish stock (or *bouillon* in which your fish has been poached), warm	6 tablespoons very finely chopped parsley
	1 egg yolk
	1 tablespoon double cream

In a saucepan, melt the butter. Stir in the flour, cook for 3 or 4 minutes (don't let it burn). Add the warm fish stock, stirring continuously, then pour in the milk—still stirring—and the salt and pepper. Simmer, stirring, until you achieve a smooth sauce. Add the parsley, simmer for 5 minutes more. Just before you serve the sauce, whisk in the egg yolk and cream very quickly.

Again, Floyd has other suggestions to flavour the sauce—capers or mushrooms instead of parsley—or reduce the sauce before the addition of flavouring by about a quarter (continue to simmer and stir until more liquid evaporates and the sauce thickens) and add a few lightly cooked mussels (meat only) and some fresh prawns. *That's* something to pour over a piece of freshly poached white fish, halibut or turbot, or even a good piece of cod or haddock.

Roux-based sauces are a mixture of flour or starch and fat (usually but not necessarily butter), cooked a little, to which is blended an amount of liquid. With milk or cream, you have a bechamel; with stock, you have a velouté. Clearly, the more fat the richer the sauce; the more flour, the thicker the sauce; the more liquid, the thinner the sauce. The longer it is cooked the more liquid will be evaporated, so you will get a thicker sauce. Generally, proportions are

Sauce to pour:
30g/1oz butter to 30g/1oz flour to 750ml/24fl.oz liquid
Sauce to coat:
30g/1oz butter to 30g/1oz flour to 500ml/16fl.oz liquid
Sauce to bind:
30g/1oz butter to 30g/1oz flour to 250ml/8fl.oz liquid

For a bechamel, the milk may be warmed and flavoured with a bayleaf, and an onion stuck with cloves, or a blade of mace.

GARLIC AND ANCHOVY SAUCE (BAGNA CAUDA)

This rather strong sauce is served warm and is usually eaten by dipping raw vegetables into it, but it is good with large peeled prawns.

60g/2oz unsalted butter
4 cloves garlic, finely
 chopped
1 can anchovy fillets, drained

freshly ground black pepper,
 a dash of Tabasco or a
 pinch of cayenne, to taste
180ml/6fl.oz olive oil

In a small saucepan, heat the butter, add the garlic and cook very gently making sure that the garlic doesn't brown. Add the anchovies, still cooking gently, and stirring until the anchovies 'melt'. Add the pepper or cayenne. Slowly pour in the oil, continuing to stir, and thoroughly heat through for 6–8 minutes. The sauce can be kept warm over a low spirit lamp or something similar. Serve with crisp fresh lettuce leaves and crusty bread.

GOOSEBERRY SAUCE

Hilary Spurling, the biographer, cooked for a while from a book from her husband's family library. She used the little leatherbound book, dated 1604, as the starting point for her delightful account of Elizabethan life, *Elinor Fettiplace's Receipt Book*. The following recipe was originally designed to be eaten with boiled chicken, but by changing the stock to fish you can make an excellent sauce for fish. Gooseberry sauce, of course, is traditionally had with mackerel or with herring, its slight sharpness offsetting the richness of the fish.

180g/6oz gooseberries,
 topped and tailed
1–2 teaspoons fresh or
 ½ teaspoon dried thyme
½ teaspoon ground mace
120ml/4fl.oz white wine

180ml/6fl.oz fish stock
50g/1½oz unsalted butter or
 60–75ml/4–5 tablespoons
 cream (optional)
Salt and pepper to taste

Use a food processor or blender to purée the gooseberries with the thyme and mace. Put the mixture in a small heavy saucepan with the wine and stock. Stir and simmer for 20–30 minutes when the sauce should be reduced. Whisk in the butter or cream which will thicken it. Adjust seasoning to taste.

Another method is to use the recipe for sorrel sauce on page 63, replacing the sorrel with gooseberries. Or gently cook some gooseberries in a little wine and/or stock, a pinch of thyme, whizz the mixture in a food processor and adjust the flavour to taste with a little sugar or lemon juice.

GRANVILLE SAUCE

This comes from *The First Principles of Good Cookery* by Lady Llanover, 1867, via Theodora Fitzgibbon's *A Taste of Wales*. It's rich but flavourful and is particularly good with white fish, turbot, gurnard, halibut or haddock.

1 shallot, finely chopped	6 black peppercorns
1 anchovy, mashed	Pinch of nutmeg and mace
2 tablespoons medium sherry	1 tablespoon butter
2 tablespoons white wine vinegar	1 tablespoon flour
	6 tablespoons cream

In a pan over very low heat, or in a double boiler, simmer together the shallot, anchovy, sherry, vinegar, peppercorns and spice. Cook until the shallot is soft, stir to thoroughly blend. In another pan, melt the butter, stir in the flour to make a smooth roux, add the shallot and sherry mixture, stir and mix quickly. When smooth, add the cream. Stir, strain or liquidise, and serve warm.

BASIC BEURRE BLANC

Ten-Minute Cuisine by Henrietta Green and Marie-Pierre Moine has some good simple recipes, 'the result of our love of good food and lack of time to prepare it'. Many of them depend on the use of a food processor for preparation of sauces and pastes for 'painting' on food. This is their basic beurre blanc.

In the food processor, whizz 2 shallots. In a small saucepan, simmer 150ml/¼ pint white wine with the chopped shallots until the mixture is soft and syrupy. Remove from the heat. Cut 120g/4oz unsalted butter into small pieces and whisk them into the pan, one piece at a time, until the sauce is smooth and shiny. Season lightly with sea salt and freshly ground black pepper.

GURNARD

SCASSE

Parrot
fish

aRRacuda
(BECUNE)

Pomfret

Skate

Dover Sole

Lemon Sole

John Dory

MICKY SHANE'S SUPER-RICH BEURRE BLANC

Micky Shane, muralist and interior decorator, is an enthusiastic amateur cook (frustrated chef, according to his wife), who often comes into the shop to see what looks good on the slab, and has given this recipe for Beurre Blanc which is *very* rich—and wonderful.

240ml/8fl.oz dry white wine
2 shallots or 1 small onion,
   finely chopped
1 tablespoon fresh tarragon,
   chopped
120ml/4fl.oz whipping cream

375g/12oz unsalted butter,
   cut in small pieces and
   chilled
juice of ½ lemon
salt and pepper to taste

Put wine, chopped shallots and tarragon in a saucepan over medium heat, and cook, stirring occasionally, until reduced to about one third. Add the cream, stir to blend and continue cooking until reduced to about 120ml/4fl.oz. Turn the heat to low and whisk in the butter, a few pieces at a time. The mixture must not boil or cool but remain at a constant temperature. When all the butter is absorbed, add the lemon juice and season to taste.

Strain, preferably through muslin, and serve at once—the sauce will separate if reheated.

Micky says that you could make a 'beurre rouge' or possibly 'rosé' by using a heavy red wine instead of white, and adding a pinch of dried thyme and a bay leaf to the tarragon.

GREEN SAUCE (1)

I like this recipe of Ian McAndrew's in *A Feast of Fish*. The spinach is used as the main 'colouring' agent, and you can change the fresh herbs to your taste, emphasising a particular one if you prefer.

60g/2oz potatoes (use 1 small potato, peeled and diced)
120ml/4fl.oz fish stock or water
180g/6oz spinach
50g/2oz fresh dill
50g/2oz fresh parsley
50g/2oz fresh tarragon

Salt and freshly ground white pepper
1 egg yolk
2 teaspoons Dijon or other mustard
180ml/6fl.oz light salad oil
90ml/3fl.oz single cream

Cook the diced potatoes in the fish stock until soft. Allow to cool in the stock. Remove and discard the stalks from the spinach, and wash well. Remove and discard the stalks from all the herbs. Drop the spinach and herbs into a pan of boiling salted water and cook until just soft and limp. Drain, then refresh in ice cold water and drain again.

Once cold, put all the cooked ingredients, including the potatoes, in a food processor, add a little salt and fresh ground pepper. Whizz until smooth. Add the egg yolk and mustard, and keeping the machine on, slowly add the oil as if making mayonnaise.

Remove the sauce from the machine, stir in the cream. Strain through a fine sieve or muslin, and adjust the seasoning if necessary. If the sauce is a bit thick, you can thin it down by whisking in a little fish stock or water.

GREEN SAUCE (2)

150ml/¼ pint good fish stock
120ml/4fl.oz dry white wine
60ml/2fl.oz white vermouth
1–2 shallots, finely chopped
150ml/¼ pint cream
20–30ml/4–6 teaspoons finely chopped or snipped fresh herbs, 2 or more in combination: basil, chervil, chives, coriander, dill, fennel, parsley, tarragon

60g/2oz butter, cut in pieces and chilled
Lemon juice
Salt and pepper to taste

In a saucepan, heat the stock, wine and vermouth, add the shallot. Cook together and reduce by about half. Mix in the cream, stir to blend, simmer gently until slightly thickened. Pour through a sieve to remove the pieces of shallot. Return to the pan, heat through just once, remove from the heat and beat in the butter, a piece at a time. Add the chopped herbs, stir thoroughly, put back on the heat, bring slowly back to a low boil, season to taste with the lemon juice, salt and pepper.

SALSA VERDE

This is also a green sauce. It is by Sarah Lewis and taken from the BBC's *Good Food*, and is quite sharp.

15g/½oz fresh flatleaf parsley
15g/½oz fresh basil
1 garlic clove, chopped
60g/2oz capers, washed
60g/2oz salted anchovies, washed and boned (or use canned)

1 tablespoon red wine vinegar
1 tablespoon extra virgin olive oil
½ teaspoon Dijon mustard
Seasoning

Using a food processor, roughly blend the parsley, basil, garlic, capers and anchovies. Transfer to a bowl and add the remaining ingredients.

MUSTARD SAUCE

You would be amazed at the number of recipes there are for what is supposed to be the classic sauce to serve with herring and mackerel. You can simply make a bechamel or velouté and whisk in a tablespoon or two of prepared mustard. Our choice would be the velouté. Or you could make it this way:

Melt 30g/1oz butter; stir in gradually 1 tablespoon cornflour; add 240ml/8fl.oz warm water, stir until the mixture boils; add 1 tablespoon dry mustard mixed with 2 tablespoons white wine or cider vinegar, stir thoroughly; add 2 tablespoons milk, a pinch of cayenne, bring to the boil and season to taste.

MUSTARD AND DILL SAUCE

Essential to the proper presentation of gravlax (gravad lax), the Swedish dill-cured salmon, which is a good way to prepare the usually cheaper sea trout, commonly called salmon trout. This sauce is also good with pickled herring, smoked fish, and any other dish that can handle a firmly stated flavour.

4 tablespoons good strong-flavoured prepared mustard
1 teaspoon dried mustard
2 tablespoons sugar
2 tablespoons white wine or cider vinegar

90ml/3fl.oz oil
Sprigs of dill, enough to give 2–3 good tablespoons of chopped herb

Thoroughly mix the mustards, sugar and vinegar (you can use a food processor or blender); slowly whisk in the oil until you achieve a smooth sauce. Stir in the chopped dill.

The following sauce makes a change from the usual mustard sauce and is based on one used by Anton Mosimann.

MISO AND MUSTARD SAUCE

2 egg yolks
2 tablespoons white miso paste (Japanese soy-based seasoning)
1 tablespoon rice vinegar

1 teaspoon English mustard
Dash of light soy sauce
Pinch of sugar
60g/2fl.oz clarified butter, melted

Use a food processor, and quickly whizz all the ingredients except the butter. With the machine still running, slowly pour in the butter. Keep the sauce warm. Very good with grilled or lightly sautéed seafood.

PARSLEY SAUCE

The most commonly made parsley sauce is a flour-based white sauce with added parsley (see also 'Floyd's Mum's Parsley Sauce', page 35). The following recipe is particularly suited to fish fillets cooked *en papillote* or baked with butter and lemon. It uses no flour and depends on reduction for thickening and should use the cooking liquid of whatever fish you are cooking.

2–3 shallots, finely chopped
3 tablespoons Noilly Prat
120ml/4fl.oz single cream
Cooking liquids

2–3 tablespoons finely
  chopped parsley
Salt and pepper

In a saucepan, gently cook together the shallots and Noilly Prat and reduce by about half. Stir in the cream and again reduce by about half. In a separate pan, pour in the juices from your cooked fish (120–180ml/ 4–6fl.oz) and reduce again by about half. Combine the reduced juices with the cream mixture, add the parsley, stir to blend, adjust seasoning, pour over the fish. Whisking in a little olive oil will give the sauce a gloss.

SORREL SAUCE

The simplest and probably one of the best recipes is that given by Elizabeth David in *French Provincial Cooking*:

120g/4oz sorrel, washed and
  finely chopped
15ml/½oz unsalted butter

150ml/¼ pint single or
  double cream
1–2 tablespoons fish stock

Put the sorrel and butter in a pan, stir over a low heat until the sorrel 'melts'. Gradually stir in the cream; add enough fish stock to thin as you wish.

TARATOR SAUCE

A nutty sauce from *The Complete Book of Turkish Cooking* by Ayla Esen Algar.

3 slices white bread, crusts
  removed
180g/6oz pine nuts, walnuts
  or blanched almonds
  ground
180ml/6fl.oz olive oil
1 teaspoon sea salt

2–4 cloves garlic, crushed
4–5 tablespoons lemon juice
  or white wine vinegar
  (lemon juice for pine nuts
  or almonds; vinegar for
  walnuts)

Soak the bread in water and squeeze dry. Put half each of the bread, nuts and oil in a food processor and mix; add the remaining bread, nuts and oil, salt and garlic, turning the machine on and off between each addition. Gradually add the lemon juice or vinegar and blend until smooth. Mix in a little ground black pepper if liked. Serve with shallow-fried fish.

TOMATO SAUCE

This can be as spicy and flavourful as you like.

2 tablespoons olive oil
1–2 shallots, finely chopped
1–2 cloves of garlic, finely
chopped or crushed
1 stalk of celery, ribby parts
removed and finely
chopped
1 medium can Italian
tomatoes
1 tablespoons tomato purée
2–3 tablespoons red wine or
vermouth (optional)
1–1½ teaspoons dried herbs
or sprigs of fresh herbs,
such as basil, marjoram,
oregano, thyme

½ teaspoon ground cinnamon
Tabasco to taste, or ½
teaspoon cayenne or 1 red
chilli, chopped (optional)
Juice of ½ lime or ½ lemon
½–1 teaspoon sugar
2 or 3 sprigs of parsley,
coarsely chopped
Sea salt and freshly ground
black pepper to taste

In a sauté or heavy frying pan, heat the oil, add the shallots and garlic and cook until the shallots are transparent, add the celery and cook for a further minute or two. Add all the other ingredients, stir thoroughly to mix, and simmer over a low heat for 20–25 minutes. The sauce will reduce and thicken (don't let it cook too quickly or it might start to stick to the pan). Pass the sauce through a sieve to remove the solids, pressing them against the sieve to extract all the sauce.

You can leave out some of the flavourings or increase the amount of cayenne as the mood takes you, and as you believe your final dish requires.

WATERCRESS SAUCE

This comes from Susan Hicks's *The Fish Course* and is wonderfully simple. It also points the way to using other vegetable purées to achieve a flavourful and colourful accompaniment to any fish.

1–2 bunches watercress,
trimmed
150ml/5fl.oz sour cream

Freshly ground black pepper
Squeeze of lemon juice

In your food processor or blender, whizz together the watercress, sour cream and pepper, add lemon juice to taste. It can be used chilled or gently warmed. And it looks pretty.

CUCUMBER SAUCE

Peel, deseed, and dice the cucumber, sprinkle salt over, and let stand for about 15 minutes. Rinse, drain and thoroughly dry. Mix with sour cream or yoghurt, add some snipped fresh dill, season to taste, and add a little lime or lemon juice if liked. Very similar to the *raita* served in Indian restaurants.

BASIC MAYONNAISE

In the American classic, *The Joy of Cooking*, we are told that mayonnaise was originally called Mahonnaise after a French victory over the British at Port Mahon on the Island of Minorca. The date was 1756. Why and how this sauce should take its name from this particular ignominy suffered by the British, we don't know, but there's certainly no prejudice on the part of the British regarding its use.

You can still make a mayonnaise in the classic tradition in a bowl and with a wire whisk, but use of a food processor is widespread and you can achieve an excellent result very quickly. If there is a golden rule, then it is that all ingredients should be at the same temperature. So take your eggs out of the refrigerator two hours before you use them. Also, no more than 180ml/6fl.oz oil to 1 egg yolk.

Whizz together in your food processor 1 or more egg yolks (depending on how much mayonnaise you want to make—see above) with ½–1 teaspoon prepared mustard of your choice, a pinch of fine sea salt, a few grains of cayenne (optional). With the machine still running, slowly pour in 180ml/6fl.oz (or more) olive oil until you have a thick sauce. Finish with a teaspoon of lemon juice or wine vinegar. You can increase the amount of lemon juice or vinegar if you like a slightly more acid mayonnaise.

AIOLI

The classic garlic mayonnaise used for so many dishes is also wonderful with a platter of freshly cooked prawns or crawfish. Some say there should be at least 1 clove garlic per person, so they should all be good friends.

Use a food processor to blend together:

2 egg yolks
2–4 garlic cloves, coarsely chopped (or more, if you insist)
Pinch of sea salt

With the machine running, pour in

240ml/8fl.oz olive oil

until you have a good thick mayonnaise. Finish with a squeeze of lemon or lime juice, and some freshly ground black or white pepper.

VARIATIONS ON MAYONNAISE

Once you have the basic mayonnaise you can add almost anything to it to give flavour, texture and colour. Escoffier recommends using the eggs and creamy parts of large shellfish, crayfish or prawns, anchovies or caviar, by pounding them to a purée and mixing them with mayonnaise (passing them through a fine sieve if necessary to remove any coarse bits).

You can also add crushed or chopped fresh herbs: chervil, chives, coriander, dill, fennel, tarragon; or ground spices: cardamom, coriander, cumin or curry powder; a little cayenne or paprika, or a little Tabasco, anchovy essence or grated horseradish.

Tartare sauce is a mayonnaise to which is added a mixture of finely chopped capers, gherkins and green olives. You could also add chives, coriander, parsley and a little shallot.

Sauce remoulade is similar: mayonnaise mixed with chopped gherkins and capers; finely chopped chervil, parsley and tarragon; a little anchovy essence and a little prepared mustard.

ROUILLE

To my mind a teaspoonful of this garlic and chilli-flavoured sauce is essential to bouillabaisse, bourride or any other fish soup. A 'pure' Provençal version would pound together 2 cloves garlic, 2 red chillies (seeds removed), a stale slice of white bread (crusts removed) soaked in water or fish stock and squeezed out, then slowly add 3 tablespoons olive oil. Jane Grigson recommends adding the liver of bream or red mullet if they are included in your dish and/or a little fish stock. The following is made as you would a mayonnaise:

Using a food processor whizz together:

1 egg yolk	A pinch of saffron
2 cloves garlic, coarsely chopped	1 teaspoon mustard (Dijon preferred)
1 or 2 small red chillis (to tolerance) or use half teaspoon cayenne or Tabasco	

With the machine still running, pour in

120ml/4fl.oz olive oil

until you have a thick sauce. Adjust seasoning with a little fine sea salt. Some people like to add a teaspoon or two of tomato purée to give added colour and to sweeten a little.

Another version adds to the first mixture:

½ sweet red pepper, seeded and chopped
2 tablespoons soft breadcrumbs
1 tablespoon good fish stock

STOCK

Everyone seems to have their own formula for making fish stock (also known as *fumet*): Constance Spry recommends using only Dover sole bones; Jane Grigson suggests cheap fish such as whiting; Escoffier mentions sole, whiting or brill; others simply include trimmings of firm white fish. If you have bought a whole white fish, whatever it is, you should use its trimmings: heads, tails, skin and bones. In fact, it doesn't matter what fish you use, except the oily fish, which don't make a good stock.

Crab legs, prawn shells or any leavings from shellfish will add to the flavour and richness of your stock.

The proportion of water to trimmings is *very* roughly 500ml per ½kg/ 1 pint per lb of trimmings. This will vary depending on the amount of flavouring vegetables and herbs you include. The only rule that has to be observed is that you should have enough water to cover. And water can be supplemented with a glass or two of white wine, or a couple of tablespoons of white wine vinegar with a teaspoonful of sugar.

Additions to stock can include, depending on what you have at hand: bayleaf, bouquet garni, celery, carrot, fennel, garlic cloves (unpeeled), leeks, lemon juice or rind, mushroom trimmings, onion (can be stuck with cloves), parsley, peppercorns and thyme. Add salt, if required, later.

Bring to the boil and skim. On the matter of how long to simmer the stock, 30 minutes is the minimum to get any flavour.

Of course, I'm lucky. I have at my disposal any amount and any variety of fish bones and trimmings. And I use them all. I have a very large saucepan and in they go, I cover them with water and nothing else, bring to the boil, lowering heat, then simmer until I feel there's no more protein and flavour to be extracted—about 1 to 1½ hours. I strain it and let it cool, and it sets wonderfully. Used as a base for soup or sauce, there is nothing like it. Some of my customers use it to stretch a jar of commercially made soup, particularly if they are making a quick bouillabaisse.

If you want to reduce it to strengthen and thicken it (as a base for a sauce) do so in a wide pan, a frying or sauté pan, so you have a lesser depth of stock in the pan and a greater surface area from which the water content can be evaporated.

If you don't intend to use it immediately, bring it to the boil again within the next 24 hours. Like all stocks, you can freeze it.

POACHING LIQUID (COURT-BOUILLON)

A poaching liquid can be as simple or as complex as you like. Its purpose is to enhance the natural flavour of the fish you will cook in it.

You will usually need about at least 1 litre/2 pints liquid: all water, half water/half white wine, all wine, water with a dash of vermouth, half water/half milk (particularly good for smoked haddock). Add a couple of bayleaves, 4 or 5 juniper berries, a few peppercorns, a small onion or shallot, peeled and cut in half, a piece of lemon rind or lemon pieces, a few pieces of celery or fennel, a carrot, peeled and sliced, a bouquet garni, a few sprigs of parsley or tarragon, or whatever other fresh herb you like.

Bring your poaching liquid to the boil and allow it to simmer at a low boil for at least 15–30 minutes to extract flavours. Allow it to cool.

Once the fish is cooked, the liquid you have left, of course, is a stock. Use some of it to make a sauce to accompany the fish you have just cooked; use it later as the base for a soup; or, if you are not sure what you want to do with it, reduce it, strain and freeze it.

HOW TO EAT FISH

Fish have bones. This is a fact of life. Most of the time you will be presented with fillets, cutlets and steaks, all of which will be no trouble at all, but from time to time you will have to cope with a whole fish on the bone. Do not be dismayed.

Keep calm, keep in mind the basic bone structure (see above), and be prepared to take a little time, about two minutes, to successfully remove the flesh from the bone and enjoy.

Whole fillets can be removed from some cooked firm-fleshed fish; from some fish the flesh will come away from the bone in flakes (e.g. cod) and from other whole cooked fish, such as plaice, the flesh is so soft it has to be scraped gently from the bone straight on to the fork.

Small flat fish requires that you hold the fish firmly on the plate with your fork; first make a cut across the base of the head, then at the base of the tail. Then draw the point of your knife down the centre of the fish, cutting down to the centre bone, the spine. Slide the knife under the flesh, against the rib bones on one side of the spine, along the length of the fish, and lift your first fillet—cut it away along the side. Repeat the process for the other side. You have two fillets and are faced with the naked bones, the skeleton, which you must remove, and the flesh underneath them. Slide your knife between the bones and the lower side of the fish and loosen the skeleton from the flesh. Cut through at head and tail and the whole skeleton will come free and can be set aside leaving you the underside fillets.

Flat fish have an additional set of short, rather gelatinous bones on each side of the fish. (These are, in fact, an internal extension of the fin). They can be lifted with your knife and set aside, though personally I love to chew on them to get all that lovely delicate flesh from them. Soft-flesh fish (such as plaice, flounder, dab): open the fish in the way described above, but instead of trying to remove fillets, scrape the flesh gently from the bone on to the fork (any attempt to remove a whole fillet will fail as the flesh is too soft to hold together).

Small round fish—basically the same process, though the fish lies on its side and the spine is on either the left or right of your plate.

Oily fish (herring, mackerel, sardine) have very fine rib bones. Depending on how it has been cooked, the flesh will either come away in whole or part fillets, or in flakes.

SERVING GUIDE

What is a portion? So much depends on hunger and appetite. Very roughly, 60–90g/2–3oz edible flesh for a first course; 180–250g/6–8oz for a main course. I have a customer who asks very precisely for a particular weight: 220g/7oz salmon; 150g/5oz prawns. Another factor to consider will be the density of the flesh and its 'richness', and of course how it is served (with or without a rich sauce). You could probably eat more whiting than salmon, for example, unless the whiting were presented with a rich cheese sauce.

Some fish and seafood, when bought whole, have far greater wastage than others. Lobster or crab come immediately to mind; you will buy, say, a 1kg/2lb crab but have only about 375g/12oz edible flesh. Typically, fish that are bought whole—sardine, herring, mackerel, trout, for example—result in about 25% wastage (heads, tails, gut, bone). Don't forget that you buy fish from a fishmonger at a price per kg/lb *before* gutting and other preparing, unless you buy pre-prepared steaks or fillets which will nevertheless be at a price reflecting the work the processor or fishmonger has already done.

So if you are in any doubt about how much you need for a certain number of people, *do ask your fishmonger's advice and guidance*.

The following is a guide to the *average* amounts to buy of the raw fish.

	Per Person	
	First Course	Main Course
Whole small fish, e.g. red mullet	1	1–2
Whole fish, large (to be baked, poached) e.g. salmon, bass	125–185g/4–6oz	185g–280g/6–9oz
Fillets (e.g. cod, haddock)	90–125g/3–4oz	150–250g/5–8oz
Crab (live)	250–375g/8–12oz	375g–½kg/12oz–1lb

THE LISTINGS

INTRODUCTION

'Many housewives whose allowance is strictly limited are apt to consider fish an expensive luxury, only to be indulged in at rare intervals. This is a mistaken idea; for fish, when well prepared, is wholesome and easily digested, and, if purchased with due regard to price and quality, an economical food. Needless to say, soles, salmon, whitebait and turbot cannot be afforded by those who must keep their house-bills to 10s. per head a week; but such fish as lemon soles, plaice, whiting, fresh haddock, mackerel, cod, halibut, brill, skate and sprats are not to be despised when well cooked and served.'

Mrs C. S. Peel, Ten Shillings a Head per Week, *(1902)*

Without going into scientific detail, we should like to give you some indication of the general categories of fish described and their characteristics.

White fish, flat and round All members of the cod family are lean round fish. North Atlantic cod and its cousin, the haddock, have firm sweet flesh; hake and whiting have a delicate flavour and a fine texture. Other members of the cod family, such as pollack, coley and ling, tend towards blandness, but are an inexpensive choice if a recipe calls for cheap white fish. Among flat fish it is generally accepted among seafish cooks that Dover sole and turbot have the most exquisite taste. For myself, I love a middle cut of large plaice or lemon sole, shallow fried. Plaice, lemon sole, brill, dabs and witch are all very sweet-fleshed, and their shallow bodies make them ideal for grilling or sautéeing. The bones of most flat fish are rich in gelatine, especially the turbot, so keep the bones and make a stock from them to give body to your sauces. The largest of the flat fish is the halibut, my favourite next to sea trout. Small 1–1.5kg/2–3lb fish are known as chicken halibut, and the same applies to turbot.

Oily fish Once the mainstay of the east coast fishing fleets, the herring's streamlined body is rich in protein, iodine and vitamins. Its relatives are the sprat, anchovy, shad and pilchard (the sardine is actually a young pilchard). All these magnificent fish lend themselves to grilling, frying and baking.

The mackerel family includes the bonito, tuna and swordfish, all powerful swimmers with compact muscular flesh. The mackerel is distinguished from the others by its comparatively soft texture and oily flesh.

73

They are all good to grill, braise or bake, and they are all magnificent on a barbecue. The colour of flesh in the oily fish ranges from the near white of the swordfish to the deep red of the tuna. The lighter the colour, the more delicate the flavour.

Fish from the warmer waters of the Mediterranean and elsewhere include many other species, some of which enter our waters, such as the much-prized sea bass and red mullet. The sea breams (*daurades*) include many firm lean-fleshed fish, such as the red and black sea bream, the dentex and snappers. All are wonderful fish for the table in almost any way you want them, as is the monkfish, a chef's favourite, but once shunned. Now the long garfish with its lovely delicate flesh is equally disregarded. It is extremely cheap since few see the attraction of its green bones.

Wrasse, gurnard, weavers and grey mullet are all used in the stews for which the Mediterranean region is famous. All these fish swim round the Iberian peninsula into our own home waters. The grey mullet, no relation to the red, is in my opinion one of the most under-rated fish and can be substituted for the expensive sea bass. Many of the groupers, first cousins to the sea bass, have relatively bone-free flesh, and are particularly good baked, steamed or grilled.

Shark, skate, rays What really endears these fish to fish eaters is their lack of true bones. Their skeleton is composed of cartilaginous material which separates easily from the flesh when cooked. The dogfish, huss, is of this family, a much-favoured offering in the fish and chip shop, but I would recommend trying it in highly seasoned dishes like curry. Skate, contrary to what many food writers say, has a smell of ammonia only when it is old and spoiled. Shark has a white to pink flesh with a close texture that can be compared to veal.

The term **shellfish** covers a wide variety of seafood: crustacea, such as crabs, lobsters and prawns; molluscs like scallops, mussels, clams, cockles (bivalves); cephalopods; and gastropods.

Crustacea are nearly everyone's favourites; but molluscs are often neglected by cooks. They can be eaten raw or cooked, and are wonderful in soups and stews.

The cephalopods—squid, cuttlefish, octopus—until recently were only truly appreciated in the Mediterranean and the Far East. These fish have a particularly high flesh for weight ratio as they don't have a true skeleton. They can be fried, stewed, or their bag-like bodies can be stuffed and braised.

Gastropods are the single-shell whelks and winkles, long-beloved by the British seaside holidaymaker.

Smoked fish The smoking of fish is an ancient method of preservation. Nowadays the process is retained for the resulting flavour. The fish is either cold smoked or hot smoked (see p.203–13 for further information). Hot-smoked fish can be eaten just as you buy it, but cold-smoked fish such as haddock should usually be treated as raw fish and needs further cooking. Smoked salmon is one exception to the rule. Either way, they are delicious on their own or in combination with other fish. A mixed smoked fish platter can make a wonderful start to a meal or even a meal in itself (a small glass of vodka—from a bottle that has been in the freezer—is an ideal partner).

You can't make a silk purse from a sow's ear, and you can't make a good meal from poor ingredients, particularly when it comes to fish. Only the freshest and best will do, and I do *not* mean the most expensive. A good fresh herring will make a feast while a piece of stale halibut will make a misery.

The following listing of species is divided into two main sections: Round and Flat Fish and Shellfish. It gives the following information:

- Name.
- Category (type).
- A brief description of shape and colour.
- Names in other languages where appropriate—French, German and Spanish.
- Waters: the region or regions where the fish is caught for the British market.
- An indication of price at the time of writing on a comparative basis. For example, very low (herring), low (coley), moderate (haddock), high (monkfish), very high (lobster). In general, the price of a particular fish will vary according to whether your fishmonger has been able to find a good supply in the wholesale market that morning, which in turn depends on whether the trawlers have had a good catch of that particular fish. Price may also be affected by restaurant demand (for example, all restaurants now want monkfish on their menus) and by the desirable size of the fish.
- Market size (the average size range it is available to the retailer and the customer, and the minimum legal size it can be sold).*
- How it is usually sold to the customer (whole, fillet, cutlet/steak).

* In order to guard against over-fishing, the EEC has produced a schedule of minimum sizes that can be sold of particular species of fish. These sizes are expressed in cm and are marked in the text with +, and are valid at the time of going to press. We believe that it is of interest to the consumer to be aware of these regulations.

- Market availability is an assessment of the likelihood of your local fishmonger being able and wanting to supply it (poor, fair, moderate, good, very good).
- Seasonal availability is what time of year the fish is usually available and, where applicable, the best time of year for quality of that particular fish, usually outside the breeding season. Many species, even those thought of as 'British', can be and are imported from other areas at times when they would not normally be considered 'in season' in this country.

The fish listed are those generally available—fresh—in the United Kingdom, and *include* imported fish. From the responses to a questionnaire circulated to a number of fishmongers in various regions of the country it appears that some of the imported *fresh* fish (the 'exotics') are more likely to be found in the south east, though they may be readily available frozen in large city shops and markets in the rest of the country. While saying that, I know that importers of fresh fish are busy expanding their business up and down the country.

There are other fish not included in this book which are imported from all over the world with wonderful-sounding names—but all are *frozen*. They will usually only be found on stalls and in shops in large cities and, because they are frozen, they will be cheap. If you want to try them I am sure you will be able to find out about them from the traders.

Country or region of origin is indicated where a fish is imported. Other remarks might include suitability for a particular cooking treatment and any other relevant information or item of interest.

Recipes or guidance notes for preparation are given under some but not all species. Where they are omitted a note is included recommending that they be treated as another fish.

There is a third section on Smoked and Preserved Fish and Shellfish and Other Delicacies which also contains useful preparation techniques and recipes.

ROUND AND FLAT FISH

Albacore See **Tuna** (Albacore).

Angler fish See **Monkfish**.

Anchovy

French: *Anchois*
German: *Sardelle*
Spanish: *Anchoa, Boqueron*

Category: Round, oily (herring family).
Waters: Home waters (south west) and Mediterranean.
Shape and colour: Similar to but much smaller than the sardine, its back is a dark green-blue with a silver belly.
Price: Moderate.
Market size: Up to 15cm/6in.
Sold: Whole, fresh.
Market availability: Poor to fair, fresh.
Seasonal availability: Year round.
Remarks: Anchovies are an absolute delight when they are fresh, with an excellent strong flavour. However, they deteriorate quickly so I don't often have them on display. Fresh fish are imported from France and Portugal, but in the United Kingdom they are best known and more frequently used as canned skinless salted fillets. They can sometimes be found filleted and kept in oil, and sold by weight. Eat them just as they are.

Salted fillets can be used in many other ways too. As a butter (see p.50) to spread on toast or a crumpet (with a poached egg on top is highly recommended) or to put on a poached or steamed fillet of fish (halibut, for example), combined with a little lemon or lime juice and cayenne. The commercial version is known as *Patum Peperium*, 'Gentlemen's Relish'. They are marvellous on pizzas, in *Salade Niçoise* and in sauces.

JANSSON'S TEMPTATION

There aren't many dishes that depend entirely upon anchovies for flavouring, but this Swedish specialty does. There are several variations, but this one is based on the recipe included in Time-Life's *The Cooking of Scandinavia*.

1kg/2lb boiling potatoes,
   peeled and cut into thin
   chips, about 5cm/2in long
   and 0.5cm/¼in thick
2 tablespoons oil
30g/1oz butter
2–3 large onions, thinly
   sliced

Approximately 16 anchovy
   fillets, or 2 tins, drained
Ground white pepper
2 tablespoons fine dry
   breadcrumbs
60g/2oz butter
240ml/8fl.oz cream
120ml/4fl.oz milk

Preheat the oven to 200°C/400°F. Keep the potato chips in cold water to prevent discolouring. In a frying or sauté pan heat the oil and butter. When the foam subsides, cook the onions, stirring frequently, until they are translucent and soft, but not brown.

Butter a baking dish large enough to hold all the potato and onion. Drain the potatoes and dry them thoroughly with kitchen paper or a teatowel. Arrange a layer of potatoes in the dish, and then alternate layers of onions and anchovies, ending with potatoes. Sprinkle each layer with a little white pepper. Scatter the top with the breadcrumbs and dot with the rest of the butter. Heat the cream and milk together until barely simmering, then pour over the potatoes. Bake for about 45 minutes or until the potatoes are cooked through. Serves 4–6.

With a green salad, this makes a delicious supper.

ALAN DAVIDSON'S FRESH ANCHOVIES AU GRATIN

First find your fresh anchovies, though you can substitute fresh sardines or small herring, and it would probably work rather well with sprats.

Take 1kg/2lb of fish, washed and gutted, with heads, tails and backbones removed (see p.27). Arrange them in a shallow oiled dish, pour over 120ml/4fl.oz oil, then sprinkle them with 2–3 cloves of garlic, finely chopped, a little sea salt and some freshly ground black or white pepper. Chop 2 or 3 sprigs of parsley and mix with 3–4 tablespoons of breadcrumbs and 1 tablespoon olive oil, and spread the mixture over the fish. Bake in a hot oven for 15 minutes. Serves 4–6.

Mr Davidson also recommends an alternative method, covering the fish with a mixture of chopped garlic, parsley, salt and pepper, and oregano.

You could vary these flavourings by using coriander instead of parsley, and thyme or basil instead of oregano.

Barracuda

French: *Brochet de Mer*
Spanish: *Espeton*

Category: Round white.
Waters: Most warm waters.
Shape and colour: An elongated fish with a slowly tapering tail, large eyes on a pointed head with a very fierce-looking jaw. Its back and sides are grey/bronze and it is white-bellied. It can grow up to 150cm/5ft.
Price: Moderate, frozen; high, fresh.
Market size: 45–120cm/18–48in.
Sold as: Whole fish or cutlets from large fish.
Market availability: Fresh, fair; frozen, good. Also available smoked.
Seasonal availability: Year round (imported).
Remarks: Barracuda is known primarily as a game fish with a fighting nature, but its flesh is quite firm and tender and it is becoming very popular as a fish to barbecue, bake or casserole. It is imported from the Mediterranean and the Indian Ocean region (East Africa/Seychelles) from where a smaller related fish known as Becune is also imported. On a recent holiday in Florida Keys, I caught a 15kg/30lb barracuda. It was magnificent, and I let it go. Unfortunately, the photograph didn't come out either. True, I swear.

Bass (Sea Bass)

French: *Bar Commun/Loup de mer*
Spanish: *Lubina*
German: *Wolfbarsch, Seebarsch*

Category: Round white.
Waters: Southern home waters and Mediterranean.
Shape and colour: A really beautiful fish with a magnificent streamlined body, steel-grey on its back going through silver sides to a white belly, covered in large scales.
Price: Very high.
Market size: 36–75cm/14–30in (no legal minimum size for farmed fish).
Sold as: Whole fish and cutlets from large fish.
Market availability: Good.
Seasonal availability: All year, best June to February.
Remarks: Now a much desired fish for its wonderful texture and flavour and easily handled bone structure. It is caught around most United

Kingdom coastlines, but mainly in the south, and is increasingly being brought in from the Mediterranean and from fish farms in France, Greece and Egypt. It was the first fish I caught on my old second-hand rod and reel and, sadly, I never caught one again. If you ever visit the London fish restaurants, 'Cibo' and 'L'Altro', you will be given a whole fish (about 500g/1lb) per person.

It is a superb fish and best cooked in the simplest ways: steamed, with oil, soy sauce, slivered ginger and spring onions, or smothered with rock salt and baked.

SEA BASS IN SALT

There are a number of good simple recipes for sea bass, but none quite so simple as baking the bass in salt. All the flavour stays in the fish itself. There are just a few rules: the fish must be as fresh as you can get it; take care you don't buy a fish that won't fit your oven (it is better to buy two or more); and it should be cleaned through the gills to prevent salt getting into the belly cavity. You don't have to have it scaled, though it is best to trim the fins. And you will need at least 2kg/4lb coarse sea salt to cover a 1kg/2lb fish, more if your fish is larger. Buy more than you think you might need; you can always use it. A 1kg/2lb fish will serve 2–3.

Choose a fairly deep baking dish that will take the fish quite neatly with not too much space around it. Pour in salt to a depth of about 2.5cm/1in, put the fish on top, then continue to pack it around with salt until the bass is completely buried with a similar thickness on top.

You will need to cook it at quite a high temperature. Preheat the oven to 215°C/425°F and cook the fish for about 25 minutes for a 1kg/2lb fish (approximately 15 minutes per 500g/1lb).

To serve, take the dish to the table and crack open the salt crust. Remove the pieces carefully to expose the whole fish. Remove the skin from the top half, and you can start serving.

You could have a sauce of your choice, something quite simple, to pass around.

Bonito See **Tuna (Bonito)**.

Bream, Sea

There are various sea breams now being seen more regularly on fish-mongers' slabs. They can be divided roughly into two types: those which are found off the south coast of Britain in the summer (Red and Black Sea bream); and those which are imported from the Mediterranean and tropical waters (Dentex, Bogue, Salema, Gilthead, Black-banded, Emperor, *Capitaine Blanc*, *Capitaine Rouge*, etc.).

All breams and snappers have sharp spiny fins and particular care should be taken first to cut off the fins before doing anything else to the fish.

● *Bogue* (Sea Bream)

French: *Bogue*
German: *Gelbstriemen*
Spanish: *Boga*

Category: Round white.
Waters: Mediterranean.
Shape and colour: Small narrow fish with a greenish-yellow/silver body with big eyes on a small head, and small scales.
Price: Low-moderate.
Market size: 15–25cm/6–9in.
Sold as: Whole fish.
Market availability: Poor to fair.
Seasonal availability: All year (imported).
Remarks: A lot of people will have eaten and enjoyed this fish while on holiday in the Mediterranean area, particularly Malta (where it is known as *Vorpa*) and Morocco. It is now imported fresh to the United Kingdom. Excellent slightly sardine-like flavour, it is particularly good for the barbecue, and for grilling and baking. Distribution is spreading throughout the country, but it is more likely to be found in the south east.

An easy way to cook this fish is to grill it. Allow 1–2 per person, depending on size and appetite. Clean, slash two or three times on each side, brush with a herbed oil (rosemary and thyme, for example), grill on a preheated rack or in a baking dish for about 5–7 minutes on each side until the skin is browned and the flesh cooked through. Test with a knife. A squeeze of lemon or lime, a green salad, and the result is a good meal.

● *Bream* (Black-banded)
Category: Round, laterally flattened, white.
Waters: Indian Ocean.
Shape and colour: A really striking fish in appearance. Compressed oval body, silver with vertical black bands, and yellow fins and tail.
Price: Moderate.
Market size: 20–30cm/8–12in.
Sold as: Whole fish.
Market availability: Fresh, fair; frozen, good.
Seasonal availability: Year round.
Remarks: Excellent quality fish with firm white flavourful flesh. As all fresh sea bream, this is a first-class fish and should be tried. It is well-suited for frying, grilling, baking and steaming, though it looks so pretty it seems almost a pity to cook it.

BAKED BREAM

1–2 black-banded bream (or other sea bream)	3–4 sprigs of fresh coriander, freshly chopped
Sea salt and pepper	1 standard can tomatoes
Oil	1 teaspoon ground coriander
Juice of 1 lime or lemon	½ teaspoon cayenne or Tabasco

One for 1 or 2 people, depending on the size of the fish. Clean, slash three or four times on each side, season the cavity with a little salt and pepper, brush with a mixture of oil, half the lime or lemon juice, and finely chopped coriander leaves, making sure that the mixture is brushed into the cuts. Let the fish stand for 30 minutes.

Lightly oil a baking dish. Make a mixture of the tomatoes (strained—reserve the juice), the rest of the lime or lemon juice, ground coriander, cayenne or Tabasco and a little sea salt. Spread half the mixture in the baking dish, lay in the fish, spread the remaining mixture over the fish.

Bake in a high preheated oven for about 15 minutes. Check whether the sauce is drying out, and if so add a little of the reserved tomato juice. Bake for another 5 minutes. Test if done (it should be) with the point of a knife.

● *Bream, Black Sea*

French: *Griset*
Spanish: *Chopa*

Category: Round, laterally flattened, white.
Waters: Home waters and Mediterranean.
Shape and colour: Compressed oval body with small head and spiny dorsal fin. Dark grey back and sides, with large scales.
Price: Moderate.
Market size: 23+–40cm/10+–16in
Sold as: Whole fish.
Market availability: Fair in season.
Seasonal availability: March to August. Outside this period they are available from the Mediterranean at a much higher price.
Remarks: Not a very pretty fish, but its white flesh has excellent texture and flavour. The large bones are easily handled. More usually found in warmer waters, but comes north to the English and Irish coasts in summer. A much under-rated fish (also the second fish I caught with rod and line); more likely to be seen and eaten in the south. Can be grilled, baked or steamed.

At the time of writing it is quite cheap, but I believe it will probably become more expensive when restaurants realise how good it is.

You will usually need one fish for two people. At home we like to marinate it for about half an hour in olive oil, garlic, ginger and sweet paprika before grilling it. Slash the sides two or three times first to allow the flavour to penetrate the flesh. This is quite delicious, and a method that can be used for any firm-fleshed white fish to be grilled or barbecued.

● *Bream* (Capitaine Blanc)
Category: Round, laterally flattened, white.
Waters: Indian Ocean.
Shape and colour: Oval compressed silver-grey body with hint of orange on the spiny fins, and thick broken lines on cheek.
Price: Moderate–high.
Market size: 15–30cm/6–12in.
Sold as: Whole fish and cutlets.
Market availability: Fresh, fair; frozen, fair.
Seasonal availability: Year round, imported.
Remarks: Another fine quality full-flavoured fish imported from the Seychelles (hence its French name) with moist white flesh well suited for most forms of cooking. Large easily handled bones. Its younger sister is

called 'Sweet lips' because of its prominent red mouth, and it's also apparently rather shy since it's not often seen.

Good on the grill or baked. Try it steamed too: slash the flesh two or three times on each side, brush with a mixture of oil, soy sauce and lime or lemon juice, sliver a couple of scallions over it, and steam for about 15 minutes or until cooked through.

● *Bream (Emperor)*
Category: Round, laterally flattened, white.
Waters: Indian Ocean and Arabian Gulf.
Shape and colour: Compressed round/oval body, with head sloping forward to mouth and large eyes; grey-green body with red-edged gill cover, and spiny fins. Quite pretty.
Price: Moderate to high.
Market size: 15–30cm/6–12in.
Sold as: Whole fish and cutlets.
Market availability: Fresh, fair; frozen, good.
Seasonal availability: Most of year, imported.
Remarks: Another good quality fish with firm white flavourful flesh. Usually imported fresh from the Indian Ocean, so it is high priced, but worth it. It is more often seen in the south east though its distribution is spreading throughout the country.

This is one of the smaller bream so, depending on size, you could serve one per person as a main meal. It is best left whole, though you could cut off the head(s) for stock. Treat it simply, as you would the other bream.

To bake in foil, keep the head on. Clean and slash three or four times on each side. Preheat oven to about 190°C/375°F. Brush with oil pieces of foil large enough to totally enfold each fish. Season the cavity with sea salt and pepper, and lay in a sprig of fresh fennel or rosemary. Lay each fish in its piece of foil, pour over each 1 tablespoon medium/dry sherry, 1 teaspoon ginger juice, 1 teaspoon lime or lemon juice, a pinch of paprika. Fold the foil loosely around fish, making sure each package is sealed. Bake for about 25–30 minutes.

● *Bream (Gilthead)*

French: *Daurade*
German: *Nordische Meerbrasse*
Spanish: *Dorada*

Category: Round white
Waters: Mediterranean, Indian Ocean, most warm water.
Shape and colour: Narrow oval body, grey-black body paling through sides to belly. There are dark markings on the back of the head, yellow-gold band between the eyes and markings on the cheek. An attractive fish.
Price: High.
Market size: 30–40cm/12–15in.
Sold as: Whole fish.
Market availability: Fair, owing to imports.
Seasonal availability: Year round.
Remarks: Probably the best of the sea bream, it is highly prized in mainland Europe. Most frequently known in this country by its French name, *Daurade*. Although the gilthead swims in warm waters, it is occasionally found in the English Channel. It is an extremely attractive fish with a juicy white flesh and large, easily handled bones. Because of the imports, we can enjoy this fish all the year round, grilled, baked or fried.

It is particularly popular among those of my customers who run Italian restaurants. Use any of the recipes given for sea bream. One fish should be enough for two or three people.

SEA BREAM EN PAPILLOTE

We like this recipe from Anna Del Conte's *Secrets from an Italian Kitchen* because it is so simple and keeps all the flavours in the package.

For 4:
4 sea bream, each about 225g/8oz, gutted and scaled, but retaining head and tail
2–3 tablespoons mixed fresh herbs, such as parsley, basil, fennel, marjoram, rosemary, 1–2 sage leaves, thyme

1 small clove or ½ large clove garlic, peeled
Salt and pepper
Juice of a ½ lemon
3 tablespoons extra virgin olive oil

85

Rinse the fish well and pat dry, inside and out, set aside. Preheat the oven to 200°C/400°F. Finely chop all the herbs and the garlic. Transfer to a bowl, season with salt and pepper, add the lemon juice, then gradually beat in the oil to thicken.

Cut four squares of greaseproof paper or foil, each large enough to wrap around a fish. Brush with a little oil. Lay a fish on each square, spoon a little sauce inside and around the fish. Fold the paper or foil around the fish and twist the edges to seal.

Put the parcels in a baking tin and cook in the oven for 15 minutes. Serve by placing the parcels on individual plates and open by cutting off the twisted edge.

Miss Del Conte recommends eating the fish with plenty of crusty white bread and followed by a salad.

● *Bream, Red Sea*

French: *Commune*
German: *Nordische Meerbrassen*
Spanish: *Besugo, Esparido*

Category: Round, laterally flattened, white.
Waters: Home waters, Mediterranean.
Shape and colour: Compressed round/oval body. Orange-rose back paling to a pink belly and with a distinctive large smudge behind the head. It has sharp spiny fins and large scales.
Price: High, fresh; moderate, frozen.
Market size: 25–40cm/10–15in.
Sold as: Whole fish.
Market availability: Fresh, fair to good in season; frozen, good.
Seasonal availability: June–December, fresh; year round, frozen.
Remarks: Definitely one of my favourites with firm white flavourful flesh. Large bones make easy eating. It is very good baked in foil or steamed.

Clean and scale, slash three or four times on each side. Rub over the surface and into the cuts, a mixture of 1 tablespoon dry sherry, 1 tablespoon ginger juice, 1 teaspoon sea salt. Let the fish stand for about 30 minutes. Prepare your steamer. If you use a bamboo steamer, line it with *bok choi* or lettuce leaves. Lay your fish in the steamer, pour over it a mixture of 1 tablespoon soy sauce, 1 tablespoon vegetable oil (which can have a few drops of sesame oil added), and sprinkle over a few slivers of finely sliced spring onion. Put the lid on your steamer and steam for about 15–20 minutes. Test with the tip of a knife. Serve direct to table. A 1kg/2lb fish will serve 2–3 people.

Brill

French: *Barbue*
German: *Glattbut, Kleist*
Spanish: *Remol*

Category: Flat.
Waters: Home waters.
Shape and colour: Round disc-like body; light brown to grey back and white underside; small scales.
Price: Moderate to high.
Market size: 30+–50cm/12–20in.
Sold as: Whole fish and fillets.
Market availability: Fair to good.
Seasonal availability: Year round, but best in summer months.
Remarks: An under-rated fish with creamy moist flesh and a super flavour. Anything you can do with the expensive turbot, you can certainly do with brill. It's becoming more popular at the time of writing, so the price will probably jump. To tell the difference between brill and turbot touch the top dark side—turbot has little nodules while the brill has a smooth skin. Some might feel that while the flesh is not as fine as that of the turbot, it has more flavour.

There are a number of recipes that recommend combining strips of salmon with brill. Well, it might look pretty, but I don't believe it does either fish any favour.

The Victorian chef, gourmet and traveller, Alexis Soyer, was a man of extraordinary and eccentric talent, and of firm opinions. The following recipe appeals particularly because of its name and the unusual spelling in the text.

BRILL À LA BILLINGSGATE

'Broil the fish as for brill à la meunière *and dish it without a napkin; then have ready the following sauce—blanch a pint of muscles [sic], beard them and take out the black spots, then put two chopped eschalots in a stewpan with one ounce of butter, pass it over the fire five minutes, then add half a tablespoon of flour, mix with it the liquor from the muscles, half a pint of milk, and half a gill of cream, a saltspoonful of salt, a little white pepper, and some grated nutmeg, boil it until rather thick, pass it through a tammie, then add two pats of butter, a few drops of essence of anchovy and the muscles; pour over the fish and serve very hot.'*

It is quite a simple dish. The mussel sauce is not difficult to achieve, and is extremely good.

1 medium-size brill
(approximately 750g/
1½lb), cleaned and left on
the bone, or in 4 fillets
1–2 tablespoons olive oil or
30g/1oz butter (to grease
dish)
Pinch of sea salt
Fresh ground white pepper
500g/1 pint mussels (in shell)
30g/1oz butter

2 shallots or 1 small onion,
chopped
1 tablespoon flour
120ml/4fl.oz milk
60ml/2fl.oz cream
Few gratings of nutmeg
Essence of anchovy (quite
strong, use only 4 or 5
drops to start, add more to
taste)

Rinse and pat dry the brill. Rinse and debeard the mussels, discarding those that don't close when tapped. Butter or oil an ovenproof dish, preferably one you can take straight to the table. Lay in the brill, drizzle over a little oil or melted butter, sprinkle with a little sea salt and a few grindings of white pepper. Cook in a preheated oven (190°C/380°F) for approximately 15 minutes or until fish is just cooked through. Remove from the heat and keep warm.

While the fish is cooking, put the mussels in a saucepan with a little water, cover and put over a high heat for 2 or 3 minutes or until all the mussels are open (discard those that don't open). Strain the mussels, reserving all the liquid; remove the mussel flesh and reserve.

In a saucepan over low to medium heat, melt 30g/1oz butter, add the shallots or onion and, stirring, cook until they are soft and transparent. Add the flour, stirring and cooking gently to make a roux. Add the reserved mussel liquor, stir to blend; add the milk, stir to blend; add the cream, stir to blend. Add a few gratings of nutmeg and the essence of anchovy, and some white pepper. Continue cooking, stirring occasionally, to reduce and thicken.

Strain the sauce (though some people don't mind having the chopped shallots in the sauce), add the mussels, stir, test for seasoning, add sea salt/pepper/anchovy essence to taste. Pour over the brill and serve immediately. Serves 4.

Or, brush a baking dish with butter or oil, lay in the brill fillets, brush with butter, season with sea salt and pepper (or paprika) and bake for about 15–20 minutes. Remove from the oven and serve immediately with a piece of anchovy or other flavoured butter of your choice on top. Serve with steamed beans or broccoli.

BRILL WITH RED WINE AND SHALLOTS

A wonderfully simple recipe from the chef, Ian McAndrew, published in his *A Feast of Fish*. People don't often think of using red wine with fish, yet there is no good reason for not doing so. While brill is used here, it would work equally well with other fillets, such as John Dory or turbot, but cheaper fish could also be used.

4–6 fillet steaks of brill (or other fish), about 180g/6oz per person
240g/8oz shallots, finely sliced
Salt and freshly ground white pepper

180ml/6fl.oz red wine
600ml/1 pint good fish stock
180g/6oz cold butter, cut into smallish cubes
Sprigs of chervil, coriander or parsley to garnish

Butter an ovenproof pan large enough to take the fillets without over-lapping. Sprinkle the sliced shallots over the bottom of the pan, lay the fish on top, season with salt and pepper. Add the red wine and the stock, and cover the pan with foil or buttered greaseproof paper. Heat on top of the stove bringing the liquid to a bare simmer—quivering point. Transfer to a moderately warm oven (preheated to 160°C/325°F) and cook for a further 4–6 minutes without allowing the liquid to boil until the fish is opaque and just cooked through. Remove the fish and shallots from the pan, cover and keep warm.

Transfer the cooking liquid to a saucepan, boil to reduce by about half. Lower the heat slightly and gradually add the cubes of cold butter, beating with a small whisk until all the butter has melted. The sauce should not boil again after the butter has been added.

Either on a platter, or divided between individual plates, serve the fillets on top of the shallots and pour the sauce around. Garnish with your chosen herb. Serves 4–6.

Mr McAndrew has another similar recipe with a *rich* red wine sauce which omits the shallots and uses fish stock and veal stock (rarely to hand in the domestic kitchen) and a pint of red burgundy. He recommends the best quality you can afford. I'm not sure I would have the heart to cook with it.

Carp, Common

French: *Carpe*
German: *Karpfen*
Spanish: *Carpa*

Category: Round, freshwater.
Waters: Home and European fresh waters.
Shape and colour: Round deep plump golden-brown body, large heavy scales and soft fins, the mouth bearing barbels.
Price: Low.
Market size: 30–50cm/12–20in.
Sold as: Whole fish.
Market availability: Fair.
Seasonal availability: Year round, except April and May when spawning. Farmed and imported all year.
Remarks: Carp available in British shops are usually farmed in Holland or Israel, especially mirror carp, and normally weigh less than 2.5kg/5lb. They are rather bony, but the flesh has a good flavour. It is a bottom feeding fish and wild carp need careful cleaning to eliminate any 'muddy' flavour. It is very common and eaten regularly in mainland Europe. I think my mother cooked the best carp.

Take a whole, cleaned fish, cut as if into steaks but without cutting through the backbone. Put in a very lightly buttered or oiled baking dish and surround with peeled and sliced potatoes, carrots, onions and celery. Season—with pepper and sugar if you would like it Romanian-style, or pepper and salt if in the Polish fashion. Cover with fish or chicken stock and a little white wine and cook until the vegetables are cooked through. A 1–1.5kg/2–3lb fish will serve 4.

Another way to cook a carp is to have it cleaned through the gills (ask your fishmonger) and stuff it with a mixture of cheap white fish, seasoned with salt, pepper and a pinch of fresh or dried herbs, combined with an egg to bind and a spoonful of dry breadcrumbs or matzah meal. Cut the stuffed fish as above, place in a lightly buttered or oiled baking dish, add a little stock, a little wine and a few chopped vegetables, cover and bake for about 30–40 minutes, checking from time to time that it doesn't dry out, and adding more stock or wine as necessary.

CARP

Izaak Walton's *Piscator* tells us how to deal with a carp, and an amazingly

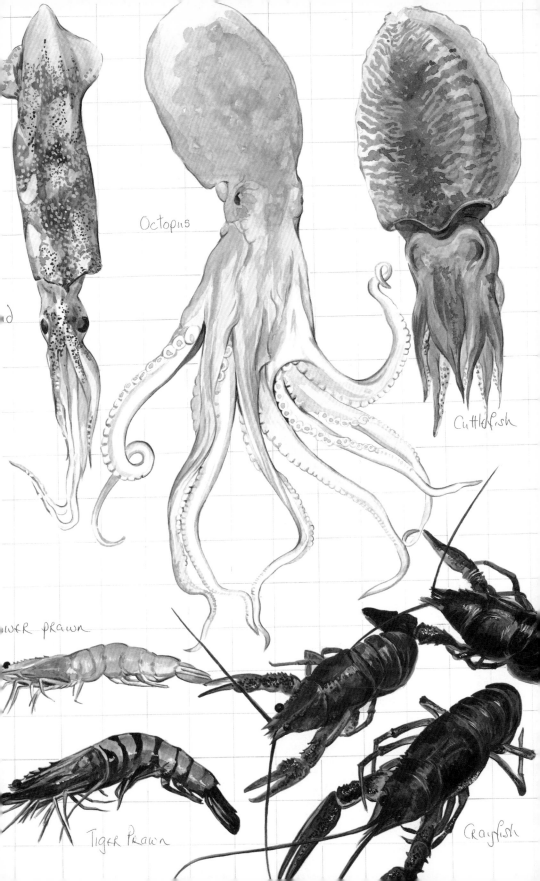

Octopus

Cuttlefish

...d

...wer Prawn

Tiger Prawn

Crayfish

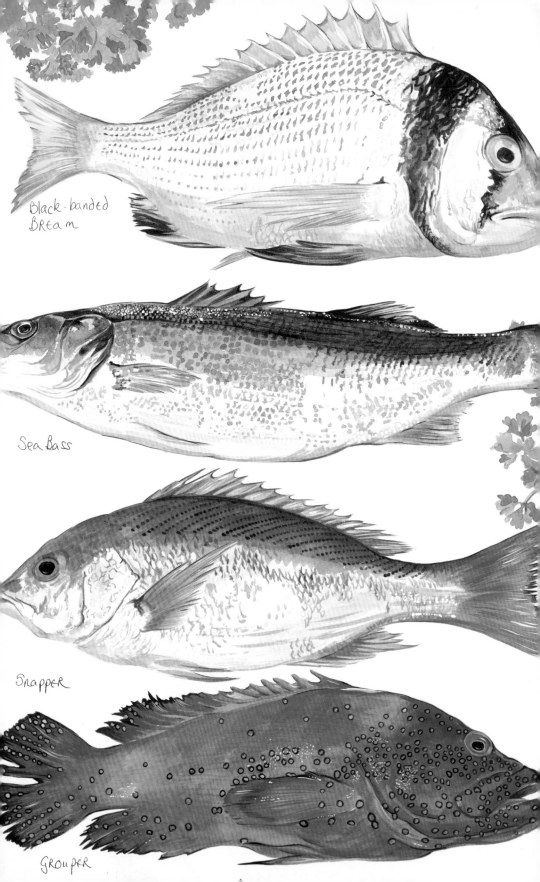

Black-banded Bream

Sea Bass

Snapper

Grouper

complex dish it must have been: 'Put him . . . and his liver . . . into a small pot or kettle; then take sweet marjoram, thyme, and parsley, of each half a handful, a sprig of rosemary, and another of savory, bind them into two or three small bundles, and put them to your carp, with four or five whole onions, twenty pickled oysters, and three anchovies. Then pour upon your carp as much claret wine as will only cover him, and season your claret well with salt, cloves, and mace, and the rinds of oranges and lemons; that done, cover your pot and set it on a quick fire till it be sufficiently boiled; then take out the carp and lay it with the broth into the dish, and pour upon it a quarter of a pound of the best fresh butter, melted and beaten with half-a-dozen spoonfuls of the broth, the yolks of two or three eggs, and some of the herbs shred; garnish your dish with lemons, and so serve it up, and much good do you.'

The writer James Bentley spends half his time in France and has written a delightful account of *Life and Food in the Dordogne*. In it he includes Curnonsky's (Maurice Edmond Sailland, the French writer and gastronome) relatively simple, though these days outrageously expensive, recipe for stuffed carp which seasons that modest fish with cognac, stuffs it with chopped *foie gras*, and studs it with truffle. It must be very, very good.

Dr Bentley also gives us a much simpler way to deal with this fish which he learned from his farming neighbours.

CARP STUFFED WITH MUSHROOMS

Morilles, the mushrooms traditionally used, are not easy to find fresh in Britain, but you can buy them dried though they are fiendishly expensive. Soak in a little water for about 15 minutes.

For one medium-sized carp—about 1kg/2lb—you need the soft crumbs of 2 slices bread, 125g/¼lb morilles (or substitute field mushrooms), finely chopped, a beaten egg, and some thyme. Mix them together thoroughly, season with a little salt and pepper or cayenne, and stuff the fish, fastening it with toothpicks.

Put the fish in a buttered baking dish, brush with a little olive oil, add a glassful or two of white or red wine and a sprig of thyme. Cover loosely and bake in a preheated oven for 25–30 minutes until the fish is cooked through. Remove the fish to a serving plate, and use the cooking juices to make a quick sauce with a sautéed chopped shallot, a teaspoonful of mustard and some chopped parsley. Serves 3–4.

This dish was washed down with the excellent local *red* wine.

Catfish

French: *Loup*
German: *Katfisch*
Spanish: *Lobo*

Category: Round freshwater.
Waters: Some European freshwaters.
Shape and colour: Dark scaleless elongated body with a flat head, and around its mouth a set of six barbels or whiskers.
Price: Moderate.
Market size: Up to 45cm/18in.
Sold as: Whole live fish and fillets.
Market availability: Fair.
Seasonal availability: Year round (farmed).
Remarks: Usually imported. Catfish can live out of water for some time and that is why they can be bought live (in Chinese communities they can sometimes be found kept live in tanks). The flesh of catfish is white, moist and quite soft, and has a mild flavour. Depending on the waters from which it has been taken, catfish can sometimes have a slightly earthy flavour. If you think this is the case, rinse it thoroughly in vinegared water, or water with lemon juice. I don't normally stock it, but I do get it on order for some of my Chinese clients. Supermarkets sometimes stock catfish fillets.

Skinned fillets are very good rolled in seasoned flour—add a little paprika and a pinch of dried herb—and shallow fried in olive oil or a mixture of oil and butter until golden brown. Or dress in egg and seasoned dry breadcrumbs. Serve with a sauce of your choice, or pour off the excess oil in the frying pan and deglaze with half a glass of white wine or vermouth, add some snipped fresh dill or chopped parsley or coriander, and pour over the fish.

Char

French: *Omble*
German: *Saiblinge*
Spanish: *Salverino*

Category: Round freshwater.
Waters: Most northern cold waters of the United Kingdom.
Shape and colour: Closely resembles the trout and salmon with a streamlined body. Its colouring is similar to brown trout, a dark brown

body going to dark gold sides and belly with numerous spots over back and sides.

Market size: 25–35cm/10–15in.
Sold as: Whole fish and fillets.
Market availability: Poor to fair.
Seasonal availability: All year, farmed.
Remarks: Though it resembles the trout and salmon, char has a less distinctive flavour. It is being farmed increasingly nowadays and I believe it will become an important food in the future.

An average char will serve 4–6 people. Treat as salmon: poach or bake.

Season with salt and pepper, put sprigs of fresh dill or fennel and a bayleaf in the cavity, lay on oiled foil with a few more sprigs of fresh herb and 2 quarters of lemon, and pour 2–3 tablespoons white wine or vermouth over the fish. Enfold the fish in the foil leaving space around the fish, but making an airtight package, and bake for 25–30 minutes. Let the fish rest for 5–10 minutes after removal from the oven, then open the foil package and transfer to a serving dish with the juices. Skin if you prefer. New potatoes and a steamed fresh green vegetable complete an excellent dish.

Cod

French: *Cabillaud, Morue*
German: *Kabeljau, Dorsch*
Spanish: *Bacalao*

Category: Round white.
Waters: Home waters.
Shape and colour: Small-scaled fish with greenish-grey back with mottling, paling to lightish grey on the sides and a white belly.
Price: Moderate.
Market size: 35+–100cm/14+–36in.
Sold as: Fresh whole fish (codling), fillets, cutlets/steaks; dried, salted and smoked fillets.
Market availability: Excellent.
Seasonal availability: Year round, best in winter months.
Remarks: Firm white flesh, with good flavour; large bones, easy to handle.

Cod is the most popular fish in the United Kingdom and there is some fear that it is being over-fished. It is a good fish on which to try your strength if you use a rod and line; its colours change very rapidly when it is taken out of the water from green to grey.

There are probably as many ways to prepare cod as there are weeks in the year. It combines well with other fish in soups and stews, and in pies. Whatever you can do with a cod fillet or steak, you can do with fillets or steaks of coley, haddock, hake, ling or whiting. The head chef at Blake's Hotel even fries codskins to use as a garnish.

Alexandre Dumas stuffed a small cod with pounded whiting and anchovies, laid it in a dish with butter and parsley, covered it with Parmesan cheese and breadcrumbs, cooked it in a bottle's worth of white wine, then suggested you served it with 'any sauce you think fit'. Doesn't sound too bad.

Cod cheeks and tongues are also sold in some regions of the country. I don't stock them myself—they are most popular north of the Wash—they are considered quite a delicacy. They would probably be very good served in a cheese-flavoured white sauce.

And don't forget the seasonal fresh cod's roe which appears between November and March. Because they are large, they are normally boiled by your fishmonger to enable him to slice off the amount that you want. They make very good fish cakes, either on their own or mixed with other fish.

COD CUTLETS EN PAPILLOTE

4 cod cutlets (allow 180–250g/6–8oz each, depending on appetite) 50g/2oz butter	Juice of half a lemon or lime Salt and pepper Coarsely chopped coriander or parsley for garnish

Preheat the oven to 180°C/375°F.

Butter four pieces of greaseproof paper or aluminium foil each big enough to parcel a cod cutlet. Place a cutlet in the middle of each paper, dot each cutlet with butter, pour over each a little lemon or lime juice and season with salt and pepper. Fold the paper or foil around each cutlet making four parcels, place on a baking tray and cook for 20 minutes. To serve, put a parcel on each plate, open and garnish with coriander or parsley. A dash of Tabasco adds a fillip. Serves 4.

Alternative fish: coley, haddock, salmon.

BAKED COD WITH SAFFRON AND RED PEPPERS

Saffron is expensive and can be omitted, but the richness of colour and depth of its flavour would be lost. The amounts given of garlic, saffron, cayenne and salt can be adjusted to taste.

4 cod steaks (180–240g/ 6–8oz each)
Lemon juice
150ml/5fl.oz olive oil
1 large red pepper, seeds removed, cut into small chunks or diced
3 garlic cloves, finely chopped
Pinch (about ¼ teaspoon) saffron threads dissolved in a teaspoon of water
½ teaspoon cayenne
½ teaspoon sea salt
½ teaspoon dried thyme
Sea salt and ground black pepper to taste
2 tablespoons finely chopped parsley

Rinse the fish and thoroughly pat dry. Sprinkle with a little lemon juice and set aside.

In a frying pan heat 120ml/4fl.oz olive oil, add the red pepper and cook until it is soft—about 10 minutes. Add the garlic, saffron, cayenne and salt, stir and cook very briefly.

In a baking dish large enough to hold the fish in one layer, spread the mixture and lay in the fish, turning once to ensure that both surfaces of the fish are coated in the pepper mixture. Sprinkle the rest of the olive oil over the fish, the dried thyme and additional salt and the ground pepper to taste. Bake in a preheated oven (180°C/350°F) for 20 minutes or until the fish is cooked through. Sprinkle with the parsley and serve. Serves 4.

Alternative fish: coley, conger eel, halibut.

Coley (Also known as Coalfish, Blackjack, Saithe)

French: *Lieu Noir, Colin*
Spanish: *Polero, Carbonaro*
German: *Kohler, Seelachs*

Category: Round white.
Waters: Home waters.
Shape and colour: Similar to cod. Blackish or dark green back paling towards the silverish underside.
Price: Low.
Market size: 60–100cm/2–3ft.
Sold as: Fillets and cutlets.
Market availability: Very good.
Seasonal availability: Year round, though better in summer.
Remarks: Has been an unfairly despised fish though it is becoming more popular with a matching increase in price. Its greyish flesh turns white on cooking and in all ways it can be used as one uses cod. Particularly good to eat with strong-flavoured sauces or butters, it is also very good curried or prepared with a mix of soy and spices.

It is sometimes confused with pollack which has slightly different marking; the young of both fish are sometimes known as 'billet'.

SPICED COLEY

One of Jackie's favourites, and equally good hot or cold. It can be served as a starter or as a hot main dish with rice. The fillet does not need to be skinned.

1–1.5kg/2–3lb coley fillet, part of a large fillet is best as it's thicker
90ml/3fl.oz oil
60ml/2fl.oz dark soy sauce
Juice of 1 lime or lemon
½ small red capsicum, finely chopped
2 shallots, finely chopped
1 large clove garlic, finely chopped or crushed
1 red or green chilli, finely chopped

2.5cm/1in piece of ginger, finely chopped
½ teaspoon ground coriander
Fresh coriander or parsley, finely chopped, about 3 tablespoons
2–3 tablespoons dry breadcrumbs
Coriander or parsley to garnish

ROUND AND FLAT FISH

Lay the fish in a shallow baking dish. Combine in a bowl the oil, soy, lime or lemon juice, chopped capsicum, shallots, garlic, chilli, ginger, ground coriander and chopped coriander or parsley. Pour the mixture over the fish and let it stand for about 15 minutes. Sprinkle the breadcrumbs on top. Bake in a moderate preheated oven for 15–20 minutes or until the fish is cooked through, or put under the grill, but watch that the breadcrumbs don't burn. Garnish with sprigs of coriander or parsley. Serves 6.

Conger Eel (Conger)

French: *Congre*
German: *Congeraal, Meeraal*
Spanish: *Congrio*

Category: Round white.
Waters: Home waters.
Shape and colour: Powerful serpent-like body with a flattened tail; black back, blue- or brown-grey sides and white underside; no scales.
Price: Low to moderate.
Market size: 50cm–3m/2–9ft.
Sold as: Cutlets.
Market availability: Very good.
Seasonal availability: Year round, better during summer months.
Remarks: An old-fashioned fish, mainly bought by appreciative grannies and grandads (no doubt the young will learn in time). I've caught a few in my time on rod and line and it has firm, well-flavoured flesh which keeps longer than most other fish. The tail is very bony and is best used for soups and stock. A poached cutlet with parsley sauce is excellent.

Dab

French: *Limande*
German: *Scharbe, Kliesche*
Spanish: *Limanda, Limanda Nordica*

Category: Flat.
Waters: Home waters.
Shape and colour: Perhaps the smallest flat fish sold. It has a coarse sandy-brown back and a white underside.
Price: Low.
Market size: 15–25cm/6–10in.
Sold as: Whole fresh fish.

97

Market availability: Fair to good.

Seasonal availability: Year round.

Remarks: A very under-rated fish. Its flesh is sweet and tender though a degree of care is necessary in handling the small bones. One of my favourite fish when shallow fried.

You don't need to do anything much to it except clean, rinse and pat dry. Dip in seasoned flour and fry in olive oil. Sprinkle with finely chopped parsley and coriander and serve with a slice of lemon.

We used to a catch a lot of dabs off the south coast. They are quite long-lived out of water, and a large one is quite a find.

Dolphin Fish (Mahi-Mahi)

French: *Dorado*
Spanish: *Lampuga, Dorado*

Category: Round, laterally flattened.

Waters: Mediterranean, Indian Ocean.

Shape and colour: A marvellous looking fish, its large compressed elongated body tapers quickly to a forked tail, and its dorsal fin runs the whole length of the body. Gender is distinguished by the shape of the head: the male's forehead is square, and the female's slopes back. The blue-green back pales to a yellow-white underside, and occasionally the fish is spotted overall.

Price: Moderate–high.

Market size: 1–1.5m/3–5ft.

Sold as: Cutlets and fillets; frozen cutlets.

Market availability: Fair (fresh); good (frozen). Has been seen in supermarkets prepared in battered portions ready for cooking.

Seasonal availability: Most of year.

Remarks: The flesh is dark and very succulent.

This fish is absolutely no relation to that delightful mammal, the dolphin. Probably seen more frequently in the south east, but its popularity is spreading, and it is sometimes seen in some of the larger supermarkets as fillets or as pieces ready breadcrumbed. I have been gratified to note that some supermarkets are honest enough to announce on the label when the fillets have been frozen.

I ate a lot of this fish while on holiday in Florida, mainly fillet simply grilled or barbecued with lemon squeezed over.

At the time of writing mahi-mahi had started to be imported from the United States as either fresh whole fish or large fillets.

GRILLED MAHI-MAHI WITH CORIANDER SAUCE

We found this recipe in the beautiful *A Visual Feast: The Year in Food* by Arabella Boxer and Tessa Traeger. It's a wonderfully simple way to cook a piece of fish and would suit any firm-fleshed fish.

For 4–6, using 1 steak of approximately 2.5cm/1in thickness per person. Preheat the grill or barbecue. Brush the steaks on each side with olive oil, and grill them for 4 or 5 minutes on each side until cooked through. In the meantime mix thoroughly 4 tablespoons olive oil and 1 tablespoon lemon juice, then stir in about 3 tablespoons chopped fresh coriander. Serve the sauce in a small jug with the grilled steaks laid on a platter and garnished with coriander.

You could substitute lime for the lemon juice and slightly increase the amount if you wish; or make the mixture slightly more aromatic with a ½ teaspoon ground coriander or ground cardamom; or give it a bit of zip with a pinch of cayenne.

Dover Sole

French: *Sole Commune*
German: *Seezunge*
Spanish: *Lenquado*

Category: Flat.
Waters: Home waters and Mediterranean.
Shape and colour: Its blunt-nosed body is dark brown on the back with a white underside.
Price: Very high.
Market size: 25–55cm/10-20in. Sole of 20–25cm/8–10in are called 'slips'; those of 15–20cm/6–8in are called 'tongues'.
Sold as: Whole fish, fresh.
Market availability: Very good, fresh and frozen.
Seasonal availability: Year round.
Remarks: A highly prized and popular quality fish with good flavour and texture. Some believe it is best left a day or so for the flesh to soften and the flavour to develop. It has a very hard coarse skin and should be skinned before cooking. Restaurants, or perhaps more accurately, waiters, love it because it comes off the bone so easily after cooking. It is frequently filleted, in which form Escoffier lists more than 180 ways to cook it.

I think it should be cooked as simply as possible.

For example, whole slip sole, skinned, brushed with egg white, dipped in lightly seasoned flour, then shallow fried in butter or a mixture of oil and butter for 2–3 minutes on each side could hardly be bettered.

In 1935, (John) Quaglino presented to the public *The Complete Hostess*, intended 'to help all wives and housekeepers' and to give 'not only recipes but the details of how to order and how to buy, so that every housewife may know how to entertain'. Well, half his intention—the bit about ordering and buying—is shared with our own endeavour. But his assumptions about the contents and capabilities of the average domestic kitchen seem totally at odds with today's realities. Quaglino's *Delice de Sole* Royal Jubilee takes fillets of sole (laid on 'a marble table'), piped with raw mousseline of sole, filled with a slice of cooked lobster, a mushroom and a slice of truffle and cooked with stock and white wine. The sauce was thickened with hollandaise and cream, and the fish placed on a mixture of crab meat and apple, sauce poured over and the whole lightly browned.

SOLE MIMI

Some years ago, a small book appeared which was a collection of recipes drawn mainly from two quite substantial households and their cooks. Fortune Stanley edited these collections which became *English Country House Cooking* and the following simple dish comes from it. While it specifies sole, the method could be applied to any skinned fillet of white fish.

4–6 fillets of sole (or other white fish)	30–60g/1–2oz grated mature cheddar cheese
60g/2oz butter	150ml/¼ pint double cream
Ground black or white pepper to taste	1 teaspoon Dijon mustard
	1 teaspoon Worcester sauce
4–6 tablespoons good dry breadcrumbs	1 teaspoon anchovy essence

Rinse the fish and pat thoroughly dry. In an ovenproof serving dish, melt the butter, lay the fillets in, turning once to coat them with the butter. Season with pepper. Sprinkle with the breadcrumbs and the cheddar cheese. Bake in a preheated oven 200°C/400°F for about 20 minutes until the top is golden. Whip together the cream, mustard, Worcester sauce and anchovy essence, and serve the sauce with the baked fish. Serves 4–6.

If you want to reduce the fat content of the sauce, replace the cream with *fromage frais* or yoghurt.

Eel

French: *Anguille*
German: *Aal, Flussaal*
Spanish: *Anguila*

Category: Round.
Waters: Home fresh waters, with some New Zealand imports.
Shape and colour: Dark green to black snake-like body with pale belly.
Price: Moderate.
Market size: 24–75cm/10–30in.
Sold as: Whole fish (live), fillets or pieces, and smoked.
Market availability: Very good.
Seasonal availability: Year round (with imports).
Remarks: Eels spend most of their lives in rivers, but the silver (adult) eels migrate to the Sargasso Sea to spawn in the autumn and to die. The young eels return to the rivers their parents came from. As every schoolchild learns, they are known as elvers and are about 7–8cm/3in long. Occasionally seen on the fishmonger's slab. For the adventurous and insomniac, catching eels at night is known as 'babbing'.

I remember gingerly eating my first jellied eel when I was 15 years old at Tubby Isaac's in Petticoat Lane market, with spiced vinegar and lumps of fresh bread. I have been a firm fan ever since. The famous oysterage at Orford Ness in Suffolk also supplies smoked eel, a great treat with a little horseradish and a sprinkle of lemon juice.

COLIN WILLOCK'S RICHMOND EEL PIE

Brown 2 small onions or shallots in butter. Add parsley, salt, pepper, nutmeg, 2 glasses sherry (or substitute Noilly Prat). Add 750g/1½lb skinned eels, chopped into 2.5cm/1in pieces, cover with water and bring slowly to boil, reduce the heat and simmer for 5 minutes. Remove the eel pieces and arrange in a buttered or oiled pie dish. Make a sauce with the strained liquor using 60g/2oz butter, 60g/2oz flour and the juice of a lemon. Add 2 sliced hard-boiled eggs, bacon and mushrooms. Cover with puff pastry and bake for 1 hour. Serves 4–6.

If you want your eel skinned it is best done by your fishmonger, but there is an instruction on p. 31.

Eels cut in 2.5cm/1in lengths, tossed in seasoned flour, and fried in oil flavoured with bacon and herbs, drained of excess oil on kitchen paper, make an excellent meal. Or curry them.

Flake See **Huss**.

Flounder (Fluke)

French: *Flet*
German: *Flunder, Butt*
Spanish: *Platija*

Category: Flat.
Waters: Home waters.
Shape and colour: Brown or greenish back and white underside. Same group as plaice and dab, but smooth-skinned. Can also be found in rivers, particularly estuaries.
Price: Low.
Market size: 15–40cm/6–15in.
Sold as: Whole fish.
Market availability: Fair to good.
Seasonal availability: Year round, but best in winter months.
Remarks: Rather watery flesh; not as good as plaice, but given its comparatively low price a good choice for using in any recipe calling for a cheap white fish fillet. The bones are ideal for the stockpot. To tell the difference between plaice and flounder, rub your finger across their heads—the plaice has bony nodules where the flounder is quite smooth.

The book *British Cookery*, sponsored by the British Farm Produce Council and the British Tourist Authority, gives the following recipe for flounder.

FLOUNDER WITH SORREL

---

16 small flounder fillets	60–90ml/2–3fl.oz fish stock
250g/8oz sliced onions (or use shallots)	500g/1lb sorrel
	50g/2oz butter, melted
60–90ml/2–3fl.oz dry white wine	Salt and pepper

Arrange the fish fillets in a baking dish, cover with the sliced onions or shallots, pour over them the wine and stock and cover with buttered greaseproof paper. Bake in a preheated oven for 25–30 minutes until the fish is cooked through. Meanwhile, put the sorrel in a saucepan with a little water, bring to the boil and cook until the sorrel is limp. Drain well and chop finely. Stir in the melted butter, season with salt and pepper. Spread the sorrel mixture over the cooked fish and serve. Serves 6–8.

You could substitute sole, dab or brill, and use spinach instead of sorrel in which case you could use the ready chopped frozen spinach to which we would add a little grated nutmeg or ground coriander.

Garfish

French: *Orphie*
German: *Hornhecht*
Spanish: *Ajuga*

Category: Round.
Waters: Home waters.
Shape and colour: A strange elongated needle-snouted slender fish with a beautiful green or dark-blue back and silver sides and belly.
Price: Low.
Market size: 30–60cm/12–24in.
Sold as: Whole fish.
Market availability: Fair.
Seasonal availability: Summer months.
Remarks: Sometimes known as 'needle' or 'pipe' fish, it is much under-rated as its flesh has a good flavour and texture. Unfortunately it is subject to prejudice because its bones are green both before and after cooking. I find this rather attractive and certainly a conversation piece. I stock it now and again to try to break the prejudice. Use it for grilling, baking or frying.

I have recently come across *The Great Book of Seafood Cooking* by Giuliana Bonomo which has been translated from Italian. It contains a number of excellent recipes among which is:

GARFISH BRAISED IN RED WINE

---

2 garfish, about 500g/1lb each (or 1 fish, 750g–1kg/1½–2lb)
Flour for dredging
60ml/2fl.oz olive oil
1 small bunch parsley, finely chopped

2 cloves garlic, finely chopped or crushed
1 small onion, finely chopped
Juice of 1 lemon
120ml/4fl.oz dry red wine
Salt and freshly ground white pepper

Clean the fish, discarding any roe, cut off the heads, and cut into large, even-sized slices. Rinse and pat dry. Coat the fish pieces with flour, shaking off excess.

103

Heat the oil in a large frying or sauté pan, add the parsley, garlic and onion, and sweat the mixture over a low heat. Add the pieces of floured fish and sauté lightly, turning once with tongs or a fish slice. Sprinkle with lemon juice, add the wine, season with salt and freshly ground pepper. Simmer, uncovered, for about 15 minutes over moderate heat. The fish should be tender but not sloppy; increase the heat to reduce liquid.

Greenland Halibut (Mock Halibut, Black Halibut)

French: *Fletan Noir*
German: *Schwarzer Heilbutt*
Spanish: *Hipogloss Negro*

Category: Flat.
Waters: North Atlantic.
Shape and colour: A large flat fish, but much smaller than a true halibut. It is greenish-grey on both sides.
Price: Moderate.
Market size: from 60cm/24in.
Sold as: Steaks, cutlets or fillets.
Market availability: Good, mainly frozen.
Seasonal availability: Year round (imports).
Remarks: Mock halibut is a name sometimes used in the trade. It should not be confused with chicken or small halibut. The difference is in the skin: true halibut is dark on one side and white on the other; Greenland halibut is dark on both sides and the flesh is perhaps a little coarser and drier. But it can still be used as a true halibut and baked, grilled, fried, steamed or poached.

Nearly all the smoked halibut you see is Greenland halibut.

In *The Fish Course* Sue Hicks gives the following recipe for halibut which I think does equally well for Greenland halibut.

4 steaks or fillets (1 per
person)
A little sunflower oil
2 young leeks, trimmed and
very finely sliced (use as
much as you can)
Freshly ground black pepper
Juice and grated rind of
1 lemon, lime or orange

2 large ripe tomatoes, peeled
and sliced
Sprigs of fennel, or finely
chopped parsley and
snipped chives
Garlic mayonnaise (*aioli*) to
serve on the side

Preheat oven to 200°C/400°F. Brush with oil four pieces of foil, each large
enough to make a generous parcel. Rinse the fish and pat dry. Divide half
the chopped leeks between the four pieces of foil and place the fish on top.
Season each piece with freshly ground black pepper and sprinkle over a
little fruit juice and the grated rind. Top with the remaining chopped leeks
and arrange the sliced tomatoes on top. Season again with a little more
pepper and sprinkle with the remaining juice. Gather up the sides of the
foil and crimp to make loose but airtight parcels. Put them on a baking tray
and bake for about 25 minutes.

To serve, place the parcels on warmed plates, peel back the foil and
garnish with the herbs. Or allow each person to open their own parcel.
Pass the garlic mayonnaise separately. Serves 4.

Grey Mullet

French: *Muge, Mulet*
German: *Meerasche*
Spanish: *Lisa, Mujol*

Category: Round white.
Waters: Home waters.
Shape and colour: Flat head and a heavy scaled wedge-shaped body,
medium-grey back and silvery underside.
Price: Low.
Market size: 20+–40cm/8–15in.
Seasonal availability: Year round with imports.
Remarks: Very good value. Around the world there are several different
varieties of grey mullet and all have wonderful white moist flesh and easily

handled large bones. It usually has a delicate sweet flavour, but if taken from estuaries it might have a slightly muddy flavour and should be washed well and rinsed in vinegar before cooking. It is a much under-rated fish and could be a substitute in most sea bass recipes. The roe of the grey mullet is used to make the true *taramasalata*. According to a colleague, the gizzard of a very large mullet can be treated like chicken—split and carefully cleaned to remove waste, then lightly cooked—and is considered a great delicacy. He didn't say by whom.

I remember watching my father skin the mullet roe, cream it with a dinner fork (hard work), then add stale crustless bread (first soaked in milk and squeezed), olive oil and lemon juice. So much nicer than ready made *taramasalata*.

As a short cut you can buy ready prepared the *tarama*, the mullet roe mixed to a paste with salt, and then add the rest of the ingredients to your own taste: usually an equal amount of soaked and squeezed stale white bread plus a little finely chopped onion or garlic.

Small grey mullet cook very well on a barbecue or grill. Add a few herbs and some salt and pepper.

The following recipe for Stuffed Grey Mullet with Bacon and Sage is based on one in Jane Grigson's *Fish Cookery*. Allow about 250g/½lb fish per person, so for four people you could have 2 mullet whole of about 500g/1lb+ each, or for six 2 mullet of about 750g/1½lb+ each. Scale and clean the fish, rinse thoroughly and pat dry inside and out. Slash each fish three or four times on each side, and season inside and out with a little salt and pepper.

Stuffing:

1–2 tablespoons oil	50g/2oz soft breadcrumbs
1 shallot or small onion, finely chopped	Ground black pepper to taste
	50–75g/2–3oz butter
4–6 slices of smoked bacon, finely chopped or minced	120–150ml/4–5fl.oz dry vermouth (Noilly Prat)
About 12 sage leaves, chopped	

In a small frying pan heat the oil and sauté the shallot or onion until transparent. With a slotted spoon remove and reserve. Add the chopped bacon to the pan and quickly fry until any fat is transparent, add the chopped sage leaves and stir quickly to combine.

In a bowl put the breadcrumbs, add the reserved shallot, the bacon mixture, a little ground pepper, and mix thoroughly. Stuff the fish with the mixture and fasten with a toothpick or two.

Grease a baking dish with the butter, and put the stuffed mullet into the dish. Bake in a preheated oven (180°C/350°F) for 15 minutes. Add the vermouth. Return to the oven and cook or a further 10–15 minutes. You could then add, if you like, 90–120g/3–4oz double cream, yoghurt or *crème fraîche*, in which case return to the oven for a further 3 minutes.

Alternative herbs (or even mix them): coriander, parsley, tarragon, thyme.

STEAMED GREY MULLET

---

2 small grey mullet (about 360g/12oz each) or 1 large fish	2 tablespoons oil (you could add a drop or two of sesame oil)
1 teaspoon sea salt	1 tablespoon dark soy sauce
4 spring onions, cut into 5cm/2in lengths and sliced	1 tablespoon slivered ginger (optional)

Wash and dry the fish, slash three or four times on each side, rub a little salt into the cuts and inside the fish. Set up a steamer. Put half the spring onion, oil, soy sauce and optional ginger into the belly cavity of the fish, the remaining half on top. Steam for about 15 minutes or until the fish is cooked through. Serves 2.

Alternative fish: bass, sea bream, grouper, snapper.

Groupers

Groupers come in all shapes and colours and are now being seen more on the British fishmonger's slab, fresh and frozen. All species come from warm or tropical waters; fresh fish are imported from the Mediterranean, the Indian Ocean and the United States as well as the Arabian Gulf and the Caribbean. All have a very deep body, large head and a mouth that looks upwards. Below are descriptions of just a few of my favourites, but *all* have an excellent flavour and firm texture. Apparently some groupers can grow bigger than a man, but usually those species that are eaten grow only up to 10kg/20lb. People have been hesitant about buying these 'exotics', perhaps because most of them are not included in general cookbooks. We are trying to change that.

- *Croissant* (Coral Trout, Crescent Tail Grouper)

Shape and colour: Heavy oval body, eyes high on head, mouth pointing upwards, and large crescent-shaped tail; bright red with pale spots, fins edged in yellow; small scales.

Price: Moderate.

Market size: Up to 60cm/24in.

Sold as: Whole fish.

Market availability: Fair (fresh imports).

Seasonal availability: Year round (imports).

Remarks: A versatile fish that can be used any way you like and, like all groupers, a really top quality fish in texture and flavour that can be grilled, poached, baked or fried.

It's a beautiful fish to look at with its bright red skin and is a show stopper at a party when presented whole. Like all groupers, it has a different flavour when eaten cold. Very popular with my customers.

- *Grouper* (Leopard Coral Trout)

Shape and colour: Heavy oval body, eyes high on head, mouth pointing upwards; bright red with dark-edged blue spots; small scales.

Price: Moderate.

Market size: Up to 45cm/18in.

Sold as: Whole fish.

Market availability: Fair (fresh and frozen imports).

Seasonal availability: Year round (imports).

Remarks: An excellent quality fish with firm white succulent flesh. This fish is also quite spectacular in appearance, and impressive at a dinner party, no matter how you cook it.

- *Grouper* (Vieille Maconde or Honeycomb Grouper)

Shape and colour: Heavy oval body, eyes high on head, mouth pointing upwards; brown and white honeycomb design over body and fins; small scales.

Price: Moderate.

Market size: Up to 45cm/18in.

Sold as: Whole fish.

Market availability: Fair (fresh and frozen imports).

Seasonal availability: Year round (imports).

Remarks: This fish doesn't sell as fast as other groupers because it isn't as pretty as some of its cousins and people tend to buy with their eyes, but nevertheless it is an excellent quality fish with firm white flesh and easily handled bones. Another all rounder.

- *Grouper* (Vieille Rouge or Red Grouper)

Shape and colour: Heavy oval body, eyes quite high on head, mouth pointing upwards; red all over; small scales.

Price: Moderate.

Market size: Up to 45cm/18in.

Sold as: Whole fish.

Market availability: Fair (fresh and frozen imports).

Seasonal availability: Year round (imports).

Remarks: An excellent quality fish with firm white flesh. It keeps its colours when cooked (baked or steamed), as do all groupers, and looks most attractive on the table. Perhaps you could decorate it with holly and try it for Christmas!

GROUPER IN HOT HERB SAUCE

1 × 1–1.5kg/2–3lb grouper, cleaned and scaled	Sprigs of coriander, finely chopped
Sea salt and freshly ground black pepper	1 red chilli, finely chopped (or use just half, depending on tolerance and the chilli)
120ml/4fl.oz olive oil	
Juice of 1 lime or lemon	3–4 canned anchovy fillets, finely chopped
8–10 basil leaves, finely chopped	60ml/2fl.oz dry white wine
3–4 sage leaves, finely chopped	

Rinse the fish and dry thoroughly with kitchen paper. Slash on each side three or four times. Season with a little sea salt and freshly ground pepper. Lay in a baking dish. In a bowl, whisk together the olive oil and lime or lemon juice, add the chopped herbs, chilli and anchovy, and mix thoroughly. Pour the mixture over the fish making sure it enters the slashed flesh. Sprinkle the white wine over. Bake in a moderate preheated oven for 15–20 minutes, basting if necessary. Serves 3–4.

Serve with rice and a salad.

A very simple method of cooking any medium-sized whole fish (up to 1–1.5kg/2–3lb), grouper, John Dory, sea bream or snapper.

Cut a large lemon in very fine slices. Clean, scale, rinse and dry the fish; slash each side three or four times, sprinkle a little sea salt on the fish and on slices of lemon and set aside for at least half an hour. Rinse and dry. Brush with oil a piece of greaseproof paper (parchment) large enough to enclose the fish. Lay on the paper 3 or 4 slices of lemon, and cover with a light sprinkling of freshly ground black or white pepper. Then add the fish, a little more pepper, and more slices of lemon. Sprinkle over about 1 tablespoon oil, and fold the paper around the fish. Bake in a moderate preheated oven for 15–20 minutes.

Serve with the cooking juices poured over. Serves 2 or 3.

As a variation add a little ginger juice to the fish as it stands, and a little freshly ground coriander to the pepper.

Gurnard

French: *Grondin Gris, Rouge or Perlon* (yellow),
Trigle (sometimes confusingly called *rouget*)
German: *Knurrhahn*
Spanish: *Rubio*

Category: Round white.
Waters: Home waters.
Shape and colour: There are three gurnards on the market, the red, grey and yellow (which is rather like the red but bright blue on the rear of the pectoral fin). All have large bony heads with spines, and fast-tapering bodies and wing-like fins.
Price: Low to moderate.
Market size: 25–40cm/10–15in.
Sold as: Whole fish.
Seasonal availability: Year round.
Remarks: Another under-rated fish with good-flavoured firm and sweet white flesh. It is well suited for poaching, frying and baking. The head is particularly good for stock and soup, and gurnard makes an excellent contribution to bouillabaisse. Yet another candidate for discovery by the restaurant trade, and consequent price increase. In the meantime some customers assume it can't be very good because it is so cheap. And it's often used as bait for crab and lobster pots. As Chris Leftwich of Fishmongers' Hall says, 'Lucky old crabs and lobsters.'

110

MADAME PRUNIER'S GRONDINS BEURRE BLANC

In her *Fish Cookery Book* Madame Prunier recommends poaching gurnard fillets in a well-flavoured poaching liquid. The fillets (1 per person) should be removed and kept warm and 2 litres/4 pints of the liquid, with some chopped shallot, rapidly reduced (use a sauté pan or deep-sided fry pan) to about 120ml/4fl.oz. Add, a piece at a time, 60g/2oz chilled butter, over the heat, stirring constantly. When all the butter has been combined and the sauce thickened, pass through a fine sieve and season with salt and pepper. Serve with steamed or new potatoes and hand the butter around separately.

Haddock

French: *Aiglefin, Eglefin*
German: *Schellfisch*
Spanish: *Eglefino*

'. . . *Now to cook the haddock* [which, apparently, she did with sausage].'
Virginia Woolf, *Diaries*, 1941

Category: Round white (cod family).
Waters: Home waters.
Shape and colour: Smaller than the cod, the haddock has a dark grey back and silver underside with a 'thumb print' on the side, behind the head and below the first dorsal fin.
Price: Moderate to high.
Market size: 40–75cm/15–30in.
Sold as: Usually steaks or fillets, but also whole.
Market availability: Very good.
Seasonal availability: Year round, but best during winter months.
Remarks: Softer flesh than the cod and, like that fish, one of the most popular fish in the United Kingdom and at risk from over-fishing. It has white flaky flesh and a good flavour. It is also available smoked.

I haven't seen jumbo haddock (the size for steaks and cutlets) for some time. This would seem to confirm what I noted when on the *Margaret H* in the North Sea—haddock is over-fished and few large ones are left. If you are lucky enough to see a large haddock it is probably from Iceland.

Haddock roe appears between November and March. It is much smaller than cod's roe, and is usually sold raw. But use it in much the same way: fry it as a fishcake or mix it with other fish.

111

HADDOCK AU GRATIN

A good simple supper dish, so long as you can make something approaching a bechamel or velouté sauce. The recipe was found in an old handwritten notebook, so its source is lost, though there are probably dozens like it.

Haddock fillets, approximately 180g/6oz per person
30g/1oz butter
Salt and pepper, paprika or Tabasco or cayenne
240g/8oz button or other mushrooms, lightly cooked in a little oil and butter

Approximately ½ litre/1 pint of good seasoned white sauce, made with milk or stock (fish/chicken) or a mixture of both
30g/1oz breadcrumbs
60g/2oz grated cheese (cheddar/Parmesan)

Butter a baking dish and lay in the fillets, season with ground black or white pepper, a little paprika, Tabasco or cayenne. Cover with the cooked mushrooms, then pour over the sauce. Mix together the breadcrumbs and the cheese and sprinkle over the top. Bake in a moderate oven until the top is browned, 20–30 minutes. Serves 4–6.

Hake

French: *Merlu*
German: *Seehecht*
Spanish: *Merluza*

Category: Round, white (cod family).
Waters: Home waters, Mediterranean.
Shape and colour: Long slow-tapering body with large pointed head, black mouth and ferocious jaws and teeth. The whole body is dark grey and has large loose scales.
Price: Moderate to high.
Market size: 30+–100cm/12–36in.
Sold as: Steaks or whole fish, sometimes fillets.
Market availability: Good.
Seasonal availability: Year round.
Remarks: A fish much appreciated in mainland Europe, especially Portu-

gal and Spain, where the small 'pin' hake is often deep fried. The flesh is white, soft and creamy and some care is needed when handling so as not to damage it. Treat as cod.

In Israel, we were once promised a special treat in Old Jaffa and were taken to what was little more than a broken-down hut. We sat at a rickety table and were amazed to see very expensive cars roll up containing extremely well-dressed and affluent people. Then we discovered why. We were served the best hake I have ever tasted, simply battered and deep fried.

PROVENÇAL BAKED HAKE STEAKS

This dish has a strong Mediterranean flavour with the combination of olive oil, garlic and lemon.

4 thick hake steaks or cutlets, 180–250g/6–8oz each
Sea salt
Juice of 2 lemons
180ml/6fl.oz olive oil
2–3 shallots or 1 onion, finely chopped
2–3 cloves garlic, finely chopped or crushed
3–4 large tomatoes, peeled and chopped
2–3 bayleaves
1 teaspoon paprika
Freshly ground black pepper
Pinch of sugar
4–5 sprigs of parsley, finely chopped

Rinse the fish, and thoroughly pat dry. In a dish large enough to take the steaks in one layer, put the fish and sprinkle over a little sea salt and half the lemon juice. Set aside.

In a frying or sauté pan, heat half the oil and gently cook the shallots and garlic until translucent and just starting to turn brown. Add the tomatoes, bayleaves, paprika, a little salt and pepper, and the sugar. Cook for 3 or 4 minutes, adjust seasoning to taste. Add the chopped parsley, stir to blend, cook for a further minute and remove from the heat.

Lightly oil a baking dish large enough to take the fish in one layer, spread half the tomato mixture into the dish, put in the fish and top with the remaining tomato mixture. Quickly whisk together the remaining oil and lemon juice and pour over the whole dish. Cover the dish with foil and bake in a preheated oven (180°C/350°F) for 20–25 minutes. Uncover and bake for a further 8–10 minutes. Serve with salad and some crusty bread to soak up the juices. Serves 4.

Alternative fish: cod, coley, conger eel, whiting.

Halibut

French: *Fletan*
German: *Heilbutt*
Spanish: *Halibut, Fletan*

'TO THE IMMORTAL MEMORY OF THE HALIBUT
On which I dined this day, Monday, April 26, 1784 . . .
Peace, therefore, and good health, and much good fish
To him who sent thee! and success, as oft . . .
Thy lot thy brethren of the slimy fin
Would envy, could they know that thou wast doom'd
To feed a bard, and to be praised in verse.'
William Cowper

Category: Flat.
Waters: Most northern waters.
Shape and colour: The most magnificent and largest of all flatfish. Grey to olive-green back and white underside.
Price: High–very high.
Market size: The average size your fishmonger will buy it from market will be from 60cm/2ft up to 150–200cm/5–6ft, though the halibut can grow up to 200kg/400lb. Smaller fish would be known as 'chicken' halibut.
Sold as: Steaks, cutlets, fillets.
Market availability: Very good around April, May, June, otherwise sporadic, though some fresh halibut is imported from the north-east coast of the United States, but it is very expensive. It is now starting to be farmed, particularly in Norway. Very good frozen with frozen imports.
Seasonal availability: Year round.
Remarks: Highly prized, and no wonder. It has white moist flaky flesh and even though it's more expensive, most of my customers prefer the fresh to frozen. It is extremely versatile when it comes to cooking. My personal choice is to have it à la Florentine.

Smoked halibut is usually the Greenland or mock halibut.

HALIBUT FLORENTINE

This is one of my favourite dishes. Halibut has a wonderful flesh, but the recipe can also be used for much cheaper fish such as cod, coley, conger eel, hake or whiting.

500g/1lb fresh spinach (or use frozen)
1 teaspoon ground coriander
4 tablespoons single cream
60–90g/2–3oz grated hard cheese

Ground white or black pepper to taste
4 halibut steaks (each about 180g/6oz)
30g/1oz butter
Paprika

Wash and trim the spinach and cook in a little boiling water for 4–5 minutes. Drain and squeeze out all excess water, then finely chop. (If using frozen spinach, heat in a small pan with a little butter until fully defrosted.) Put the spinach in a pan over low heat, add the ground coriander, single cream and grated cheese and stir until the cheese melts. Set aside. Dot the halibut steaks with butter and cook under a hot preheated grill for 3–4 minutes each side. Spread the spinach and cheese mixture on one side of each cutlet, dust with a little paprika, and return to the grill to brown.

Another version would be to serve the grilled fish on a bed of cooked spinach and pour a cheese sauce over it.

Herring

French: *Hareng*
German: *Hering*
Spanish: *Arenque*

> '*Be not sparing,*
> *Leave off swearing;*
> *Buy my Herring*
>   *Fresh from Malahide,*
>   *Better ne'er was try'd.*
> *Come eat 'em with pure fresh Butter and Mustard*
> *Their Bellies are soft and white as a Custard.*
> *Come, Sixpence a Dozen to get me some Bread,*
> *Or, like my own Herrings, I soon shall be dead.*'
>   *Jonathan Swift,* '*STREET CRIES*'

Category: Round, oily.
Waters: Home waters.
Shape and colour: A really handsome streamlined fish, dark blue-green back becoming silver on the sides and belly. A reddish tint around the eyes.
Price: Low.

Market size: 20–25cm/8–10in.

Sold as: Whole fish and fillets. (Known as Sild, when canned.)

Market availability: Very good with fresh and frozen imports.

Seasonal availability: Year round (except after spawning in spring).

Remarks: Surprisingly, the fresh fish is very fragile and needs careful handling. Excellent strong flavour and creamy texture, though care should be taken to avoid the small pin bones. Herring spawn once a year in either spring or autumn; there follows a period of starvation when the fish are quite lean and are known as 'spents' or 'shotten'. According to folklore, if the first herring caught in the season is female the fishing will be good, but if a male fishing will be bad.

The herring appears in many forms: bloaters, kippers, pickled, salted and soused. Personally I am surprised not to see herrings on restaurant menus. I guess it's too cheap. Restaurants seem to prefer the more expensive fish and don't bother too much about price and flavour.

Soft herring roes (milts) are available year round, mainly because of the frozen imports from Canada. Not only are they good for you (full of Vitamin D), but they can also be delicious fried with a little dried tarragon, and a squeeze of lemon juice, on toast or not.

Alexis Soyer, the Victorian chef and gourmet, had a nice way with a red herring (salt-cured): 'Well wash and clean a red herring, wipe it dry and lace it in a pie-dish, having cut off the head, and split it in two up the back; put a gill or two of whisky over the herring, according to size, hold it on one side of the dish, so that it is covered with the spirit, set it alight, and when it goes out the fish is done.' Man-about-town, Jeffrey Bernard, once mentioned in his column in the *Spectator* a Marquis of Hastings who breakfasted on a dish called 'Fixed Bayonets', herring poached in gin. A less intoxicating method would be to poach them in a mixture of white wine and water, with a bayleaf and a few juniper berries.

Fresh herring, like sardines, grill beautifully. Using one fish per person, gut and clean the fish, slash them diagonally three or four times on each side. Steep them for about half an hour in a simple marinade of oil, soy sauce, lemon juice; or orange juice, oil, salt and pepper; or any other mixture you like; or just rub the cuts with a little salt and lay fresh bayleaves and rosemary on the fish. If you are going to grill them on a barbecue, lay the herbs on the oiled grid, then lay the fish on top. Then under (or over) high heat, grill for about 5 minutes on each side. You will be able to test when the flesh is cooked through by using the tip of a knife blade.

Herring with mustard sauce is a good old-fashioned British dish and was apparently a favourite of King Edward VII who had several favourite dishes, we hear.

The Scottish method is also particularly good dipped in oatmeal and cooked in bacon fat. Theodora Fitzgibbon, Jane Grigson and Richard Stein all give instructions for this method.

HERRING DIPPED IN OATMEAL

For four people:

1 herring per person (about 240g/8oz each), gutted and boned, and patted dry
125g/4oz coarse oatmeal
½ teaspoon sea salt
Few grindings of black or white pepper

2 tablespoons oil or clarified butter
4 rashers of good streaky bacon (preferably smoked), each cut into 3 or 4 pieces
Parsley, finely chopped
1 lemon, cut into wedges

Roll the herrings in the oatmeal seasoned with the salt and pepper. In a frying pan, heat the oil or butter, fry the bacon until lightly browned, but not hard. Remove with a slotted spoon and reserve. Fry the herring for about 3 or 4 minutes on each side. Serve still sizzling on a hot plate with the reserved bacon, a sprinkling of parsley and wedges of lemon. This is also a good way to cook small trout.

A soused fillet is another popular way of serving herring, hot or cold. Use the method for mackerel (p.127).

The Sea Fish Industry Authority makes available to fishmongers for passing on to their customers leaflets describing specific fish and how to cook them. Some of their suggestions are included in this book and are marked (SEAFISH).

HERRING WITH MUSTARD (SEAFISH)

For 2:

2 herring, cleaned, head off
4 tablespoons dry white wine
2 teaspoons Dijon mustard
1 shallot or small onion, chopped

1 teaspoon chopped chives
1 teaspoon dry breadcrumbs
Salt and freshly ground pepper

Preheat the oven to 220°C/435°F. Put the cleaned herring in an ovenproof dish. In a small saucepan, bring the wine to the boil and cook for 2 minutes, then mix in the mustard, shallot and chives. Pour the sauce over the herring, sprinkle with the breadcrumbs, season to taste, and bake for 15 minutes.

Jacks

Throughout warm and tropical waters there are many members of the Jack family, or the Corangidae family. Many of these fish have compressed bodies and therefore the ratio of edible flesh to size is low. Today many species are imported to the United Kingdom in fresh and frozen form, and some of them have become an important part of fishmongers' sales, especially the Trevally. Here in the south-east we are exceptionally lucky in seeing many members of the Jack family in their fresh state— Queenfish, Leatherskin, Rainbow Runner, Golden Trevally, Pompano, Pomfret. They are all strong fish with a slightly dark oily firm flesh. If you see any of them on your fishmonger's slab, try them. They are very good fried, grilled or steamed.

Horse Mackerel See Scad.

Huss (Flake or Rigg, Dogfish or Rock Salmon, Piked Dogfish, Spurdog)

French: *Aiguillet, Chien de Mer*
German: *Dornhai, Dornfisch*
Spanish: *Mielga, Galludo*

Category: Round (shark family).
Waters: Home waters.
Shape and colour: A typical shark-shaped body with sandy-brown spotted back fading to white underside.
Price: Low to moderate.
Market size: 50–100cm/20–40in.
Sold as: Skinned, steaks or fillets.
Market availability: Very good.
Seasonal availability: Year round.
Remarks: Flavoursome flesh. Yet another under-rated fish for reasons unknown. Ideal for soups, kebabs, curries—anything that requires a firm flesh that holds together. I always suggest it to my customers as an alternative to the now exorbitant monkfish.

HUSS KEBABS

500g/1lb huss fillets
1 green pepper, seeds and ribs removed, and cut into 2.5cm/1in chunks
1 red pepper, prepared as green pepper
120g/4oz prawns in shell
120g/4oz mushrooms, button or field

Marinade:
2 tablespoons oil
1 tablespoon dark soy sauce
1 tablespoon white wine vinegar
Pinch of cayenne or dash of Tabasco
1 teaspoon ground coriander

Cut the huss fillets into 2.5cm/1in cubes. Using 8 small or 4 large skewers, thread in turn huss, peppers, prawns, and mushrooms. Lay the kebabs in a shallow dish. Mix together the marinade ingredients, brush the mixture over the kebabs and allow to stand for about 30 minutes.

Preheat your grill, cook the kebabs for approximately 15 minutes, turning and basting from time to time. Serve immediately.

A salad of finely chopped onion and tomato, mixed with salt and a little lemon juice can be served on the side. Serves 4.

Alternative fish: monkfish or any other firm-fleshed white fillet. Or use just prawns.

CURRIED HUSS

750g–1kg/1½–2lb skinned huss, cut in 5cm/2in chunks
Flour for dredging
3 tablespoons light oil
1 shallot or ½ onion, finely chopped
1 large clove of garlic, finely chopped or crushed
1–3 teaspoons (to taste) prepared curry paste of your choice, Indian or Thai

1 teaspoon ground coriander
1 red chilli (seeds removed, if preferred), finely chopped
Small piece of ginger, finely chopped
½ teaspoon sugar
Juice of ½ lime or ½ lemon
1 tablespoon dark soy sauce
150ml/5fl.oz fish stock or water
Sprigs of coriander to garnish

Rinse and thoroughly dry the pieces of huss. Lightly dust with flour, shaking off any excess. Set aside.

In a frying pan, sauté pan or wok, heat the oil. Add the shallot and garlic and cook until starting to colour. Add the curry paste and ground coriander, stir thoroughly and cook together for a minute or two. Add the chilli, ginger, sugar, lime juice and soy, and stir. Add the pieces of fish, coat thoroughly with the mixture, and cook for a further minute or two. Add the fish stock or water and simmer for 5–6 minutes, turning the fish occasionally until it is thoroughly cooked through.

Remove the fish to a serving platter. If the sauce is too liquid, reduce a little over high heat, if too dry, add a little more liquid. Pour the sauce over the fish and garnish with sprigs of coriander.

John Dory (St Peter's Fish)

French: *St Pierre*
German: *Herringskonig, Petersfich*
Spanish: *Pez de San Pedro*

Category: Irregular.
Waters: Home waters, Mediterranean.
Shape and colour: Compressed grey body with distinctive 'thumb print' behind the head which is large and ugly. Tough spines and fins.
Price: Moderate to very high, depending on size.
Market size: 20–50cm/8–20in.
Sold as: Whole fish and fillets.
Market availability: Good.
Seasonal availability: Year round.
Remarks: The Greeks think so highly of this fish they call it 'Zeus'. In the opinion of the connoisseur, it is one of the best eating fish to come out of our waters. It is much sought after by good restaurants for its firm white moist flesh and excellent mild sweet flavour. The proportion of flesh to whole fish is very low, therefore it is very expensive, especially when sold as fillets. The one-third head and bones are good for stock and soup.

Another versatile fish when it comes to cooking—it will steam, bake or fry.

Some people are mistakenly put off buying the John Dory because of its appearance.

JOHN DORY WITH VERMOUTH AND CREAM (SEAFISH in conjunction with *Woman's Realm*)

A microwave recipe. If your fishmonger doesn't have John Dory, ask him what he might recommend as a substitute.

4 × 240g/8oz John Dory fillets	2 tablespoons dry vermouth
	150ml/5fl.oz double cream
1 tablespoon fresh *lemon* thyme, chopped	1 teaspoon cornflour

Put your fillets in a shallow dish, sprinkle with thyme, cover and microwave for 5 minutes or until the fish is cooked through. Drain, reserving the juices, and transfer the fish to a serving dish. Cover.

Mix together the vermouth, cream and cornflour and the reserved cooking liquid. Microwave uncovered for about 1 minute. Pour the sauce over the fish and serve. Serves 4.

Britain is fortunate in playing host to some of the great chefs of our time—Nico Ladenis, Anton Mosimann and the Roux brothers—as well as our own Alastair Little and Marco-Pierre White, among others. All of them seem fond of fish and make it an important part of their menus.

Anton Mosimann, the Swiss chef, is devoted to fish and has produced *Anton Mosimann's Fish Cuisine* as well as making television presentations of buying and cooking fish. This, very slightly adapted, is one of his recipes. I don't know why it lacks a name, but it doesn't matter a bit as it is such a good and simple dish.

JOHN DORY FILLETS WITHOUT A NAME (*Filets de St Pierre Sans Nom*)

4 fillets of John Dory (each about 200g/7oz), scaled but skin on	1 tablespoon olive oil
	200g/7oz good quality tomatoes, skinned, seeds removed, and diced
30g/1oz butter	
200ml/7fl.oz fish stock	Salt and freshly ground pepper, to taste
60ml/2fl.oz dry white wine	
150ml/¼ pint double cream	4 sprigs chervil, to garnish
Lemon juice to taste	

121

Season the fillets, lay them in a lightly buttered heatproof casserole or deep sauté pan that has a lid. Add the stock and white wine, bring to the boil, reduce the heat, cover and poach gently for 4–6 minutes until the fish is just cooked through.* With a slotted spoon or fish slice, transfer the fish to a warm platter and keep it warm.

With rapid boiling, reduce the cooking liquid by half. Add the cream, stir to blend, and bring to the boil. Remove from the heat and either liquidise or use a hand blender to beat until it is light and frothy. Add a little lemon juice to sharpen to taste and adjust the seasoning.

In a small pan, heat the oil, and gently sauté the diced tomatoes for 3 or 4 minutes, and season with salt and pepper.

To serve, divide the tomatoes between four warmed plates, arrange the fillets on top, pour the sauce over and/or around, garnish with the chervil. Serves 4.

Alternative fish: almost any fillet or steak of white sea fish: brill, cod, conger eel, halibut, plaice, sole, witch or whiting.

Kingfish

French: *Thazard*
German: *Konigsmakrele*
Spanish: *Carita*

Category: Game fish.
Waters: Most warm waters.
Shape and colour: Large fish with a long round streamlined muscular body, a pointed head and the body slowly tapering to its tail. Blue-black and shiny.
Price: Moderate to high.
Market size: From 1 metre/3ft.
Sold as: Cutlets and steaks.
Market availability: Fair, fresh; good, frozen.
Seasonal availability: Year round (imports).
Remarks: Usually imported from the Indian Ocean and other warm waters. A delicious rosy pink flesh with one centre bone. It is one of my favourites, marvellous grilled or barbecued, with a similar flavour to swordfish. Probably more likely to be seen fresh in the south east, but

* The original recipe suggests poaching in a 200°C/400°F oven for 4–5 minutes. If you are using the oven for other cooking, this is fine; otherwise it would be a little wasteful to heat the oven just for this. If you have a microwave, you could use it for this step, timing depending on your machine.

distribution is spreading rapidly. A real favourite with my customers not only for its flavour but also because it tapers so slowly one can have all steaks and cutlets of similar size.

It has quite a dense flesh and you need steaks of about 120–180g/4–6oz per person. Brush with oil or clarified butter, sprinkle over a few chopped herbs (coriander, for example), a little ground pepper, and grill for about 5 minutes on each side. Serve with a sauce on the side: soy and ginger, spiced tomato, or with a dab of a flavoured butter and a squeeze of lemon or lime.

Lemon Sole

French: *Limande Sole*
German: *Echte, Rotzunge*
Spanish: *Mendo Limon, Lengua Lisa*

Category: Flat.
Waters: Home waters.
Shape and colour: Plump oval body, mainly light sandy-brown back, but with indistinct vari-coloured mottled markings, and a small head, white underside.
Price: Moderate.
Market size: 25–40cm/10–16in.
Sold as: Whole fish, fillets.
Market availability: Very good.
Seasonal availability: Year round, best March to December.
Remarks: Very good flavour and creamy texture. Versatile, and can be used as a substitute for the unrelated and more expensive Dover sole. My wife loves it grilled with a little butter and sweet paprika. In fact, I think we both prefer a fresh lemon sole to Dover.

Two people can tackle a 500–750g/1–1½lb lemon sole. It is up to you whether you prefer to keep the head on, and you don't have to skin it, just scale it lightly on the white underside. Put the fish white side down on an oiled grill or in a buttered baking dish, sprinkle with a little paprika, dot with butter, and under the grill it goes. Turn it once. A green salad and a few new potatoes and it is a meal for princes.

One of the high points of my year is the annual visit to Leith's School of Food and Wine where I talk to the students, one group in the morning and another in the afternoon, about fish. Naturally, I use a lot of visual aids which I've brought fresh from the market that morning. The School then uses my 'aids' on the course.

Prue Leith and Caroline Waldegrave have produced *Leith's Cookery Bible* in which the recipes have been rigorously tested by all 96 students. I am particularly endeared by their statement 'Recipes have been unashamedly adapted from magazines, newspaper articles and other cookery books.'

The *Bible* includes two recipes for lemon sole, one with blanched, chopped cucumber which has been quickly fried, and the following:

LEMON SOLE WITH BURNT HOLLANDAISE

For 4, you need 12 fillets of lemon sole, skinned.

Stock: skin, bones and trimmings from the fish
     1 onion, sliced
     1 carrot, sliced
     450ml/15fl.oz water
     2 slices lemon
     6 peppercorns
     1 bay leaf
     pinch of salt
     1 parsley stalk

Then: 150ml/5fl.oz hollandaise sauce
     45ml/3 tablespoons double cream

Put all the ingredients for the stock in a pan. Bring to the boil and simmer for 25–30 minutes. Strain and allow to cool. Preheat the oven to 180°C/350°F.

Roll up the fillets, skin side inside. Lay them in an ovenproof dish or roasting pan and pour the stock over them. Cover and poach in the oven for 15–20 minutes. Alternatively, poach them carefully on the hob.

While the fish cooks, heat up the grill and make the hollandaise sauce, which must be very thick. Drain the fish well and arrange the rolled fillets on a heat-resistant serving dish. Mix the hollandaise sauce with the cream and coat each fillet with a spoonful. Brown quickly under the grill and serve immediately.

Leith's recommend this dish is served with a white burgundy.

Ancient Rome should not just be remembered in culinary terms for that rather strong fish condiment. The epicure Apicius, via Michelle Berriedale–Johnson in *The British Museum Cookbook*, has also left us with the following way of dealing with a lemon sole:

SOLE IN WHITE WINE WITH HERBS

6 small lemon sole or 3 large (about 1–1.5kg/2–3lb in all)
2 tablespoons olive oil
6 young leeks, trimmed and finely sliced
6 sprigs of fresh coriander, chopped
300ml/10fl.oz dry white wine

Freshly ground black or white pepper
Sea salt
1 teaspoon chopped fresh mint or lovage
1 teaspoon chopped fresh oregano (or ½ teaspoon dried)
2 egg yolks

Clean the fish and pat dry. Put the oil in a large sauté or similar pan. Lay in the fish, sprinkle the leeks and coriander over. Pour in the wine, cover the pan and cook gently for 15 minutes or until the fish is opaque and just cooked through. With a large fish slice, remove the fish, skin the dark underside and fillet the fish. Lay the fillets on a serving dish, cover and keep warm. Add pepper and salt to season and the herbs to the pan. Stir to mix. Drop in the egg yolks, stir to blend, and cook over a very low heat until the sauce thickens. Adjust the seasoning, and pour the sauce over the fish.

Serve with rice or boiled potatoes. Serves 6.

Ling

French: *Lingue*
German: *Leng, Lengfisch*
Spanish: *Maruca*

Category: Round white.
Waters: Home waters.
Shape and colour: An elongated member of the cod family. Greenish-brown heavily mottled back, grey underside.
Price: Low to moderate.
Market size: From 75cm/30in.
Sold as: Fillets; also dried and salted.
Market availability: Fair.
Seasonal availability: Year round.
Remarks: Quite good flavour, though a little watery. Can substitute for cod. It is particularly good for fish cakes, and in any recipe that calls for a

125

cheap white fish. However, I am given to understand that most of the ling caught is split and salted and sold as *bacalau* to southern Europe.

If you do happen to find it, use it in fish cakes or fish pies (see page 217 and 218) or have it cut in steaks and grill or bake it with a spiced sauce.

Mackerel

French: *Maquereau*
German: *Makrele*
Spanish: *Caballa*

Category: Round, oily.

Waters: Home waters and Mediterranean.

Shape and colour: A really beautiful fish. Elegant, streamlined body, glistening green-blue back with distinctive dark waved lines, white underbelly.

Price: Low.

Market size: 30–45cm/12–18 in.

Sold as: Whole fish, fillets or smoked whole fish and fillets.

Market availability: Very good, fresh or frozen.

Seasonal availability: Year round.

Remarks: Rich dark flesh, excellent pronounced flavour and texture. Like all oily fish it deteriorates quite quickly, so the fresher the better. This is another wonderful fish that you don't see in restaurants.

A large fish between two, or a whole fish each, slashed, rubbed with a little seasoning and grilled is an incomparably fine dish, especially if it's a good fresh Cornish mackerel.

Back in the seventies you could hardly go to a dinner party without being served a mackerel pâté, smoked or otherwise, to start, while twenty years earlier smoked mackerel would hardly move off the slab. Fashions change.

PHIL'S SOUSED MACKEREL

2 large mackerel, filleted	10g/¼oz mixed pickling spice
180ml/6fl.oz malt vinegar	2 bayleaves
120ml/4fl.oz water	1 clove garlic, crushed

In a small saucepan, bring to the boil the vinegar and water, add the spice, bayleaves and garlic. Boil the mixture for 3–4 minutes. Remove from the heat and set aside.

Cover the grill rack with aluminium foil and preheat the grill. Grill the mackerel fillets for about 3 minutes each side, or until the fish is cooked through. With a fish slice or spatula, carefully lift the fillets and put them in a deep serving dish. Pour the marinade over the fillets (the marinade shouldn't quite cover the fish), and put them in the refrigerator for at least six hours, turning the fish gently just once. Serve with a salad garnish. Serves 4.

You can souse any grilled or fried fish, such as herring, whiting, witch.

BAKED MACKEREL WITH CIDER AND ORANGE

This SEAFISH recipe originally used herring.

4 medium-sized mackerel fillets	150ml/5fl.oz dry cider
2 oranges	Salt and pepper

Grate the orange rind, cut the oranges into slices and arrange the slices on the bottom of an ovenproof dish. Fold the mackerel fillets and place them on top of the orange slices. Pour the cider over the fish, season to taste, and sprinkle the grated orange rind over the fish. Bake in a preheated oven for about 25 minutes until the skin is crisp and golden.

You could add a couple of bayleaves or cloves to the dish before baking.

According to Francois-Pierre La Varenne, who wrote *Le Cuisinier François* in the 17th century, mackerel 'must be roasted with fennel; once cooked, open them and take out the backbone, and make a good sauce with butter, parsley and gooseberries; when it is all seasoned, bring it to a boil, let it bubble for a moment, then serve your mackerel with your sauce'.

Megrim (Meg, Whiff, Scarborough Whiff, Scarborough Sole)

French: *Cardine*
German: *Scheefschnut, Flugelbutt*
Spanish: *Gallo, Lliseria*

Category: Flat.
Waters: Home waters and Mediterranean.
Shape and colour: Sandy-brown body with barely discernible spots, white underside.
Price: Low–moderate.
Market size: 25–40cm/10–16in.
Sold as: Whole fish.
Market availability: Fair.
Seasonal availability: Year round.
Remarks: Not a very distinguished fish and it can be a little watery, but very useful nevertheless. Can be substituted for any flatfish, particularly in a well-seasoned dish. Try it with a spicy tomato sauce or with a pesto, or grilled and topped with a strong-flavoured butter.

At the time of writing the Sea Fish Industry Authority is making a promotional effort for this fish, but curiously I have not found it easy to get from the wholesalers.

MEGRIM WITH SAGE (SEAFISH)

Simple fried fish fillets, and you could use any white fish, round or flat.

4 × 240g/8oz megrim fillets
2 teaspoons dried sage
120g/4oz breadcrumbs
Flour seasoned with salt and
  pepper

2 eggs, beaten
4 tablespoons oil
4 lemon or lime wedges to
  garnish (optional)

Rinse the fillets and pat dry. Mix the sage with the breadcrumbs. Dip the fillets first in the flour, covering both sides, then in the beaten egg, and finally in the breadcrumbs. Heat the oil and shallow fry for 4–5 minutes until golden. Drain thoroughly and serve immediately with a wedge of lemon or lime if liked. Serves 4.

Monkfish (Angler Fish, Angler)

French: *Lotte, Baudroie*
German: *Seeteufel, Angler*
Spanish: *Rape*

Category: Irregular.
Waters: Home waters, North Atlantic and Mediterranean.
Shape and colour: One of the ugliest fish you will encounter. An enormous horny head with a huge mouth, and a very fast-tapering tail, brown mottled skin without scales and a white belly.
Price: High to very high.
Market size: 30–75cm/12–30in.
Sold as: Tails only (with or without skin), sometimes cheeks from the head at a much reduced price.
Market availability: Very good.
Seasonal availability: Best in winter; though more plentiful in spring and summer.
Remarks: Monkfish has just one central bone and dense firm flesh with a delicious flavour. If you can persuade your fishmonger to get you a whole fish, the head is marvellous for soup or stock. Only a few years ago the quality of monkfish was one of the best-kept secrets. It substituted for lobster or scampi for a fraction of their price and was largely shunned by the average cook. What a different story now. It has become the darling of the new breed of chef and hardly any restaurant of repute omits it from the menu, and because of that the price has rocketed. However, just between you and me, if you see monkfish cheeks on the slab, buy them—they should be much cheaper. The Japanese in particular consider them the choicest meat.

David Wilson, chef at the Churchill Hotel in London, was good enough to give us this recipe.

STEAMED MONKFISH WITH GINGER AND OYSTER SAUCE

750g/1½lb filleted monkfish
8 spring onions, green ends only
250ml/8fl.oz bottled oyster sauce
60g/2oz unsalted butter
2 tablespoons fish stock or white wine
120g/4oz ginger root, slivered into matchstick pieces
Ground pepper to taste
4 sprigs of fresh coriander

Make sure that all the membrane is removed from the monkfish. Slice into roundels, about 1cm/½in thick. Each portion should have about five slices. With a sharp knife, and leaving one end of each whole, sliver the pieces of spring onion and drop them into iced water so the cut ends will curl.

In a small saucepan, pour the oyster sauce, and slowly heat. Add the butter and stir to blend, add the fish stock or wine.

Set up a steaming apparatus using a pan large enough to take a serving dish. On the serving dish lay the slices of monkfish in a decorative fashion, and cover with the pieces of ginger. Steam for about 15 minutes or until the fish is cooked through.

Remove from the steamer, pepper lightly, pour the oyster sauce over the fish, garnish with the sprigs of coriander and the spring onions. Serves 4.

Parrot Fish (Cacatois)

French: *Perroquet Vieillard*
Spanish: *Vieja Colorada*

Category: Round white.
Waters: Indian Ocean, Mediterranean.
Shape and colour: A very pretty fish that wears a coat of many colours. Deep heavy oval body with large scales, a distinctive parrot beak-like mouth. Its name derives from its various brilliant colours—blues, greens, reds—as well as its beak.
Price: Moderate.
Market size: 20–45cm/8–18in.
Sold as: Whole fish.
Market availability: Good, fresh; very good, frozen.
Seasonal availability: Year round.
Remarks: A real eye-catcher, with a firm white flesh, but not as succulent or flavoursome as some of the other fish imported from the region. It is becoming very popular throughout the country. The colour doesn't fade when the fish is baked. It is best with a well-seasoned sauce or dressing.

The Seychellois method of seasoning this and other fish is to half lift a fillet on the whole fish, insert the spices, replace the lifted flesh, then cook.

Perch

French: *Perche*
German: *Barsch, Flussbarsch*
Spanish: *Perca*

Category: Round, freshwater.

Waters: Home and European fresh waters.

Shape and colour: One of the most handsome British coarse fish. There are many colour variations, though largely they are greenish-gold, some with red fins, and their bodies are heavily scaled.

Price: Low.

Market size: 15–30cm/6–12in

Sold as: Whole fish.

Market availability: Fair.

Seasonal availability: July–March. Farmed and imports, year round.

Remarks: A considerable proportion imported from Holland. It has a good flavour, though bony and should be scaled as soon as possible. Could be substituted for trout.

One of the most famous dishes in Geneva is *Filets de perche du lac*, filleted and fried in the lightest batter and best eaten at one of the excellent restaurants overlooking the Lake itself. Anton Mosimann recommends double-frying them.

Pike

French: *Brochet, Brochet du Nord*
German: *Hecht, Flusshecht*
Spanish: *Lucio*

'First open your Pike at the gills . . . keep his liver, which you are to shred very small, with thyme, sweet marjoram, and a little winter-savory; to these put some pickled oysters, and some anchovies, two or three; both these last whole, for the anchovies will melt, and the oysters should not . . . let him be roasted very leisurely; and often basted with claret wine, and anchovies, and butter, mixt together . . .

This dish of meat is too good for any but anglers, or very honest men.'
Izaak Walton

Category: Round, freshwater.

Waters: Lakes and rivers, home and abroad.

Shape and colour: Round elongated body tapering slowly to the tail, with a heavy-toothed duck-like jaw on a narrow head. Back is dark grey-green, paling on the sides to a yellowish belly.

Price: Low to moderate.

Market size: 50–115cm/20–45in.

Sold as: Whole fish, cutlets and fillets.

Market availability: Fair, with fresh and frozen imports.

Seasonal availability: July–March. Farmed and imports, year round.

Remarks: Young pike are known as 'jacks'. Much of the pike available in the United Kingdom is imported from Holland. It is much more popular in central Europe where freshwater fish is particularly appreciated.

Despite the mouth-watering description of Izaak Walton's stuffed pike, a small whole fish fries or bakes very well. You need to use a roasting pan or something similar to take the whole fish and, if you fry it on top of the stove, over two rings. If the fish is still too large either cut the head off (make stock) or cut the fish in half, cook the halves side by side, and reassemble on the serving platter.

First, clean your pike. Wash it thoroughly using a little lemon juice or vinegar. Dry it equally thoroughly, score it several times on each side, and season with salt and pepper inside and out. Dredge in seasoned flour and shake off the excess. In your pan, heat about 100ml/3fl.oz oil and fry 4 or 5 slices good streaky bacon, preferably smoked, until it is crisp. Remove the bacon and add 60–90g/2–3oz unsalted butter. When the butter has melted, lay in the floured fish, and fry for about 6 or 7 minutes on each side, basting occasionally, until it is golden brown all over. This can also be done in a hot oven. Carefully remove the fish—use two fish slices—to a warm serving platter and squeeze over it some lemon juice. In a small pan, heat 6 tablespoons clarified butter until it bubbles, then add and mix 4–5 tablespoons finely chopped parsley, pour over the fish and serve.

On my last visit to the Loire I asked for a pike. A huge fish was presented to our group of four, simply poached and served in a similar way to salmon—gently lifted from the bone. Then Madame appeared with an enormous bowl of *beurre blanc* which she spooned generously over each portion. That and a bottle of Chablis . . .

My mother brought with her from Romania a recipe for stuffed pike. It was always a family favourite. Unfortunately, it is time-consuming and rather complicated, though the result is worth the time and effort. It has something in common with the classic French *quenelles de brochet*, but is served whole and has a more concentrated flavour using as it does the skin and head. Nor does it use herbs or spices, the flavour being derived from the vegetables, salt and sugar, and the cooking method.

1 × 1.5kg/3lb
  (approximately) pike
1 medium onion, finely
  grated or minced
1 carrot, finely grated
3 eggs, separated
240ml/8 tablespoons
  vegetable oil
1–2 teaspoons salt
1–2 tablespoons sugar
3–4 tablespoons medium fine
  matzah meal

For the stock:
2 medium onions, coarsely
  chopped
240ml/8 tablespoons
  vegetable oil
4 medium carrots, trimmed
  and sliced lengthways
1 teaspoon salt
1 tablespoon sugar
Water to cover

The first part is the tricky bit, but a fishmonger would be happy to do it for you. The pike should be scaled, gills removed. Cut off the head, remove the eyes, and clean it thoroughly. Gut the fish from the head end, removing any roe, and *making sure the skin is not damaged.* Rinse thoroughly and trim the tail.

Now, insert the forefinger between skin and flesh and the head end of the body and gently separate the skin, pulling it back as you might remove a sock. Any flesh remaining on the internal surface can be scraped away later. Continue to peel back the skin using your fingers to separate it from the flesh and being careful not to tear the skin, until within 1cm/½in of the tail. Then cut the body away so you are left with the skin complete with tail, albeit inside-out. Set aside.

This was the point when my mother used to take up an old serrated knife from which she wouldn't be parted to scrape the flesh from the backbone. Take up any implement you feel comfortable with and, working downwards from the head end, scrape away as much flesh as possible from the spine, removing all the ancillary or rib bones. Put the scraped flesh into a large mixing bowl. Set aside the cleaned backbone. Carefully scrape any flesh still adhering to the skin and add to the bowl. Set aside the cleaned skin.

Use a fine mouli or old-fashioned mincer, mince the flesh, removing any left-over bones (a food-processor would pulp it too finely, and a degree of texture is required.) Put the minced flesh in a bowl and, one at a time, add the finely grated onion and carrot, egg yolks, oil, salt and sugar, mixing thoroughly after each addition. Add the matzah meal and mix again. To achieve a really good blend, put the mixture through the mouli again. In another bowl, lightly whisk the egg whites to soft peaks, then fold into the fish mixture and thoroughly blend. The final mixture should be the consistency of a thick grainy cream, rather like a *taramasalata*.

Using a spoon, stuff the skin with the mixture, patting it into the natural shape of the whole fish. Add a little of the mixture to the head cavity.

In a small saucepan, cook the coarsely chopped onion in the oil until the onion is transparent and starting to brown. Take a pan or small fish kettle which will take the fish complete with head (you can curl the fish in a large saucepan or cut the fish in two and reassemble after cooking as the stuffing won't fall out). Put in the cooked onion and oil, carrot, salt, sugar and the reserved backbone. Carefully place the stuffed fish and the head in the pan and cover with cold water. Bring the water slowly to a simmer, cover, and raise the heat. After 15 minutes, half-cover the pan, and allow the fish to cook at a very slow boil for about another 30 minutes. The liquid will reduce and thicken. Remove the pan from the heat and allow to cool.

Carefully transfer the stuffed fish onto a serving dish, arranging it with its head as if it were a whole fish. Strain the thickened cooking liquid through a fine mesh sieve, and pour over the fish. Cool and chill.

To serve, cut the fish across in thin slices. The cooking liquid will have set to form a glaze. Serves 3–4.

Pike Perch See **Zander**.

Pilchard See **Sardine**.

Plaice

French: *Plie, Carrelet*
German: *Scholle, Goldbutt*
Spanish: *Solla*

Category: Flat.
Waters: Home waters and Mediterranean.
Shape and colour: Brown back with distinctive orange-red spots and a white underside.
Price: Low–moderate.
Market size: 27+–40cm/11–16in.
Sold as: Whole or fillets.
Market availability: Very good, in fact, the country's most important commercial flat fish.
Seasonal availability: Year round, best from May to December.

Remarks: Excellent moist white flesh, which has a slight iodine smell when really fresh, with a good flavour, especially when cooked on the bone. A favourite of my wife because of its versatility, and a great favourite of mine when I can have a middle cut of a large fish shallow fried. The rest of the fish can be used for soup or stock. The very large plaice seem not to be very popular, but they *are* available, worth looking for, and worth *asking* for so you can get a good middle cut.

Trim and clean a whole fish (if you remove the head, use it for stock). Pat dry. Dip in seasoned flour and fry it in olive oil. Serve with watercress and slices of lemon.

GRILLED PLAICE WITH PAPRIKA AND GARLIC

2 medium-sized plaice (each about 350–500g/12oz–1lb), head removed, cleaned and trimmed	1 clove garlic, crushed
	15g/½oz paprika
	Salt and freshly ground black pepper
30g/1oz butter	

Preheat the grill. Score each side of the fish two or three times. With half the butter, lightly grease a shallow baking dish large enough to take the fish side by side, and lay in the fish, dark side up. Dot the remaining butter over the fish and sprinkle with the crushed garlic and paprika. Cook under the grill for about 5 minutes, occasionally basting. Turn and repeat.

With a fish slice or spatula, carefully transfer the plaice to a warm serving dish and pour the cooking juices over. Season to taste. It couldn't be simpler. Serves 2.

Alternative fish: any small to medium flat fish, dabs, lemon sole, slips, witch.

STUFFED PLAICE WITH ORANGE AND ALMONDS

4 plaice fillets, skinned	1 large orange
60g/2oz soft white breadcrumbs	30g/1oz butter
60g/2oz ground almonds	Freshly ground black pepper

Preheat the oven to 180°C/350°F. In a bowl, put the breadcrumbs, ground almonds, juice of half the orange and 1 teaspoon orange rind, and thoroughly mix. Spread the stuffing equally over the four fillets and either roll each fillet from head to tail, skinned side in, securing with a toothpick if necessary or simply fold the fillets over. Use half the butter to butter a shallow ovenproof dish, lay in the fillets and dot them with the remaining butter. Pour the juice of the remaining half orange over, and grind black pepper to taste. Bake for about 20 minutes or until fish is cooked through. Serves 2–4.

Alternative fish: lemon sole, sole, witch.

Pollack (Pollock, Lythe)

French: *Lieu Jaune*
German: *Pollack, Klamottendorsch*
Spanish: *Abadejo*

Category: Round, white.
Waters: Home waters.
Shape and colour: Of the cod family. Brownish-green mottled back paling to yellowish sides and belly, and a thrusting lower jaw.
Price: Low–moderate.
Market size: 40–50cm/15–20in.
Sold as: Whole, steaks or fillets.
Market availability: Fair.
Seasonal availability: Year round, best from August to March.
Remarks: An uninspiring fish that doesn't command great interest yet its flesh, like coley, rather grey until cooked, is of reasonable quality. Use for any recipe calling for a cheap white fish and for fish cakes and pies.

Pomfret (White or Silver Pomfret)

French: *Castagnoles*
German: *Brachsenmakrele*
Spanish: *Japula*

Category: Round, white, laterally flattened.
Waters: Warm and tropical waters.
Shape and colour: A member of the Jack family it has a white vertical compressed oval body with swallow-like fins and tail, tiny silver scales and a small head.

Price: Moderate.
Market size: 20–30cm/8–12in.
Sold as: Whole fish.
Market availability: Good, fresh; very good, frozen.
Seasonal availability: Year round with main imports from Indian Ocean.
Remarks: A marvellous little fish with firm white succulent flesh, easily taken from the bone. It is particularly good for steaming, but extremely versatile. I remember with great fondness eating deep-fried pomfret in a fishing village near Penang, Malaysia. It was wonderful, until I got the bill. It cost more there than in London. Distribution is spreading throughout the country. Frequently used in south-east Asian recipes.

Pomfret fillets are an excellent substitute in any recipe calling for John Dory. They have a similar flavour and texture.

FRESH STEAMED POMFRET

Fresh pomfret steamed is a very simple dish—one will serve two people. Set up your steamer. If you use a steaming basket, you might like to line it with a few leaves of Chinese cabbage or a similar green. Clean, trim and rinse the pomfret. Pat dry and slash three or four times on each side. Lay the fish on the plate or basket, and on it sprinkle:

2 spring onions, finely sliced lengthways and cut into 5cm/2in pieces

A small piece of ginger, slivered

1 fresh red chilli, slivered (optional)

1 tablespoon fish sauce

2 tablespoons light soy sauce

Juice of half a lemon or lime

A little freshly ground white pepper

Coriander or parsley, to garnish

Cover, and steam for 15–20 minutes or until the fish is opaque down to the bone (test with the point of a knife). Transfer to a serving dish and garnish with a few leaves of coriander or flat-leaved parsley.

Rabbit Fish

French: *Cordonnier*

Category: Round (tropical).
Waters: Mediterranean and Indian Ocean.

137

Shape and colour: Squarish dark grey compressed body, no scales, and a small head with a mouth shaped like a rabbit. (Not to be confused with domestic rabbit fish which has no commercial or other value at all.)
Price: Moderate.
Market size: 15–24cm/6–9in.
Sold as: Whole fish.
Market availability: Fresh, fair; frozen, good.
Seasonal availability: Most of year.
Remarks: Mainly imported from the Indian Ocean, it makes wonderful soups and lends itself well to highly flavoured or spiced dishes. Very popular in Chinese communities. Treat as the parrot fish—insert spices under a gently lifted half-fillet and replace.

Rascasse See **Scorpion Fish**.

Redfish (Bergylt, Ocean Perch)

French: *Sebaste, Chevre*
German: *Rotbarsch, Goldbarsch*
Spanish: *Gallineta Nordica*

Category: Round, white.
Waters: Home waters.
Shape and colour: Deep plump body, large head, reddish-orange colour paling to a pink belly, and large scales.
Price: Moderate.
Market size: 30–45cm/12–18in.
Sold as: Whole fish, fillets.
Market availability: Good.
Seasonal availability: Year round.
Remarks: Sometimes called Norway cod and widely available. A reasonable white-fleshed fish with good texture ideal for poaching, frying or baking, and a cheaper substitute for the more expensive sea bream. Cook whole fish as you would sea bream; the fillets are small but can be substituted for more expensive white fish.

Red Mullet (Surmullet)

French: *Rouget de Roche*
German: *Meerbarbe, Streifenbarbe*
Spanish: *Salmonete de Roca*

Category: Round.
Waters: Home waters and Mediterranean.
Price: Fresh, high; frozen, low.
Market size: 15–30cm/6–12in.
Sold as: Whole fish.
Market availability: Fair, fresh; good, frozen.
Seasonal availability: Summer months; year round, frozen imports.
Remarks: A much esteemed fish of great flavour and texture; the larger the fish the less troublesome the bones. Most are imported from the Mediterranean and, during the summer, some are available from the Cornish coast. There are many species of red mullet found throughout the world and many are brought to our tables, fresh and frozen, but I don't think they have the quality of texture and flavour of those taken from of our own home waters.

Many cookery writers recommend reserving the liver of the red mullet, sometimes called 'woodcock of the sea'. A good idea, but only possible on the larger fish of 500g/1lb or over, particularly those wonderful mullet from Cornish waters. The frozen imported fish are usually small and often pre-gutted.

It is fast becoming one of the most popular fish for grilling either in the kitchen or on the barbecue; it marinates well; and the small frozen fish are very good in fish soups. An excellent dish tasted in a German restaurant was a warm salad with fillets of red mullet that had been marinated in a gingery sauce. Fillets are a bit fiddly, so ask your fishmonger to do it for you.

Jeanne Strang's *Goose Fat and Garlic* offers a recipe called Red Mullet in a Spicy Sauce which can equally well be used for sardines. It is an *escabeche* so it should actually be left to marinate and be eaten cold, but it is also good straight from the pan. Her recipe uses a small red pepper; I have substituted a small red chilli.

RED MULLET IN A SPICY SAUCE

Clean and scale a mullet for each person (each fish 150–190g/5–6oz), roll in a well-seasoned flour and fry in 2–3 tablespoons olive oil for 4 or 5 minutes each side. Transfer to a heated serving dish and keep warm.

Using the same pan, make a sauce as follows:

Olive oil

1 medium onion or 2–3 shallots, sliced

2 cloves garlic, chopped or crushed

1 small red chilli, deseeded and chopped (or 2 if you like your sauce hotter)

Small sprig of fresh thyme, or a pinch of dried

4–5 leaves of fresh mint

2–3 tablespoons vinegar

Add a little more oil to the pan, add the onion or shallot, garlic, chilli, thyme and mint. Fry gently until the onion is translucent and starting to colour. Add the vinegar, stir well to blend and reduce slightly. Pour the sauce over the fish.

Red Snapper See **Snappers**.

Roach

French: *Gardon*
German: *Plötze, Rotauge*
Spanish: *Bermejuela, Calandino*

Category: Round, freshwater.
Waters: Most European freshwater.
Shape and colour: Deep-bodied fish with a small head, silver colour with a reddish tinge to the fins and eyes and large scales.
Price: Low.
Market size: 20–25cm/8–10in.
Market availability: Fair.
Seasonal availability: June–December (British); year round (farmed).
Remarks: This is one of the most common fish for many of Britain's coarse anglers. However, it is also used by many people for its delicate white flesh and can substitute for carp.

Roker See **Skate**.

Sailfish

Category: Game fish.
Waters: Indian Ocean, Mediterranean and all warm tropical waters.
Shape and colour: Long powerful streamlined body with a dagger-like elongated upper jaw. Its name derives from the large dorsal fin which folds down along its back when swimming fast.
Price: High.
Market size: From 150cm/5ft.
Sold as: Cutlets.
Market availability: Fresh, poor and sporadic; frozen, good.
Seasonal availability: Year round, mainly frozen cutlets.
Remarks: Dark red succulent flesh with an excellent flavour. Very firm backbone. Particularly suited to grilling on the barbecue and to bake or casserole. It can be used in any way as swordfish or tuna.

I was able to buy 30kg/60lb fish a while ago and the actor Jimmy Ellis of 'Z-Cars' fame, a very good customer, helped me to carry it into the shop.

Saithe See **Coley**.

Salema (Saupe)

French: *Saupe*
Spanish: *Salema*

Category: Round.
Waters: Mediterranean.
Shape and colour: A narrow oval fish of medium size, grey-green with yellow horizontal stripes and a small head. It belongs to the sea bream family.
Price: Moderate.
Market size: 15–30cm/6–12in.
Sold as: Whole fish.
Market availability: Fair, fresh.
Seasonal availability: Year round, best in August, September, October.
Remarks: Mainly imported from the Mediterranean. It feeds mainly on seaweeds and algae and has a distinctive and excellent flavour, and is a very pretty fish. Cook it whole, and grill, fry or bake.

Salmon

French: *Saumon*
German: *Lachs*
Spanish: *Salmon*

Category: Round game fish.

Waters: Home waters.

Shape and colour: A beautifully proportioned streamlined silvery body with scattered black markings on the back.

Price: Wild, very high early in the season becoming moderate during June/July. Farmed fish, moderate (see remarks).

Market size: 45–120cm/18–48in.

Sold as: Whole fish, cutlets and smoked.

Market availability: Wild, very good in season; very good, farmed.

Seasonal availability: Wild: February to August. Farmed: year round, but better in summer months.

Remarks: A fresh run salmon returning to its own river is a beautiful thing to behold and more than enough has been written about it. It is probably the most popular 'special occasion' fish. Those wonderful wild salmon are rightly most expensive. There is a definite difference in the texture and flavour of the wild compared with the cheaper farmed salmon, which is still a quality fish. There is also 'organic' salmon which is farmed in coastal sea water pens and claims for itself a superiority over the usual farmed salmon. The farms of the west coasts of Scotland and Ireland produce very good fish. Farming has allowed salmon to take a more habitual place on any fishmonger's slab and we should all be grateful.

Grilse are young salmon up to 3.5kg/7lb in weight making their first return from sea to river in order to spawn. During the summer months they are much cheaper than the larger adult fish.

In her *Summer Cooking* Elizabeth David says: 'Salmon with cucumber and mayonnaise is an admirable dish, but anyone visiting this country for the first time and dining out frequently, might well be excused for supposing that salmon is the only fish procurable in England during the whole of the summer. In fact, salmon is at its best in the very early spring.' Quite so.

POACHED SALMON

I am often asked to poach a salmon for a customer and I do this in the simplest way possible. Using a proper fish kettle makes the task much easier. Richard Stein in his *English Seafood Cookery* says that he prefers to poach a salmon in salted water rather than in a *court-bouillon* as he thinks that the fine flavour of the fish needs nothing added. I think he is probably right when dealing with a wild salmon, but these days so much is farmed that a *court-bouillon* gives the slightly milder flesh a bit of a boost. To flavour the *court-bouillon* I use bayleaf, a few peppercorns, a *bouquet-garni* or sprigs of thyme and parsley, and a little dry white wine. If you are going to serve the poached salmon hot, bring the liquid to the boil, then allow to cool a little before immersing the fish. You should then keep the water at simmering point for 15–50 minutes, depending on the weight and thickness of the fish (allow 4–5 minutes per lb).

Jane Grigson preferred to seal the well-seasoned salmon in oiled or buttered foil (depending on whether the fish is to be served cold or hot) and then cook it. This, she felt, preserved all the flavour in the fish.

The following recipe from David Wilson is a little extravagant, but for a special evening absolutely delicious. Follow it with something plain, like a piece of poached halibut, with a dab of anchovy butter.

SALMON TARTARE WITH CAVIAR

250–310g/8–10oz fresh salmon, skinned and boned	1 tablespoon chives, finely chopped
1 tablespoon lemon juice	1 tablespoon dill weed, finely cut
1 tablespoon good mayonnaise	Salt, pepper and cayenne to taste
1 tablespoon skinned, sweated, and diced cucumber*	60g/2oz caviar, or substitute salmon eggs, to garnish

With a very sharp knife, slice, sliver and chop the salmon very finely. Put it in a bowl and mix with the lemon juice, mayonnaise, cucumber, chives and dill. Mix thoroughly and season to taste.

To serve, use a pastry cutter. Place the cutter on a plate, pack in one quarter of the salmon mixture, remove the cutter. Repeat the process on the other three plates. Spoon a little caviar on each mound of salmon. Serves 4.

* Take a 5cm/2in length of cucumber, remove and discard the central seeds, finely chop the remainder. Sprinkle a little salt over, and leave for about half an hour. Rinse, drain and pat dry.

ROUND AND FLAT FISH

MIXED SALMON TARTARE

In their forthcoming book, *The Great National Detective Story*, Chandra and David Marsh have a variation on this which uses 250g/½lb each of smoked salmon and fresh salmon which has been marinated in lime juice and chopped fresh dill for about twenty-four hours. Drained and finely chopped, it is mixed with the chopped smoked salmon, chopped chives, more chopped dill, crushed pink peppercorns, 3–4 finely chopped radishes, a few tablespoons of strained yoghurt, lemon juice and a tablespoon of vodka.

Sand Eel (Sand Lance)

French: *Lancon, Eguille*
German: *Sandaal, Sandspierling*
Spanish: *Lanzon, Salton*

Category: Irregular.
Waters: Home waters.
Shape and colour: Small long silvery fish.
Price: Low.
Market size: 15–30cm/6–12in.
Sold as: Whole fish.
Market availability: Good when in season.
Seasonal availability: Winter months.
Remarks: It's a pity this fish isn't seen more often as it has a good flavour and fine flesh. Unfortunately it is mostly bought up by bait suppliers. A recent report reveals that the Danes use sand eels as industrial fuel.

If you are lucky enough to find them, behead and gut, cut into small pieces, toss in seasoned flour and shallow fry in oil with herbs of your choice—thyme, tarragon or fresh coriander, for example. A squeeze of lemon or lime juice, some crusty brown bread and a salad completes a good meal.

Sand Sole

French: *Sole Peleuse*
Spanish: *Sortija*

Category: Flat.
Waters: Home waters.

144

Shape and colour: Flat oblong body, freckled sandy-brown back and a white underside, similar to Dover sole.
Price: Moderate.
Market size: 20–35cm/8–14in.
Sold as: Whole fish.
Market availability: Poor to fair.
Seasonal availability: Year round.
Remarks: Not as distinguished as the Dover Sole, but nevertheless an excellent fish. The flesh is white, creamy and moist, and it can certainly substitute for its more expensive cousin, but unfortunately it is not seen very often on fishmongers' slabs because most go over to France where they are justly appreciated. One customer, after having bought and tasted a sand sole, later bought a Dover sole. He came back the next day saying the second fish hadn't been as good as the first one.

Use it as you would any sole, whole or filleted, with any sauce you care to, or simply with herb butter.

Sardine

French: *Sardine*
German: *Sardine, Pilchard*
Spanish: *Sardina*

Category: Round, oily (herring family).
Waters: Home waters (south west) in summer, Mediterranean.
Shape and colour: Smaller than the herring, blue-green back paling to a silver belly (in fact, young pilchards).
Price: Low.
Market size: 10–15cm/4–6in.
Sold as: Whole fish.
Market availability: Good.
Seasonal availability: Most of year, more prolific in summer months.
Remarks: Most are imported from Portugal, though they do swim in waters of the south west. They are most familiar as canned fish and are an important standby in the store cupboard. But a fresh barbecued sardine on a warm summer evening is a pure delight.

SARDINES PORTUGUESE-STYLE

Anyone who has taken a holiday on the Portuguese coast will have fond memories of sitting outside on a warm evening and eating sardines straight off the grill.

145

Sprinkle gutted sardines with sea salt, freshly ground black pepper and a little lemon juice. Cook them on a hot, oiled grill, basting with a little olive oil, and turning just once.

Sometimes the cleaned fish are first marinated in white wine, garlic, and salt and pepper; or brushed with a paste of olive oil, crushed garlic, chopped coriander or parsley, a little chilli or paprika, and lemon juice; or simply brushed with oil which may or may not be flavoured and grilled with sprigs of rosemary or bayleaves; or, if small sardines have been gutted through the gills, tuck a small sprig of mint or coriander or other herb in to the cavity before cooking.

You might like to stuff them before grilling with 2 or 3 teaspoons of mixed finely chopped shallot, fresh coriander or other fresh herb of your choice—basil, parsley, tarragon or thyme—a chopped mushroom or two, a spoonful of capers, a dash of Tabasco or anything else you believe will enhance or complement the fish.

Make sure that the bars of the fish grill are thoroughly oiled so the fish don't stick.

Scabbardfish, Silver (Frostfish) or Black

French: *Coutelas, Sabre d'Argent*
German: *Degenfisch*
Spanish: *Espadilla*

Category: Irregular.
Waters: Eastern Atlantic.
Shape and colour: Compressed elongated body with a pointed head and vicious teeth. It has a shiny silver to pewter or entirely black skin with no scales.
Price: Moderate.
Market size: 45–150cm/18–60in.
Sold as: Long steaks or fillets.
Market availability: Fair.
Seasonal availability: Year round.
Remarks: White moist flesh with the texture of sole and a faint flavour of sardine. The front and middle cuts carry most of the flesh. Anyone who has visited Portugal or the Canaries, where most are caught, must have eaten and enjoyed this fish which is now being imported fresh into the United Kingdom.

Season and simply grill, or bake in a sauce. I like it best on the bone in steaks.

Scad (Horse Mackerel)

French: *Saurel, Chinchard*
German: *Stocker, Bastard-Makrele*
Spanish: *Jurel*

Category: Round, oily.
Waters: Home waters and Mediterranean.
Shape and colour: Large-headed slim fish, with a row of raised hooked scales along the sides which become hard and spiny towards the tail. Dark grey-blue back with a hint of green, fading to violet-silver on the lower side and a white belly, and a black spot on the gill cover.
Price: Low.
Market size: 25–30cm/9–12in.
Sold as: Whole fish.
Market availability: Fair.
Seasonal availability: Year round.
Remarks: A member of the Jack family, it is not a very inspiring fish, but is good for a low budget. Though it is not as oily, you can treat as mackerel or use it in soups.

Scorpion Fish

French: *Rascasse, Scorpene*
German: *Drachenkopfe*
Spanish: *Rascacio, Cabracho*

Category: Round.
Waters: Mediterranean
Shape and colour: Large bony head with spines and large fan-like fins with a rosy-red colour overall.
Price: Moderate.
Market size: 20–25cm/8–10in.
Sold as: Whole fish.
Market availability: Fair for fresh; fair to good for frozen.
Seasonal availability: Most of year, imported.
Remarks: Firm sweet flesh with a very good texture and flavour. Indispensable to bouillabaisse. The head makes a marvellous stock. Because of its rather nasty spines, I suggest that the fishmonger should do all the necessary preparation. The fresh fish is seen mostly in the south east.

Curried *rascasse* is delicious, but the flesh itself is so good that a simpler treatment is also excellent. Fillets lightly sautéed in olive oil with some chopped fresh herbs and lemon juice, for instance. Or poached in their own well-seasoned and reduced stock, remembering that for the purpose you should always ask your fishmonger for the head, bones and trimmings if he has filleted the fish for you.

It is very popular in France and I think the whole of London's French population knows when I have it in the shop. It is snapped up quicker than I can turn around.

Sea Trout, Salmon Trout

French: *Truite*
German: *Forelle*
Spanish: *Trucha*

Category: Round game fish.
Waters: Home rivers and coastal waters. They are caught on their return to river waters to spawn.
Shape and colour: Similar to salmon, but with a blunter head and a thicker body with small black spots over the whole body. The tail fin is not as forked as a salmon's.
Price: Very high early in the season; moderate later in the summer months.
Market size: 30–100cm/12–36in.
Sold as: Whole fish, cutlets and smoked.
Market availability: Good in season.
Seasonal availability: February–August.
Remarks: A superb fish, indeed my favourite. Not as heavy and rich as salmon and for some tastes all the better for that.

To be precise, there is no such fish as Salmon Trout, although it is now a permitted legal definition. To make the proper distinction in my shop during the season I correctly label it 'Wild Sea Trout', and out of season you will see the label 'farmed Salmon Trout' which in fact is a large pink-fleshed trout. Sadly, I fear there is a danger of over-fishing the wild sea trout since I am aware of an increasing scarcity.

A favourite recipe for sea trout is to bake it whole, wrapped in lightly oiled foil, with white wine, bayleaves, and fresh dill.

The late Richard Pinney, who founded the Butley-Orford Oysterage in Suffolk (and go there if you ever have the opportunity—the fish is wonderful, and the town itself has a delightful East Anglian atmosphere), called the sea trout 'the champion fish'. In his *Smoked Salmon and Oysters*, the story of the oysterage, he said: 'Seven good, big sea trout represent our normal night's fishing, but what a catch! Laid out on the kitchen table, they are a sight the weary fisherman will never forget.'

Shad (Allis, Twaite Shad)

French: *Alose, Finte*
Spanish: *Sablo, Saboga*

Category: Round, oily (herring family)
Waters: Most European waters, but caught in river estuaries.
Shape and colour: Belongs to the herring family with dark blue back, silver sides and belly, similar shape to but larger than a herring. The Allis shad is a little larger than the Twaite which also has a row of distinctive spots across the back.
Price: Low.
Market size: 25–60cm/10–24in.
Sold as: Whole fish.
Market availability: Poor to fair.
Seasonal availability: Year round, but probably better in spring months.
Remarks: Rich dark flesh with a strong flavour of herring; rather bony. Not often seen nowadays but should you see it, try it. All recipes for herring will be perfect for shad. Both soft and hard roes are delicious.

Shark, Hammerhead

French: *Requin marteau*
Spanish: *Pesmartillo*

Category: Round.
Waters: Home waters, Mediterranean, Indian Ocean.
Shape and colour: Large streamlined body with fast-tapering tail, olive-brown or brownish grey back and sides with pale belly. Hammerheads have a distinctive flattened head with hammerlike lobes on each side where the eyes are located. A rough skin.
Price: Medium.
Market size: From 60cm/24in.
Sold as: Small whole fish or cutlets from larger fish.
Market availability: Poor to fair.
Seasonal availability: Year round.
Remarks: Becoming more available with increasing demands and imports, mainly from the Indian Ocean. Like all sharks it does not have a true hard skeleton, but a cartilaginous backbone. In spite of being modestly priced, there is some reluctance to buy it except in the summer barbecue season. It is good value and makes an excellent meal.

A Jamaican customer marinates his cutlet in lime juice, lemon juice and water for about half an hour, then fries it in a spicy batter.

149

Shark, Porbeagle

French: *Taupe, Lamie, Latour*
Spanish: *Marrajo*

Category: Round.

Waters: Home waters and Mediterranean.

Shape and colour: A large streamlined fish with a pointed snout and a deep body with tapering tail. Deep bluish back and sides paling to a white underbelly. Rough skin like sandpaper.

Price: Moderate.

Market size: The whole fish can be anything from 1.5m/5ft long but I buy sections or loins of approximately half that size to cut to a customer's request.

Sold as: Cutlets and pieces.

Market availability: Fresh, poor to fair; frozen, good.

Seasonal availability: Year round.

Remarks: Availability of fresh shark meat gets better with increasing demand from the public. I once saw a stall on Portobello Road with a shark weighing about 65kg/130lb. The fishmonger couldn't cut it fast enough to meet the demands of the long queue.

Shark meat is rather dry when it has been frozen, and I think it's best marinated in oil and flavourings for about half an hour, then grilled or barbecued. Makes good kebabs too.

SHARK WITH HERBS AND MUSHROOMS

The marinade can be used for other fish, steaks, cutlets or thick pieces of fillet of tuna, coley or swordfish, for example.

750g–1kg/1½–2lbs shark steaks (each about 2.5cm/1in thick)
Juice of 1 lemon
90ml/3fl.oz white wine
1–2 cloves garlic, finely chopped or crushed
1–2 tablespoons fennel bulb, finely chopped
½ teaspoon dried oregano
½ teaspoon dried marjoram
Pinch of cayenne or dash of Tabasco (optional)
3 tablespoons olive oil
1 shallot, finely chopped
240g/8oz mushrooms, button or small field, sliced
2–3 sprigs of fennel leaf, snipped

Rinse and thoroughly dry the fish. In a deep dish, mix the lemon juice, wine, garlic, fennel, oregano, marjoram, optional cayenne or Tabasco. Add the fish, spoon the marinade over. Set aside for at least half an hour, turning the fish occasionally. Preheat grill.

Remove the fish from the marinade and drain on kitchen paper, reserving the marinade. Grill for 5–6 minutes on each side, brushing with a little marinade if necessary. Transfer the fish to a warm serving dish.

In a frying pan, heat the oil and cook the shallot until transparent. Add the mushrooms, cook together, until the mushrooms start to take a little colour. Pour the marinade into the pan with the mushrooms, raise the heat, stir and cook for about 3 minutes. Pour the sauce over the fish and sprinkle the fennel leaf over.

Supermarkets are always coming up with new products, and a recent discovery is pesto with sun-dried tomatoes, 'red pesto', sold in 190g/6oz jars. It's not only good on pasta. The following suggestion is very simple to prepare and very good.

SHARK WITH RED PESTO

---

4 shark steaks, 180–250g/ 6–8oz each	1 tablespoon olive oil
	Juice of 1 lime or lemon
4–5 tablespoons red pesto	Chopped parsley to garnish

Lay the steaks in a lightly oiled baking dish. Mix the red pesto, olive oil, lime or lemon juice. Paint the mixture onto the upper surface of the steaks. Put under a preheated grill for 10–15 minutes or until the fish is cooked through. Garnish with the chopped parsley.

If you find the sauce a bit strong for your taste, you could dilute it with *crème fraîche* or yoghurt. According to the label on the jar, this would also make a very good dip, and might be good with prawns or grilled squid. Serves 4.

You could also use it on a steak of tuna, swordfish, or coley.

Skate (Ray, Roker)

French: *Raie*
German: *Roche*
Spanish: *Raya*

Category: Irregular (Shark family).

Waters: Home waters.

Shape and colour: Skates and rays have flat, kite-shaped bodies. The skate has a pointed snout and the ray a blunted snout. Colouring differs with species, but is mainly brown. The fishing industry does not differentiate between skate and ray, and the terms are used interchangeably. A Thornback ray has, as the name suggests, raised thorny knobs along the back.

Price: Moderate.

Market size: from 250g/8oz wings.

Sold as: Mainly skinned wings as the body doesn't have much useful flesh, except perhaps for skate nobs.

Market availability: Very good.

Seasonal availability: Year round, best in winter.

Remarks: This is a cartilaginous species with pink moist flesh, a good flavour and firm texture. Some writers have claimed that a strong smell of ammonia is natural to skate. This is wrong; any very slight odour should disappear on washing, and if it doesn't the fish is 'off'.

It is mainly only the skinned 'wing' that is eaten. The rest of the fish is left with the processor to do with as he will. Skate nobs, when you can find them, can be good eating.

The classic way of serving skate is with black butter and caper sauce. It is very simple (though the black butter requires a little care and attention) and, of course, should be made with a good piece of the freshest possible skate. A sauce made with butter and lime is also extremely good, and Anton Mosimann poaches the skate and serves it with fresh garden vegetables, blanched, then lightly glazed in butter, salt and sugar, with melted butter and chopped parsley and lemon juice mixed and poured over. Very simple, very good.

SKATE WITH BLACK BUTTER AND CAPERS

A classic sauce that does not have to be used with just skate. Try it with any simply grilled or poached white fish.

500–750g/1–1½lb skate
  wing, cut in four wedges
2 tablespoons olive oil
Small knob of butter
Juice of 1 lemon
60ml/2fl.oz white wine
  vinegar

1–2 tablespoons capers,
  whole or coarsely chopped
120g/4oz butter
Ground black pepper, to
  taste
Chopped parsley, to garnish

Rinse and thoroughly dry the skate. In a large heavy frying pan, heat the oil and the knob of butter. Fry the skate for about 3 minutes each side until done, remove and keep on a warmed plate. (If you prefer, you can poach the skate in *court-bouillon* or a mixture of wine and water for 4 or 5 minutes.)

Pour off the oil and butter mixture and wipe the frying pan with kitchen paper.

Mix together the lemon juice, vinegar and capers and set aside. The next part takes no time, and you must keep a careful eye on the pan. Over a medium heat, melt the butter and watch it change colour to a dark chestnut brown, a matter of seconds. Pour in—down the side of the pan— the lemon mixture. Stir quickly once or twice, and don't mind the smoke, and pour immediately over the fish. Add pepper if you like and throw some chopped parsley over, and serve immediately. Serves 4.

Slip See **Dover Sole**.

Smelt (Sparling)

French: *Eperlan*
German: *Stint*
Spanish: *Eperlano*

Category: Small, round (Salmon family).
Waters: Home waters, but many imported from Holland.
Shape and colour: Slim fish, light olive-green with cream belly.
Price: Moderate.
Market size: 10–15cm/4–6in.
Sold as: Whole fish.
Market availability: Fair.
Seasonal availability: Most of year.
Remarks: Good flavour. Slight smell of cucumber when really fresh, as does wild salmon. Best fried like whitebait.

Sole See **Dover Sole, Lemon Sole**.

Snapper Family

These are now seen more regularly on the fishmonger's slab both fresh and frozen, and most of what I have said about sea bream applies to snapper. There are 250 different species of snapper and a number of them are imported from warm waters, particularly from the Indian Ocean (Seychelles), including: *Bordemar*, *Bourgeois*, Therese, Red Snapper, *Job Gris*, *Job Jaune*. They all have good firm flesh with an excellent flavour, and while they can grow very large are usually imported at a medium size. They are all round, white fish mostly with slightly laterally compressed bodies. Both fresh and frozen fish are imported and because of the speed of air transport, the fish can be swimming in the ocean and on the slab forty-eight hours later. Distribution is spreading through the United Kingdom.

- *Bordemar*

Shape and colour: A large deep body, rosy red all over, its forehead slopes forward to a jutting lower lip. It has large spiny fins and large heavy scales.
Price: Moderate–high.
Market size: 30–60cm/12–24in.
Sold as: Whole fish, sometimes cutlets.
Market availability: Fair to good, fresh and frozen.
Seasonal availability: Year round.
Remarks: A delightful and versatile fish: white juicy flesh with a very good flavour which can be grilled, baked, poached or steamed.

- *Bourgeois*

Shape and colour: Handsome fish with a large head, the long forehead sloping down with a slight curve to the upper lip. Large deep rosy-pink body with black edge on its large spiny fins.
Price: Moderate–high.
Market size: 30–75cm/12–30in.
Sold as: Whole fish, cutlets or fillets.
Market availability: Fair to good, fresh and frozen.
Seasonal availability: Year round.
Remarks: In my opinion probably the best of the imported Indian Ocean snappers. It is now being imported as pre-cut fillets, as well as whole fish, and is available from most good fishmongers and a few well-known

Spiny lobster

Pacific oyster

New Zealand
green-shelled mussel

Hard-backed
or quahog
clams

Whelk

cockle
(sande)

rdes

Razor shell

Venus clam

Winkles

Cockle

Scallop

TABASCO

McILHENNY CO.
CHEF SIZE
TABASCO
BRAND
PEPPER SAUCE

Arbroath smokies

Smoked salmon

Smoked mackerel

Smoked cod's roe (undyed)

Buckling

Scotch kipper (dyed)

Manx kipper

supermarkets and department stores. A number of my customers seem to have become quite addicted to these no-trouble fillets.

A number of professional as well as amateur cooks come into the shop. Corporate chef Isabelle Aubertin has given us this extremely tasty recipe for *bourgeois*.

STEAMED BOURGEOIS WITH CHIVE BUTTER SAUCE

750g/1½lb (approximately) bourgeois fillets
2 litres/4 pints fish stock
120g/4oz unsalted butter, chilled and cut into cubes
2 shallots, finely chopped

120ml/4fl.oz dry white wine
Juice of ½ lemon
1 tablespoon double cream
Seasoning to taste
1 small bunch of chives, cut about 1cm/½in long

Cut the fish into 4 or 8 pieces and season. Set up the steamer using the fish stock as the steaming medium for flavour. Steam the fish for 8–10 minutes.

In a small pan, melt a small piece of butter and cook the shallots until they start to colour. Add the white wine and lemon juice, raise the heat and reduce the liquid to about 2 tablespoons. Add the cream and gradually whisk in the rest of the chilled butter until you have a creamy consistency. Season to taste and stir in the chives just before serving. Arrange the steamed fish on a warmed platter or individual plates and pour the sauce over. Serves 4.

You could of course use in this recipe any of the snappers, groupers or sea bass.

Job Gris

Shape and colour: Tapering oval body, rather small blunt head. Greyish-green back and sides and a pale belly. Spiny fins and large scales.
Price: Moderate.
Market size: 30–60cm/12–24in.
Sold as: Whole fish.
Market availability: Fair.
Seasonal availability: Year round.
Remarks: An excellent fish. Like its more frequently seen cousin *Job Jaune*, it looks and eats like sea bass.

155

Job Jaune

Shape and colour: Slow-tapering oval body, rather small blunt head. Rosy-brown back, lighter sides and pale belly. Spiny fins and large heavy scales. Looks like a sea bass.
Price: Moderate.
Market size: 30–60cm/12–24in.
Sold as: Whole fish.
Market availability: Fair.
Seasonal availability: Year round.
Remarks: An excellent fish, it looks and eats like sea bass, but is much cheaper and is therefore becoming extremely popular with my customers.

Therese

Shape and colour: Large deep body, with a distinctive lump behind the head from which the forehead curves and slopes to projecting upper lip. All over colour of dark rose. Large spiny fins.
Price: Moderate.
Market size: 30–60cm/12–24in.
Sold as: Whole fish.
Market availability: Fair to good.
Seasonal availability: Year round.
Remarks: Firm white flavoursome flesh. Treat as any other snapper.

Red Snapper

Category: Round.
Waters: Indian Ocean and all warm seas.
Shape and colour: Slightly compressed body, slightly pointed head. Bright red all over. An attractive fish, but with spiny fins.
Price: Moderate.
Market size: 15–45cm/6–18in.
Sold as: Whole fish, fresh or frozen.
Market availability: Fresh, poor–fair; frozen, good.
Seasonal availability: Most of year.
Remarks: A genuine red snapper is both beautiful to look at and delicious to eat. Firm white flavourful flesh of top quality. Fresh fish are imported mainly from the Indian Ocean and the Caribbean and are often cleaned before transportation which guarantees their arrival in first-class condition.

SNAPPER WITH SWEET AND SOUR SAUCE (adapted from a recipe given by Yan Kit So in her *Classic Chinese Cookbook*)

Snapper, gutted, scaled, slashed 3–4 times on each side.

Marinade:

2 tablespoons medium or dry sherry	1 teaspoon coarse salt
	1 tablespoon lime juice
Juice of piece of ginger, crushed in garlic press	

Combine ingredients, pour over the fish and rub in, and set aside while you make the sauce.

Sauce:

3 tablespoons oil	2 tablespoon lime or lemon juice
1 shallot or half onion, chopped	2 teaspoons coarse salt
1 clove garlic, chopped	4 teaspoons sugar
2 tablespoons dark soy sauce	1 teaspoon cornflour dissolved in a little water
2 tablespoons rice vinegar	
1 tablespoon dry sherry	water or stock (approximately 150ml/6fl.oz)
3 tablespoon tomato paste	

Heat the oil, gently fry the shallot and garlic, and add the remaining ingredients one at a time, stirring after each addition to blend, until you get to the water. Taste to ensure the blend is to your liking. Add enough water to achieve a smooth consistency. Cook together for a minute or two, stirring constantly until it reaches boiling point and thickens. Remove from the heat and set aside (add more water later if it becomes too thick).

Oil for frying
1 egg yolk
Flour to dust

Heat some extra oil for frying, deep or shallow as you wish. Remove fish from the marinade, pat dry, brush over with a beaten egg yolk and dust lightly with flour. Fry on both sides until the skin is crisp, about 6–8 minutes. Remove and drain on kitchen paper, then transfer to a serving dish. Reheat the sauce, adjusting seasoning and adding more liquid if necessary, and pour over the fish.

This recipe is good with grey mullet or a similar whole white fish, such as small grouper.

157

INDIVIDUAL SNAPPER PARCELS

This recipe is for small whole fish (1 per person). Clean, trim, and rinse the fish, and pat dry. Slash each fish 2 or 3 times on each side. Lightly oil pieces of foil large enough to enclose each fish and lay the fish on the foil. Cover the surface of each fish with 2 spring onions (green and white parts), finely slivered in 5cm/2in lengths, 2.5cm/1in piece ginger, slivered (put a little spring onion and ginger in the cavity), and sprinkle over it 3–4 tablespoons light or dark soy, and a squeeze or two of lime or lemon juice. Fold foil to enclose fish totally and seal. Place each package in suitably sized baking pan. Cook in a pre-heated oven (200°C/400°F) for 20–30 minutes.

Serve with a steamed green vegetable and some plain long-grained rice.

Sprat (Brisling, Sild when canned)

French: *Sprat*
German: *Sprotte, Sprott*
Spanish: *Espadin*

Category: Oily.
Waters: Home waters.
Shape and colour: Dark blue/bluish-green back with silver sides and belly. Similar to herring.
Price: Very low.
Market size: 8–10cm/3–4in.
Sold as: Whole fish. Also smoked.
Market availability: Very good in season.
Seasonal availability: September to March.
Remarks: Good flavour, but because it is so small it is very bony. However, it is cheap and can make a wonderful supper dish tossed in seasoned flour and fried in bacon fat flavoured with thyme, so don't ignore it.

To test the freshness of a sprat, squeeze the body gently between thumb and forefinger. If it is fresh it will simply slip out from your fingers.

STUFFED SPRATS

750g/1½lb sprats (you should have an even number)
120g/4oz cheddar cheese, grated
60g/2oz soft breadcrumbs
½ teaspoon dried oregano or thyme

Pinch of cayenne
1 tablespoon milk
2 eggs
60g/2oz seasoned flour

Cut off the head and tail of each sprat, split them the full length of the underside and gut. Lay each fish open split side down. Press down firmly along its back with your thumb, loosening the bones from the flesh; on turning the fish over the spine and ribs will easily come away from the flesh leaving you with a butterfly fillet. Rinse, pat dry and set aside.

To make the stuffing, thoroughly mix the cheese, breadcrumbs, oregano or thyme, cayenne, milk and 1 egg. Sandwich a little stuffing between two butterfly fillets until all the stuffing is used up. Beat the remaining egg, and dip each sprat sandwich first into the seasoned flour then into the beaten egg.

You can now cook them in one of these ways:
1. Shallow fry in oil until golden brown on both sides.
2. Bake in an ovenproof dish in hot preheated oven for 15–20 minutes.
3. Cook under a preheated grill for 5 minutes each side.
Serves 4.

Swordfish

French: *Espadon*
German: *Schwertfisch*
Spanish: *Pez Espada*

Category: Game fish.
Waters: Mediterranean, Indian Ocean, United States.
Shape and colour: Large powerful streamlined fish with a long sword-like upper jaw, hence its name. It is without scales and has a rough skin, dark brown paling to a white belly.
Price: Moderate to high.
Market size: From 125cm/4ft without sword.
Sold as: Steaks/cutlets.

159

Market availability: Fair, fresh; good, frozen.
Seasonal availability: Year round.
Remarks: Compact, nearly bone-free creamy-beige flesh with a sweet flavour. Particularly good for grilling or barbecuing and a great favourite in my home. Whole fish are being imported from the Mediterranean and the Indian Ocean; loins from the United States.

Marinate steaks or cutlets (120–180g/4–6oz each) in a simple marinade for about half an hour before cooking on a pre-oiled grill or baking in a buttered dish with a sprinkling of herbs, a dash of vermouth, and a grinding of pepper. Serve with a flavoured butter, a *salsa verde*, or a tomato sauce spiced to your taste.

Tilapia (St Peter's Fish)

Category: Round, freshwater.
Waters: Temperate fresh waters.
Shape and colour: Round slightly compressed deep body with a small head, dark grey or rosy red, heavy scales and sharp fins.
Price: Moderate.
Market size: 15–25cm/6–10in.
Sold as: Whole fish and fillets.
Market availability: Good.
Seasonal availability: Year round.
Remarks: The grey tilapia is mainly imported from Holland and Israel where it is farmed, though in fact it is bred all over the world. It has become quite popular as its flesh is firm and flavoursome. I remember first eating tilapia on the shores of Lake Kinneret in Israel. The chef of the Arab restaurant slashed the flesh, rubbed salt into the cuts, dipped the flesh into seasoned flour, then shallow fried it. Then he poured garlic butter over it. I can still taste that fish, and all that was left on my plate was a clean white skeleton. Today, many years later, fresh red tilapia is being imported from Jamaica.

Trout, Rainbow (Steelhead Trout)

French: *Truite Arc-en-Ciel*
German: *Regenbogenforelle*
Spanish: *Trucha Arco Iris*

Category: Round, freshwater.
Waters: Home rivers, in the good old days (it was introduced to this country from America), but now farmed.
Shape and colour: Blunt head on a trim body, olive-green to bluish back paling on the sides to a white belly. Back and sides finely spotted.
Price: Low to moderate.
Market size: 20–60cm/8–24in.
Sold as: Whole fish and fillets, and also smoked.
Market availability: Very good.
Seasonal availability: Year round.
Remarks: It has a delicate flavour and its flesh is white or pink depending upon whether the fish has been fed on a shrimp-rich diet. The large fish are often called, incorrectly, salmon trout.

The brown trout brought home after a day by a quiet stream is not caught commercially.

STEAMED TROUT FILLETS

---

2 trout, each about 360–420g/12–14oz, filleted Juice of ½ lemon or lime Grated rind of ½ lemon or lime	15g/½oz butter Sprigs of parsley or chervil, to garnish

On a large dinner plate, lay the trout fillets, sprinkle with the lemon or lime juice and rind, and dot with butter. Cover with a second dinner plate and steam over a saucepan of boiling water for about 8 minutes. Garnish with parsley or chervil.

You can steam any small fillet of fish this way, and you could vary the seasoning: a little orange juice mixed with soy; a teaspoon of sesame oil with slivers of ginger and spring onion. Serves 2.

In *The Seafish Cookbook*, Sue Hicks has a good simple recipe for trout with almonds on which the following is based:

Plain flour for coating	120g/4oz clarified butter
Sea salt and freshly ground	120g/4oz flaked almonds
pepper	Juice of half a lemon
4 medium trout, cleaned,	Parsley or dill, finely chopped
rinsed and patted dry	to garnish (optional)

Mix the flour with the salt and pepper. Roll the trout in the seasoned flour. In a frying or sauté pan, heat half the butter and fry the fish for 3 or 4 minutes on each side until the skin starts to brown. Transfer the fish to a warmed serving plate. Add the rest of the butter to the pan with the almonds and fry gently, stirring occasionally, until the nuts are golden brown. Add the lemon juice, a little pepper to taste, stir, heat through and pour over the fish.

Garnish with parsley or dill and serve immediately with simple steamed or boiled potatoes and steamed green beans or other green vegetable.

Trout are also good coated with oatmeal and fried with bacon (see recipe for herring, page 117).

Tuna (Albacore)

French: *Germon*
German: *Weisser Thun*
Spanish: *Albacora, Atunblanco*

Category: Round, oily.
Waters: All warm waters.
Shape and colour: Similar to but smaller than Blue and Yellow Fin Tuna, with a deep streamlined body, a pointed snout and a fast-tapering tail, with particularly long pectoral fins. Its flesh is chocolate in colour and lighter than the deep red of other tunas and is not as dense.
Price: High.
Market size: 1–1.5m/3–4ft.
Sold as: Steaks or cutlets, as required.
Market availability: Poor to fair.
Seasonal availability: Year round.
Remarks: Usually imported from the Mediterranean. It is particularly suited to barbecuing, braising, grilling and baking, and less successful steamed or poached. Some believe it has the sweetest flesh of all tunas. It's not often seen, but I have a customer who won't eat any other tuna.

Tuna (Bonito)

French: *Bonite*
German: *Bonito, Pelamide*
Spanish: *Bonito*

Category: Round, oily.
Waters: Most warm waters.
Shape and colour: Of the tuna family, so a thick deep round streamlined body with a pointed head and a fast-tapering tail. Silver-steel stripes on a blue-black back and sides with white underbelly.
Price: Moderate.
Market size: 30–50cm/12–20in.
Sold as: Whole fish or steaks.
Market availability: Frozen, good; fresh, fair.
Seasonal availability: Year round (imported).
Remarks: Imported fresh from France and the Mediterranean, and imported frozen from all over the world. Sweet and juicy dark red flesh. Like all tunas, a good fish for grilling, baking and the barbecue, and the bonito is also probably the cheapest of the tunas. It tends to bleed quite a lot so ask your fishmonger to wrap it twice.

Dried bonito flakes are used with the preserved seaweed, *konbu*, to make the Japanese stock, *dashi*.

ALAN DAVIDSON'S BASQUE BONITO

In *North Atlantic Seafood*, a bible for me and for many others, Alan Davidson describes a Basque fisherman's dish of bonito, a marmite. Mr Davidson quotes from a Spanish writer, Dionisio Perez, who says that traditionally a marmite should be cooked and eaten in the galley of a fishing boat. To continue to quote Senor Perez, via Mr Davidson:

'Whoever aspires to make a good marmite will put a casserole on the fire and in it oil, onion and garlic. He will cut into slices, not too big, a large piece of bonito. He will put these straight away into the casserole and then add the necessary quantities of water and potatoes, which should all be cooked over a moderate and measured fire. He will put in just the right amount of salt, a pinch of paprika and some canned red pimentos. If these ingredients are complemented by some cubes of bread when the cooking is well under way, he will have, at the moment of bringing the dish to table, a genuine marmite which will transport him, no matter how far away he should be, to the northern coasts when the dish had its origin.'

Now that sounds wonderful.

163

Tuna (Blue Fin and Yellow Fin)

French: *Thon*
German: *Thun, Thunfisch*
Spanish: *Atun*

Category: Round, oily.

Waters: Mediterranean, Indian Ocean, United States waters. Whole fresh fish are imported from the Mediterranean and Indian Ocean; loins from the United States.

Shape and colour: Very large streamlined fish with a pointed head, deep middle body and a fast-tapering tail. Bluish-black back and sides paling to a white belly. The difference, as names suggest, is the colour of the fins. The fish every sea angler wants to have photographed hanging beside and towering above him as proof of prowess.

Price: High.

Market size: From 90cm/3ft. Imported as whole fish or loin fillets.

Sold as: Cutlets (steaks), sometimes sliced and smoked.

Market availability: Good, fresh; very good, frozen.

Seasonal availability: Year round.

Remarks: Deep red juicy firm flesh, virtually bone free. Very good for grilling on a barbecue, but you need only small portions as it is compact and filling. Care should be taken not to overcook it.

Also very good for stir-frying, sliced into strips and quickly tossed in hot oil in which a little chopped shallot and garlic has been sautéed until golden brown. Add a red pepper cut in chunks, perhaps a few green beans, a splash of soy sauce, a little lemon or lime juice, maybe even a little chilli. Turn onto a dish and serve with boiled rice and/or a crisp green salad.

According to my Japanese customers, Yellow Fin Tuna is the best for *sashimi*.

TUNA TERIYAKI

This is for the grill or barbecue and shark or swordfish steaks can be used equally well. The marinade is quite strongly flavoured and could also be used to brush over a whole fish that you might grill or barbecue, such as red mullet or snapper.

This recipe is for 4–6 people, using 1 steak per person. Place the steaks in a dish that will take them in one layer. Mix together the following:

164

4 tablespoons light oil
(safflower/sunflower/
grapeseed)
Juice of ½ lime or lemon
2 tablespoons sherry or rice
wine

1 tablespoon light soy sauce
Small piece of ginger, finely
chopped or grated
1 clove garlic, finely chopped
or crushed
½ teaspoon sharp mustard

Pour the mixture over the steaks and leave for 45–60 minutes, turning once during this time. Preheat the grill or barbecue remembering to oil the grid. Lift the steaks from the marinade, drain and lightly dry on kitchen paper, but reserve the marinade. Cook for 5–6 minutes, turning over once, and basting two or three times with the marinade.

Turbot

French: *Turbot*
German: *Steinbutt*
Spanish: *Rodaballo*

Category: Flat.
Waters: Home waters.
Shape and colour: Large, round flat fish with a small head. Sandy or dark-brown back with small hard nodules but no scales, and a white belly.
Price: Very high.
Market size: 50–100cm/20–40in.
Sold as: Whole fish fillets and cutlets.
Market availability: Fair to good.
Seasonal availability: Year round.
Remarks: Considered the prince of the flat fish with firm, thick and moist flesh with an excellent flavour. The small fish, up to 1–1.5kg/2–3lb, are known as chicken turbot. For the price I would just as soon have a brill or lemon sole, but if you are feeling extravagant then by all means treat yourself. The bones make a wonderful stock.

The best are caught on a long line; they are also now farmed, but the farmed fish are rarely seen.

For a fishmonger, the turbot is very hard to price for besides being expensive anyway, there can be anything from a third to a half of the fish lost in wastage.

There is a recipe called 'Turbot Van Melzen' which the chef Adrian Clarke named after friends. It calls not only for fillets of turbot but also for 250g/½lb langoustine tails (plus 275ml/½ pint white wine, nearly 550ml/1 pint cream, and a dash of port). It sounds delicious, but extremely rich.

We were most intrigued by his recommendation regarding the stock, made, naturally, with the turbot head, skin and bones: it requires simmering for 3 hours! A man after my own heart. None of this nonsense about only 20 or 30 minutes. You need to get all the good you can from the head and bones, and this is particularly true of turbot whose bones are quite gelatinous.

A book for the 'Good Wife', published at the beginning of the century, suggests that turbot should be rubbed all over with a cut lemon to 'make the flesh look white when sent to table'. It is quite a good tip. It also recommends serving poached turbot with oyster sauce (*not* the bottled variety) which also sounds good.

Theodora Fitzgibbon, in *A Taste of Wales*, suggests serving poached turbot with Granville sauce (see p.58).

POACHED TURBOT WITH LEEKS

4 turbot cutlets (each about 180g/6oz), rinsed and patted dry	1 teaspoon sea salt
4 young leeks, finely sliced	A few black or white peppercorns
3–4 tablespoons coarsely chopped parsley	120ml/4fl.oz white wine (optional)
	Stock or water to cover

Use a sauté or steep-sided pan which will take the cutlets comfortably without overlapping. Lay the sliced leeks on the bottom of the pan, add the parsley, lay the cutlets on top and season with the salt and add the peppercorns. Pour in the optional white wine and enough stock or water to just cover the fish. Cover the pan and simmer gently for 15–20 minutes, until the fish is barely cooked through. Leave in the pan removed from the heat until the sauce is prepared, or remove the fish and keep it on a warm, lightly buttered plate. Strain the poaching liquid and use 2 or 3 table-spoons to add to the sauce.

Alternatively, keeping the poached fish warm, you could make a very quick velouté with 30g/1oz each of butter and flour, using the poaching liquid to thicken to the consistency you like, and add a handful of finely chopped fresh herbs of your choice. Finish with a knob of butter or a spoonful or two of cream. Serves 4.

TURBOT WITH RED CABBAGE

1 tablespoon light oil
2 shallots or 1 onion, finely
   sliced
1 small head of red cabbage,
   trimmed, coarse ribs
   removed, finely sliced
120ml/4fl.oz red wine
juice of half an orange

1–2 teaspoons orange zest
1 teaspoon sugar or honey
salt and pepper to taste
4 tablespoons olive oil
4 turbot steaks (each about
   200g/7oz), rinsed and
   thoroughly patted dry

In a heavy-bottomed saucepan, heat the oil and sauté the shallots or onion until transparent but not browned. Add the cabbage, wine, orange juice and half the zest and sugar, stir thoroughly, half-cover and cook gently until the cabbage is soft (about 20 minutes), stirring occasionally. Don't let it dry out. Adjust seasoning and add the rest of the zest.

In a frying or sauté pan, heat the olive oil and fry the turbot for 3–4 minutes on each side or until golden-brown.

Arrange the cabbage on a serving platter, the fish on top, and spoon on top a little of the remainder of the oil in which the fish was cooked.

You could also add a chopped sharp apple to the cabbage.

Alternative fish: cod, conger, halibut, swordfish.

Weever

French: *Vive*
Spanish: *Escorpion*

Category: Round.
Waters: Home waters.
Shape and colour: Tapering body, grey-brown sides to a creamy belly.
Price: Low.
Market size: 15–20cm/6–8in.
Sold as: Whole fish.
Market availability: Poor.
Seasonal availability: Year round.
Remarks: Not often seen but a good firm-flavoured flesh which is ideal for fish soups.

However, a great deal of care has to be taken to remove the poisonous spines on the gill covers and the first spine of the dorsal fin. So ask your fishmonger to do this for you.

And be careful if you walk into weever-frequented water without any footwear. The fish buries itself in mud and silt and can deliver quite a hefty sting.

Whitebait

Category: Oily.
Waters: Home waters.
Shape and colour: A mixture of small fish, the fry, of mainly herring, pilchard and sprats.
Price: Low.
Market size: Approximately 5–8cm/2–3in.
Sold as: Whole fish.
Market availability: Good (frozen); poor (fresh).
Seasonal availability: Fresh February to July, frozen all year.
Remarks: Excellent flavour. Easy to prepare for the table, and equally easy to spoil.

I remember the first time I cooked whitebait, I didn't know they should be thoroughly dried and ended up with a large ball of fish and flour.

During the 19th century there was a Whitebait Dinner to mark the prorogation or end of Parliament. *Punch* in 1844 published a waggish verse to mark the occasion.

> *'Come, list my lads, my jolly lads, and now without digression,*
> *I'll sing the speech intended for the closing of the Session;*
> *To tell official secrets, p'rhaps, is like a raw beginner,*
> *But isn't this, in double sense, quite an of-fish-al dinner.*
> > *With my whack row de riddle row, fol lol de la*
> > *Chorus: With my whack, &c*
>
> *My lords and gentlemen, we've got her Majesty's commands,*
> *To do what she is glad enough to get quite off her hands:*
> *She wishes us to tell you all—at liberty you are*
> *To go where'er you please; indeed she does not care how far.*
> > *With my whack, &c.'*

Sadly, the tune isn't given.

Alexandre Dumas was also rather impressed by this traditional London fare: 'Certainly one of the most popular dishes in London. I recall being invited by a friend to eat whitebait at Greenwich—without any other excuse or occasion but just to eat whitebait . . . The fish were washed by the handful in ice water, drained on a cloth, and set over ice for 20 minutes. Just before serving, they were rolled in white breadcrumbs, put into a napkin with a handful of flour, shaken, and poured in a sieve so fine only the extra flour could get through it. The sieve was shaken and then plunged with the fish into very hot fat. A minute was sufficient to cook them. When they turned golden, they were removed with the sieve, sprinkled with salt and a little cayenne, arranged on a folded napkin, and served immediately.

'I regret I did not keep the menu of this meal, which was composed of forty-eight dishes, twelve of them fish and each seasoned in its own special fashion.'

Whitebait were probably abundant in the Thames at the time; it is gratifying to report that edible fish once more can be taken from our greatest river.

BASIC WHITEBAIT RECIPE

500g/1lb whitebait will probably serve 4 as a starter or 2 healthy appetites for a main course.

The secret of not making a soggy mess is to ensure that the fish are dried thoroughly after rinsing, and that the frying oil is sufficiently hot (use the time-honoured test of throwing in a small piece of bread to see how quickly it becomes golden-brown).

We use a seasoned flour in which to toss the dried fish: 75–100ml/5–6 tablespoons plain flour, 2 teaspoons coarse sea salt, ½ teaspoon dried thyme, ½ teaspoon cayenne, and a few grindings of black pepper, but you can vary the seasonings as you wish.

Cook only a handful at a time—they will only take a minute or two—and drain thoroughly before serving. You could sprinkle them with deep fried chopped parsley. A few slices of lemon and additional cayenne, black pepper, and sea salt should be available on the table.

Whiting

French: *Merlan*
German: *Wittling, Merlan*
Spanish: *Merlan, Plegonero*

Category: Round, white.
Waters: Home waters.
Shape and colour: A slim silver-grey fish, silver sides and white belly. Member of the cod family.
Price: Low–medium.
Market size: 27+–60cm/11–24in.

Sold as: Whole fish, fillets, and also cured and sold as 'golden cutlets'.
Market availability: Very good.
Seasonal availability: Year round, best in winter months.
Remarks: A much under-rated fish. Traditionally recommended for those with a delicate digestion, but it has a sweet flaky flesh and is extremely versatile. Can be used for any cod recipe.

The classic whiting dish is *en colère*. You can bake it whole. A whole fish—approximately 1kg/2lb—will serve 2–3 people. Rinse a cleaned fish and thoroughly pat dry; score a few times on each side; and season inside and out (you could also put some herbs in the cavity—parsley, tarragon, a bayleaf, perhaps a little chopped fennel or celery). Put in a well-oiled or buttered baking dish large enough to take the whole fish, pour over about 150ml/½ pint liquid, which could be a combination of fish stock and white wine or vermouth; cover loosely with foil and bake in a preheated oven for about 30 minutes or until the fish is cooked through, removing the foil for the last 10 minutes. Check that the liquid does not entirely evaporate away.

Either serve the fish in the baking dish or transfer it to a warmed serving platter, add to the remaining cooking liquids a little more fish stock, a spoonful or two of cream or yoghurt and some fresh chopped herbs. Stir to blend and heat, pour over the fish.

FRIED SPICED FILLET OF WHITING

2 whiting fillets, skinned, cut in serving pieces	1 teaspoon ground cumin
1 egg, beaten lightly with about 2 tablespoons milk	1 teaspoon cayenne
4 tablespoons plain flour	1 teaspoon coarse salt
2 teaspoons ground coriander	Oil for shallow frying
	Slices of lemon or lime to garnish

Rinse the fish, pat dry. Combine the flour and the spices and salt. Dip the fish pieces first in the egg mixture, then in the flour mixture, making sure they are fully coated.

Have the oil heated to frying temperature and fry the pieces, first on one side then on the other—the fish should be cooked through when the pieces are a dark golden brown, about 1 minute each side. Serve with slices of lime or lemon. The spiced flour mixture can be adjusted or changed entirely to your taste. Serves 2–4.

Barbara Kafka in her book *Microwave Gourmet* has produced a version of whiting *en colère* with parsley sauce for the microwave. The fish is curled around as if biting its own tail. (We came across a recipe for the same arrangement of a garfish with the needle-like nose pierced through its lower belly.)

WHITING WITH PARSLEY SAUCE

1 whiting (1.25kg/2½lb), cleaned, rinsed and dried
1 tablespoon plus 1 teaspoon cornflour
150ml/5fl.oz milk
Generous 80ml/5 tablespoons double cream
30g/1oz parsley, finely chopped
2 tablespoons thinly sliced chives
1 teaspoon salt

Arrange the fish in a 2 litre/4 pint soufflé dish, spine uppermost and its head and tail meeting.

Stir together the cornflour, milk and cream and mix well. Stir in the parsley, chives and salt (you might also like to add a little pepper). Pour the mixture over the fish. Cover tightly with microwave film. Cook at 100% for about 7 minutes. Pierce film with tip of a sharp knife, then remove from the oven. Uncover and serve hot.

Witch (Witch Sole)

French: *Plie Grise*
German: *Rotzunge*
Spanish: *Mendo, Falso Lenguado*

Category: Flat.
Waters: Home waters.
Shape and colour: Oval in shape with a pale or medium-brown slightly mottled back and a white underside.
Price: Moderate to high.
Market size: 30–40cm/12–15in.
Sold as: Whole fish, fillets.
Market availability: Fair to good.
Remarks: An under-rated fish. Good quality white flesh with an excellent flavour. Skinned fillets are a favourite of mine and of my customers. And

it's hard to tell the difference between them and fillets of Dover sole. Even I might be fooled.

Witch makes a much cheaper way to try some of the more elaborate sole dishes that restaurants are so fond of.

Try skinned fillets, spread with a mixture of chopped spring onions, diced mushrooms, chopped parsley or coriander, and rolled (skinned side in) or just folded over. Secure the rolls with a toothpick, brush them with melted butter, sprinkle with dry seasoned breadcrumbs, add another small piece of butter on each roll, and bake for 15–20 minutes in a well-buttered or oiled dish with 2 or 3 tablespoons vermouth.

Alternatively, spread the oiled baking dish with a well-seasoned tomato sauce (see p.64), lay in the rolls, cover with a little more sauce, and bake for about 15–20 minutes in a preheated oven.

Witch fillets are also excellent shallow fried à la Maureen.

1 witch fillet per person	120g/4oz medium or fine
Sea salt	matzah meal
Sunflower or corn oil	2 eggs
½ onion	Salt and pepper to season

Rinse the fish under running water and pat dry. Sprinkle with sea salt and leave for 10 minutes. Rinse again, and dry thoroughly. Heat the oil until it begins to shimmer slightly. Add the piece of onion, fry it until it is brown, then remove. Meanwhile, put the matzah meal in a flat dish long enough to take the fillets, and coat each fillet on both sides with meal, shaking off the excess.

Beat the eggs in a bowl and season with salt and pepper. Dip each fillet in the egg and then again the matzah meal. Taking care that the oil does not burn, fry each fillet for about 3 or 4 minutes until golden brown, then turn and fry the other side. Drain on a rack or on kitchen paper. Serve with slices of lemon and a simple salad.

The double coating makes the egg adhere and also makes it wonderfully crunchy too.

ROUND AND FLAT FISH

Wolf Fish (officially Rockfish; also sometimes called Catfish but not to be confused with the freshwater fish of that name)

French: *Loup de mer*
German: *Katfisch*
Spanish: *Perro del Norte, Lobo*

Category: Round.
Waters: Home waters.
Shape and colour: Elongated body, dark blue/grey/greenish back with vertical bars, white belly. Massive wolf-life teeth.
Price: Moderate.
Market size: From 45cm/18in.
Sold as: Whole, skinned; fillets.
Market availability: Fair.
Seasonal availability: Year round.
Remarks: This fish comes to market headed and skinned (it is an extremely ugly fish). Good flavour, rather firm flesh, and I think it's likely to become more popular.

Use as any other white fish fillet, seasoned and shallow fried, baked with a sauce of your choice, or grilled.

Wrasse

French: *Vieille, Labre*
German: *Lippfisch*
Spanish: *Maragota, Durado*

Category: Round.
Waters: Home waters.
Shape and colour: Heavy looking fish with a laterally compressed body. It comes in many colours, but mainly green and brown. Large scales.
Price: Moderate.
Market size: 23–28cm/9–15in.
Sold as: Whole fish.
Market availability: Good.
Seasonal availability: Most of year.
Remarks: Rather bland flesh which can be an excellent vehicle for flavourings, and can also be included in fish soups. It is often recommended for inclusion in bouillabaisse.

Zander (Pike Perch)

French: *Sandre*
German: *Hechtbarsch, Zander*
Spanish: *Lucioperca*

Category: Round, freshwater.
Waters: Home and European waters.
Shape and colour: Round body, grey-brown with dark vertical bars.
Price: Moderate.
Market size: 45–60cm/18–24in.
Sold as: Whole fish.
Market availability: Fair.
Seasonal availability: Year round.
Remarks: A considerable amount imported from the continent. The bone structure is similar to bass and the flesh has a good flavour, but unfortunately it is rarely seen on the fishmonger's slab. This may change: zander has become a villain. It was introduced into our rivers not long ago and has proved to be a voracious predator and a serious threat to stocks of other river fish. So eat zander and do more than yourself a favour.

It is good baked, perhaps stuffed, and served with a sauce, or use it as part of a freshwater fish stew.

SHELLFISH

Clams

There are several types of these bivalves readily available in Britain and throughout Europe, some now imported from Mediterranean waters.

Clam (Palourde)

French: *Palourde*
Spanish: *AlmejaFina*

Category: Shellfish, bivalve.
Waters: Home waters and Mediterranean.
Shape and colour: Bivalve comprising two slightly ribbed concave shells with circular growth lines; light brown with darker mottling.
Price: High.
Market size: 3–6cm/1–2in.
Sold as: Fresh, whole and intact; sold by kg/lb.
Market availability: Fair.
Seasonal availability: Year round.
Remarks: This juicy clam is imported from France. It is much prized in mainland Europe and should be better known in the United Kingdom. Well worth the high price. I recently acquired some from southern Ireland, and they were magnificent and cheap. My local Italian restaurant uses them a great deal.

In his *Mediterranean Seafood* Alan Davidson gives a good recipe for pasta with clams (*vongole*) or mussels *cozze*. He uses vermicelli, but it can equally well be made with spaghetti or linguine.

VERMICELLI ALLA VONGOLE IN BIANCO

60ml/2fl.oz olive oil
2 cloves garlic, chopped or
crushed
Approximately 1½kg/3lb
vongole, well washed and
purged (check with your
fishmonger)

Lot of parsley, finely
chopped
Black pepper and salt
600g/1¼lb pasta

Heat the olive oil in a large pan, add the garlic and cook until starting to brown. Add the *vongole* and a sprinkling of black pepper. As the *vongole* open, remove them from the pan, take them from their shells and set aside. Continue to cook the sauce to reduce. Then return the *vongole* meat to the pan, add the chopped parsley, and cook all together for another 2 or 3 minutes. We might be tempted to add a tablespoon or two of white wine with the *vongole*.

While you're preparing the sauce, cook the pasta in lightly salted water. Strain and add part of the sauce, serving the rest of the sauce in a sauceboat. Serves 4.

Mussels will give rather more liquor so the sauce might need to cook a little longer; and you can ring the changes on the sauce by doubling the amount of olive oil and adding a large can of tomatoes, strained, with the *vongole*, making the dish *con i pelati*.

Clam, Hardshell (also known as Quahog)

Category: Shellfish, bivalve.
Waters: Home waters.
Shape and colour: Grey-beige bivalve, slightly ribbed concave shells with circular growth lines.
Price: Low–moderate.
Market size: 5–10cm/2–4in.
Sold as: Whole, intact, by the piece or kg/lb, depending on size.
Market availability: Good.
Seasonal availability: Available year round; best July–March.
Remarks: Accidentally introduced to Britain from the United States about 1960 and is flourishing here, especially in Southampton waters. One theory is that a chef on board one of the ocean-going liners threw some overboard; they liked our waters so much they decided to stay.

Good flavoured beige-yellow flesh, but the large ones can be quite chewy if eaten raw, though they can be marinated for about half an hour to soften in lemon or lime juice and water.

They are great for clam chowders (see p.227); the smaller cherrystones can be eaten raw or steamed. American Indians in the east used the shells as a form of currency, the purple coloured shells being more valuable than the white (whelk shells were also used, and on the west coast so were mussel shells).

Like oysters, they can be eaten raw with a squeeze of lemon and a dash of Tabasco, but they are very good steamed. Rinse and brush clean if necessary 500g/1lb clams (2–3 people as a starter), put them in a large saucepan with 100ml/4fl.oz water, 50ml/2fl.oz white wine, ½ stalk lemon grass, chopped (or 1 slice lemon), 1 slice orange, 2–3 tablespoons chopped parsley, a small red chilli (optional) and ground black pepper. Cover the saucepan and steam over a high heat for about 5–6 minutes or until all clams are open. Divide the clams with their juice into small soup plates.

Clam, Razorshell

French: *Couteau*
German: *Meerscheide, Scheiden-Muschel*
Spanish: *Longeiron Mubergo*

Category: Shellfish, bivalve.
Waters: Home and Mediterranean.
Shape and colour: Looks like the old-fashioned cut-throat razor, elongated glossy greenish-brown shell.
Price: Moderate to high.
Market size: 10–20cm/4–8in.
Sold as: Fresh, whole intact; sometimes available smoked, in packs of 8–12.
Market availability: Poor to fair.
Seasonal availability: Year round.
Remarks: Widely spread in United Kingdom waters but it seems they are commercially caught mainly in Scotland and the Channel Islands. They are highly prized in mainland Europe; smoked razorshells are absolutely delicious. In fact raw razorshells are very sweet and tender—a squeeze of lemon juice and you need nothing else. If cooking them, they should be done very quickly or they will start to shrink and go hard, as do any shellfish. I'm glad to say the demand for this excellent creature is increasing.

Clam, Venus Shell

French: *Verni*
Spanish: *Saverina*

Category: Shellfish, bivalve.
Waters: Home waters and Mediterranean.
Shape and colour: Reddish-brown, concave shells with a very high sheen, slightly ribbed with circular growth lines.
Price: Low to moderate.
Market size: 5–7.5cm/2–3in.
Sold as: Whole, intact; by weight or the piece depending on size.
Market availability: Fair.
Seasonal availability: Year round, including imports.
Remarks: Probably seen in your fishmonger's under the name 'Verni'. Often eaten raw, but the larger ones tend to be chewy and are better cooked. Sometimes harvested off the south-west coast and the Channel Islands and are also imported from France. Probably more often seen in the south-east.

Clam, Warty Venus

French: *Praire*
Spanish: *Almeja*

Category: Shellfish, bivalve.
Waters: Home waters and Mediterranean.
Shape and colour: Beige/brown circular shells, distinctly ribbed and with circular growth lines.
Price: Low.
Market size: 3–6cm/1–2½in.
Sold as: Whole/intact, usually by weight.
Market availability: Fair.
Seasonal availability: Year round, mainly imported.
Remarks: Another variety more highly prized in mainland Europe. They could also be found on the beaches of south and west coasts of the United Kingdom if you look for them. Your fishmonger may sell them under the name 'Praire'.

Cockle (Clam)

French: *Coque*
German: *Herzmuschel*
Spanish: *Berberecho, Croque*

Category: Shellfish, bivalve.
Waters: Home waters and Mediterranean.
Shape and colour: Small bivalve, grey-beige concave shells, quite heavily ribbed in fan design.
Price: Low.
Market size: In shell, around 2–3cm/1in.
Sold as: Most often pre-cooked and shelled, fresh or frozen, by the pound or pint measure; in shell, by weight.
Market availability: Pre-cooked very good; in shell, poor–fair.
Seasonal availability: Year round, best in summer.
Remarks: Usually available pre-cooked and shelled, preserved in brine or vinegar, or dry salted. They are also available frozen, pre-cooked and shelled, but are becoming increasingly available fresh in the shell. Recently I sautéed some in garlic butter until the shells opened and ate them with brown bread and butter. Wonderful. Cockle meat can be substituted for the increasingly popular *vongole*.

Cockles have always been a mainstay on stalls in British seaside resorts, usually served on small paper plates with a little two-pronged wooden fork. A splash of vinegar and a dash of ground white pepper, and the average British holidaymaker is happy to wander along the seafront with a very tasty snack. A more sophisticated taste might prefer a squeeze of lemon juice and a hint of cayenne, but I'm a traditionalist at heart . . .

They are also a marvellous addition to many dishes, such as fish pies, soups, seafood salads and pizzas, as well as making a particularly good sauce for a simple white fish.

In summer, blanch some samphire, and while it is still hot, throw in a handful of frozen unsalted shelled cockles. Let stand for a few minutes, and toss lightly. I call this Pam's passion, after a good friend and customer served this to a party and received rave reviews. Samphire and clams are natural partners. Steam some large clams in shell until they open. Mix the clam meat and juices with blanched or steamed samphire. You could add a little melted butter, and a grinding of black pepper.

Dog Cockle (Clam)

French: *Amande de mer*
Spanish: *Almendra de mar*

Category: Shellfish, bivalve.
Waters: Home waters and Mediterranean.
Shape and colour: Beige concave shell with a zig-zag pattern.
Price: Low to moderate.
Market size: 3–5cm/1.5–2in.
Sold as: Whole intact, usually by weight.
Market availability: Fair.
Seasonal availability: Year round, with imports.
Remarks: The dog cockle is a slightly larger creature than the more commonly seen cockle, to which it is not related. It is seen in the United Kingdom more usually in the south east, but it is not fished commercially in our waters. It is encountered in France and Spain and is imported to England, and often sold under its French name, *amande*.

Crab (Edible Crab)

French: *Crabe, Torteau*
German: *Taschenkrebs*
Spanish: *Cangrejo*

Category: Shellfish, crustacean.
Waters: Home waters.
Shape and colour: Oval hard rigid shell, reddish brown back with yellowish-white underside. One large front claw and three legs on each side of the animal. The shell of the male (cock) is quite flat and the 'tail' on the underside is narrow; it also has larger claws than the female (hen) whose upper shell is slightly domed and the tail, or apron, on the underside is broadly triangular.
Price: Moderate to high, depending on size and season; the male is usually more expensive.
Market size: 12–40cm/5–16in. The minimum legal size is 11cm/4in across the broadest part of the back, but there are regional variations which require larger sizes.
Sold as: Whole, live; whole, cooked; dressed (meat extracted and re-arranged into top shell); claws only; white meat or brown meat only fresh or frozen; or in 500g/1lb packs of half white, half brown meat, unmixed.
Market availability: Very good.

Seasonal availability: Main crab fishing season is from March to September and peaks in May/June. There are fewer to be found during the winter months as they become lethargic in very cold water.

Carolyn Cavele runs her public relations company *Food (and Other) Matters* with enormous flair and skill and is also an enthusiastic fish cook. This is one of her recipes.

CAROLYN'S HOT BUTTERED CRAB

---

4 medium sized cooked crabs	Dash of Tabasco/cayenne
1 small clove garlic	pepper to taste
2 anchovy fillets	60g/2oz fresh white
120g/4oz butter	breadcrumbs
4 tablespoons white wine	Salt and pepper to taste
Juice of 1 lemon	Small bunch of parsley, finely
¼ teaspoon ground nutmeg	chopped

Extract all the meat from the crabs, wash and reserve the shells. Chop finely the garlic and anchovies, and fry them gently in a little of the butter for about 3 minutes. Add the wine, lemon juice and remainder of the butter, the nutmeg, tabasco or cayenne. Stir in half the breadcrumbs and the crab meat. Season to taste. Stir to blend and cook for about 5 minutes. Add most of the chopped parsley, reserving a little for garnish. Transfer the buttered crab mixture to the shells. Sprinkle each with the remaining breadcrumbs and parsley. Finish under the grill.

This will serve 4, or 8 as a starter if the crab mixture is served on hot buttered toast.

Crab, Spider (Spiny Crab)

French: *Araignée de mer*
German: *Seespinne*
Spanish: *Centolla*

Category: Shellfish, crustacean.
Waters: Home waters and Mediterranean.
Shape and colour: The spider-like appearance of this creature is due to the shape and arrangement of the legs and the rather pear-shaped prickly and 'hairy' body. The shell is reddish-brown and the claws are not disproportionately larger than the legs.

Price: Low to moderate.
Market size: From 15–30cm/6–12in width of shell.
Sold as: Whole, live; whole, cooked; or just claws and legs.
Market availability: Fair.
Seasonal availability: Year round, except winter months when the waters are cold and the crab becomes lethargic.
Remarks: There is little meat in the body, nearly all coming from the claws and legs. It is very moist and sweet to my palate, and I probably prefer it to the more common crab. Sadly, it's less appreciated here than in mainland Europe and most British spider crab is exported, to Spain in particular.

Crawfish (Spiny Lobster or Rock Lobster)

French: *Langouste*
German: *Languste*
Spanish: *Langosta*

Category: Shellfish, crustacean.
Waters: Home waters, where the Gulf Stream warms the coast, the Mediterranean, and all warm waters.
Shape and colour: Unlike the lobster, the crawfish has no large claws. Though colour and shape can differ according to the water from which it is taken, its shell is usually dark reddish-brown which becomes bright orange-red on cooking. It is very spiny and has two large horns to protect its eyes and two very long antennae.
Price: Very high.
Market size: 20–50cm/8–20in.
Sold as: Whole, live or cooked; tail only, fresh or frozen imports which tend to be a little cheaper.
Market availability: Fair, fresh, except during winter months.
Seasonal availability: Year round.
Remarks: Not to be confused with the small crayfish, a fresh-water crustacean. Considered a great delicacy. Provides 50% edible flesh to body weight. Some cooks say it is not as good as lobster; well *I* think it's better, *and* it's better value as you get more flesh for your money. Unfortunately the price is rising rapidly since most of the crawfish caught in British waters are being sold abroad.

Crayfish

French: *Ecrevisse*
German: *Edelkrebs, Flusskrebs*
Spanish: *Cangrejo de rio*

Category: Shellfish, crustacean (freshwater).

Waters: Most fresh waters.

Shape and colour: This small shellfish, related to the lobster, is the largest freshwater invertebrate to be found in Britain. The European crayfish is grey; the American crayfish is dark brown/maroon.

Price: Moderate/high.

Market size: 5–7.5cm/2–3in.

Sold as: Whole, fresh or frozen; whole, cooked.

Market availability: Fair, fresh; good, frozen.

Seasonal availability: Most of year, except winter months.

Remarks: It is quite rare to find the native crayfish and those available are mainly imported from Turkey, Kenya or the southern United States. The good news is that there are some crayfish farms being established in the United Kingdom. I sometimes keep them live in an aquarium in the shop; it keeps the children amused. Try them. You won't be disappointed.

This recipe is taken from Jeanne Strang's *Goose Fat and Garlic: Country Recipes from South-West France*. Mrs Strang tells us that the people of that region don't consider a crayfish worth having unless it's taken from a local stream and she is lucky enough to have a good clean crayfish stream not far from her home.

CRAYFISH IN THE PEASANT STYLE (Les Ecrevisses à la Nage ou à la Paysanne)

---

32 crayfish	3 shallots, chopped
400ml/¾ pint dry white wine	Bouquet garni, including
3 medium carrots, chopped	celery leaves and leek tops
3 medium onions, chopped	Salt and pepper

In a deep saucepan, cover the crayfish with the wine and put over a gentle heat. The fish will eventually turn a dark red. Take them off the heat. In another pan make a *court-bouillon* with the vegetables and seasonings covered with water, and simmered for 45 minutes. Strain the *court-bouillon*, reheat the crayfish and when the wine comes to a boil, add the *court-bouillon*. Cover and cook for a further 6 or 7 minutes over high heat, then check the seasoning and serve fish and broth in soup bowls. Serves 4.

Mrs Strang tells us that in the Auvergne the broth is thickened with a roux (*beurre manié*), the seasoning adjusted, and enriched with egg yolks and cream. And that sounds very good too.

According to Anne Willan in *Great Cooks and Their Recipes From Taillevent to Escoffier*, the Renaissance Italian cook Martino had all the right instincts regarding ingredients: 'Salmon is a most agreeable fish, most natural boiled . . . all fish are much better cooked whole than in pieces.' However, crayfish weren't treated with the same deference. They were cooked and opened, the meat mixed with ground almonds, lemon juice, egg yolks, Parmesan cheese, herbs and seasoning, then packed back into the shells and sautéed, and presented with the heads popped back on.

Very good, I'm sure. But can't help thinking life's too short to stuff a crayfish.

Cuttlefish

French: *Seche*
German: *Sepia*
Spanish: *Jibia, Sepia*

Category: Mollusc, cephalopod.
Waters: Home and Mediterranean.
Shape and colour: Oblong sac with a fringe of swimming fins running round the body, and grey or brown zebra pattern stripes. The protruding head has eight short and two long tentacles.
Price: Low to moderate.
Market size: 5–25cm/2–10in.
Sold as: Whole, fresh and frozen.
Market availability: Very good.
Seasonal availability: Most of year.
Remarks: The smallest cuttlefish (about 5cm/2in long and usually imported) are sometimes available ready cleaned, otherwise ask your fishmonger to clean them for you. If possible, tell him if you want to keep the ink, which is in a small sac; ink can also be bought separately in small sachets.

They are particularly popular for some Italian dishes, and the ink is also used to give colour and flavour. They can be poached, fried, stuffed, and barbecued. And if you keep a budgerigar, ask for the bone.

Dublin Bay Prawn (Norway Lobster or Scampi)

French: *Langoustine*
German: *Kaisergranat*
Spanish: *Langostina*

Category: Shellfish, crustacean.
Waters: Home waters, Mediterranean.
Shape and colour: Shaped like a lobster, but with a slender orange body and long orange and white claws.
Price: Moderate–high.
Market size: 7–15cm/3–6in body length.
Sold as: Whole fish (fresh or frozen); tails (scampi), fresh or glazed or breaded, frozen.
Market availability: Good, fresh; good, frozen.
Seasonal availability: Year round.
Remarks: Until the 1950s, British fishermen usually threw back Dublin Bay prawns, but they started to become popular when people began holidaying on the Mediterranean. Since then their popularity exploded and they are eaten in Britain mainly as scampi (the tails); but 'langoustine' is now on most bistro menus. Once again, because of their popularity in mainland Europe most of our home-caught fish are exported.

A customer once came into the shop asking for 1kg/2lb 'fresh' langoustine. When I put them on the scales they started to move about and my customer leaped back crying, 'I said *fresh*, young man, not *live.*'

Raw langoustines are best cooked by plunging into boiling salted water. Bring water back to a rolling boil, then remove the fish and allow to cool. Or cook for a further 2 minutes, remove the fish and plunge immediately into iced water.

During the summer months, the langoustines may moult—the shells become soft and the flesh less firm.

Lobster (European)

French: *Homard*
German: *Hummer*
Spanish: *Bogavante*

Category: Shellfish, crustacean.
Waters: Home waters and Mediterranean.
Shape and colour: Live—dark blue with light orange spots; (turns red on cooking). Two large claws at the front; two long antenna arching back-

185

wards to the end of the tail. The female has smaller claws than the male and a wider tail.

Price: Very expensive, probably the highest; imports a little cheaper.

Market size: 24+–60cm/10–24in overall.

Sold as: Whole, live or cooked.

Market availability: Good, with imports during winter months.

Seasonal availability: See below.

Remarks: Maybe I'm a peasant but I don't know what all the fuss is about. Yes, it's good, but *great*? Imports from Canada of the American (Maine) lobster, which is larger, are available during winter when our native lobster becomes lethargic and is harder to catch. Some think the American is not as good as the European. Lobster is priced by weight, and the ratio between edible flesh and weight is low (about 35:100) and this makes it extremely expensive. But it is 'rich', and even a little can go quite a long way. Best served in the simplest ways. There is a division of opinion regarding the most humane method of killing live shellfish, including lobster. See pages 32–34.

If you have ever been to the north-east coast of the United States—Maine or Rhode Island—you might have had plain boiled lobster with drawn (clarified) butter. You are presented with a whole split or a very large half freshly cooked lobster, a pair of crackers, a lobster pick and a pot of warm butter and left to get on with it. A bib or a very large napkin to tie around the neck is a good accessory.

The flathead lobster (*cigale*) is occasionally imported from Saudi Arabia and I believe has a better flavour, but it is rarely seen.

Mussel (Blue Mussel)

French: *Moule*
German: *Miesmuschel*
Spanish: *Mejillon*

Category: Shellfish, bivalve.

Waters: Home waters and Mediterranean.

Shape and colour: A bivalve with a dark blue or nearly black shell, the animal inside being creamy beige and orange with a brownish-black edge.

Price: Very low to moderate.

Market size: 2–8cm/1–3in.

Sold as: Live, whole by the kilo/pint, sometimes pre-bagged, or cooked and frozen out of shell.

Market availability: Very good.

186

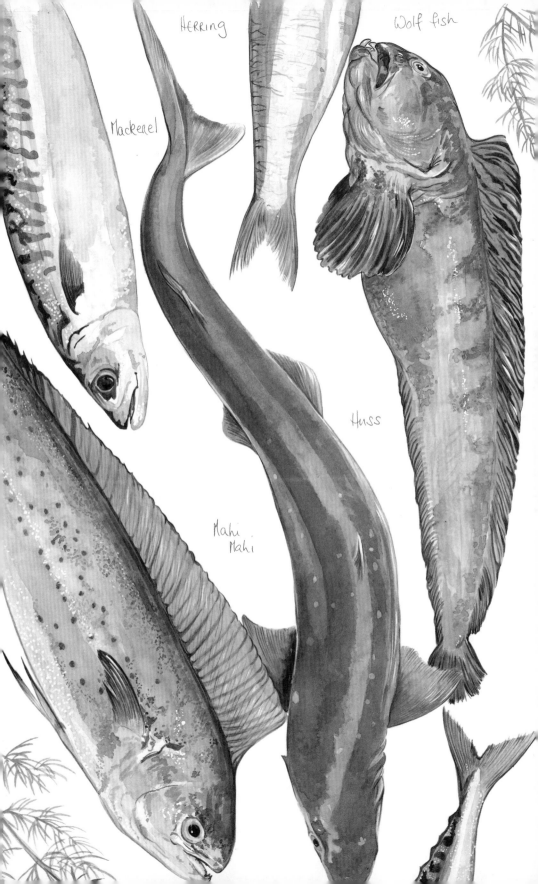

Mackerel

Herring

Wolf fish

Huss

Mahi Mahi

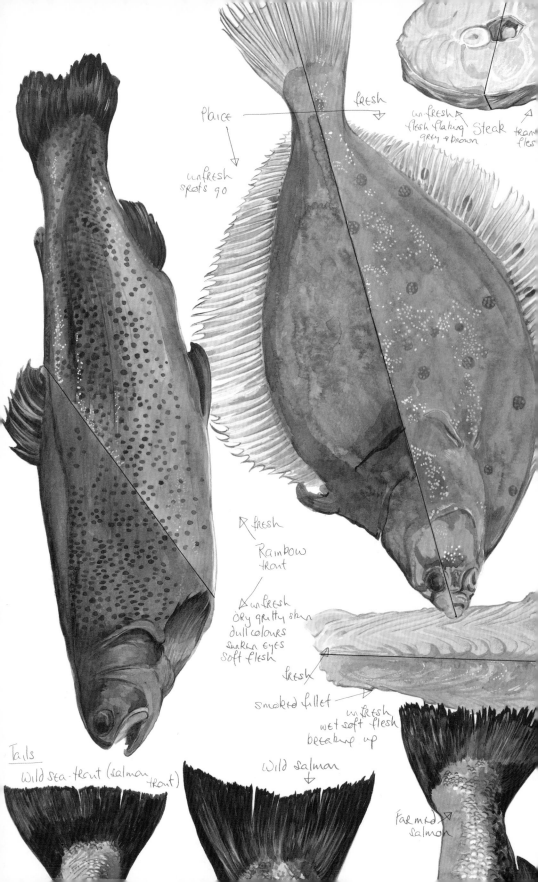

Plaice

fresh

unfresh
flesh flaking Steak
grey & brown

tran-
flesh

unfresh
spots go

fresh
Rainbow
trout

unfresh
dry gritty skin
dull colours
sunken eyes
soft flesh

fresh

smoked fillet

unfresh
wet soft flesh
breaking up

Tails

Wild sea-trout (salmon trout)

Wild salmon

Farmed
salmon

Seasonal availability: September–April; United Kingdom-farmed plus Mediterranean imports, all year round.

Remarks: Perhaps now one of the most popular shellfish. I remember the first time I ate them raw in the south of France in a platter of *fruits de mer*, sprinkled with a little garlic-flavoured wine vinegar they were just wonderful. Increasingly available is the larger green-shelled mussel imported from New Zealand which has a particularly elegant and beautiful shell with a blue-green edge—they are more expensive. We have also seen them sold out of the shell.

I was puzzled when a number of my customers complained that their mussels died after they had tried to feed them overnight. Dr Eric Edward, the director of the Shellfish Association of Great Britain, confirmed that the mussel is a salt-water animal and unless it is kept in its proper environment, it will die. So don't throw your mussels in a bucket of tap water overnight and expect them still to be clicking their shells in the morning.

MUSSEL SOUP WITH SAFFRON

This recipe gives a simple soup enriched with egg and with a very pleasing colour. Saffron is an expensive spice, but you need very little and it is well worth the cost. Instructions for soup for 4 are taken from Liz and Gerd Seeber's *Simple Food: A Menu Book For All Seasons*.

1.5kg/3lb live mussels
30g/1oz butter
1–2 shallots, finely chopped
  (to give 2 tablespoons)
Sprigs of fresh thyme or
  1 teaspoon dried
450ml/¾ pint good dry white
  wine

Salt and pepper to taste
Mini packet of saffron (about
  125mg)
4 egg yolks
550ml/1 pint double cream

Thoroughly clean and rinse the mussels, discarding those with broken shells and any that don't close on receiving a sharp tap. In a large sauté or saucepan, heat the butter, and gently cook the shallots with the thyme until soft and translucent. Add two-thirds of the white wine, bring to a light boil, add the mussels, reduce the heat, cover, and steam the mussels for about 5 minutes with an occasional shake.

Strain over a bowl to reserve the liquor. Discard any mussels that haven't opened, cool, then remove the mussels from their shells and set aside. Strain the mussel liquor through muslin or a very fine sieve. Reheat the liquor, add the saffron dissolved in a little hot water and the remaining wine. Adjust the seasoning.

In a bowl, whisk together the egg yolks and cream. Gradually whisk in a ladleful of mussel liquor, then slowly pour the contents of the bowl into the mussel liquor, whisking to blend. Heat, but do not boil. Test again for seasoning. Add the mussels, heat through for a couple of minutes, and serve immediately. Serves 4.

PHIL'S SPECIAL MUSSELS

2kg/4lb live mussels (about 4 pints)
60g/2oz butter
2 tablespoons oil
1 large onion, cut in rings
120g/4oz tomato purée
275ml/½ pint water
275ml/½ pint Dubonnet or red Martini

4 cloves garlic, crushed
1 each red, green and yellow peppers, seeds and ribs removed and thinly sliced
Handful of parsley, finely chopped, to garnish

Discard all broken or damaged mussels, and those that don't close on giving them a sharp tap. Scrape and clean the remainder, rinse thoroughly and set aside.

In a large saucepan (with a lid) heat together the butter and oil, and sauté the onions. Add the tomato purée, water, Dubonnet or Martini, and bring to the boil. Then add the garlic and sliced peppers. Stir to blend. Cook for 5 minutes, reduce heat, cover and simmer for a further 10 minutes. Turn up the heat, add the mussels, cover again, cook for 5–6 minutes. Remove the lid, and stir bringing the mussels at the bottom of the pan to the top, until all the mussels are open. Remove the saucepan from the heat. Using a slotted spoon, divide the cooked mussels between 4 serving bowls.

Reheat the sauce and pour it over the mussels, and finish by sprinkling with the chopped parsley. Serve with crusty bread. Serves 4.

Norway Lobster See **Dublin Bay Prawn**.

Octopus

French: *Poulpe*
German: *Krake, Tintenfisch*
Spanish: *Pulpo*

Category: Mollusc, cephalopod.
Waters: Home waters and Mediterranean.
Shape and colour: Mainly a head with eight tentacles, each lined with one or two rows of suckers, depending on the species.
Price: Low.
Market size: 5–40cm/2–16in.
Sold as: Whole fish, fresh or frozen.
Market availability: Good.
Seasonal availability: Year round.
Remarks: Octopus feeds exclusively on shellfish and therefore its white flesh is mild and sweet. Anyone who has holidayed in Spain is probably familiar with the dish of octopus in its ink, or cooked with garlic and peppers served in Spanish bars. While octopus is often sold ready cleaned and tenderised (though you still need to cut out the eyes and any gristle), some of the larger animals need to be bashed about a bit to tenderise them—beat with a mallet or a rolling pin or some people throw them a few times against the sides of the kitchen sink. I have even seen a recommendation to bake it for six hours on the lowest heat before eating.

Octopus provençal is a wonderful dish.

Claudia Roden in *The Food of Italy* has a very good version that serves 4:

500g/1lb octopus meat (baby octopus if possible)	300ml/10fl.oz dry white or red wine
2 tablespoons olive oil	Salt and pepper
2 cloves garlic, chopped	2 teaspoons sugar
3 tomatoes, peeled and chopped	Bunch parsley

Boil some water and blanch the octopus for a minute to thoroughly clean and be rid of any scum; the octopus will become firm and curl up. Chop it coarsely. In a sauté or steep-sided frying pan, heat the olive oil and gently fry the octopus. Add the chopped garlic and when it begins to brown slightly, add the tomatoes, wine, salt and pepper to taste, and a little sugar. Stir. Add enough water to just cover; lower the heat, cover the pan, and simmer for between 30 and 45 minutes depending on whether small or larger octopus are used. Test for tenderness. Sprinkle with chopped parsley and serve.

You can make a spicier version by adding a couple of chopped anchovies, a chilli or two (according to taste and tolerance), some Tabasco and a spoonful or two of capers.

Oyster

French: *Huître*
German: *Auster*
Spanish: *Ostra*

'I think oysters are more beautiful than any religion . . . They not only forgive our unkindness to them; they justify it, they incite us to go on being perfectly horrid to them. Once they arrive at the supper-table they seem to enter thoroughly into the spirit of the thing. There's nothing in Christianity or Buddhism that quite matches the sympathetic unselfishness of an oyster.'

Saki, The Chronicles of Clovis

Category: Shellfish, bivalve.
Waters: Home waters, Mediterranean.
Shape and colour: A very rough-styled oval/circular beige-grey bivalve, the upper shell being rather flat and the lower more bowl-shaped and thicker. The annual growth rings are clearly visible. The creature within is creamy beige, sometimes with a slightly green tinge.
Price: High to very high, depending on size and where they come from.
Market size: Natives are sold as Nos. 1, 2, and 3 according to relative size; the French also grade the Gigas according to weight.
Sold as: Live, whole; by the half-dozen, dozen or individually; also available frozen, meat only, mainly from Japan.
Market availability: Fair for native in season; farmed, very good all year.
Seasonal availability: Native, September–April (prohibited 14 May–4 August). Farmed, year round.
Remarks: There are various kinds of oyster and afficionados are fierce in their loyalties. In the United Kingdom, Whitstables, Colchesters and Helfords have been the best-known, but Whitstable is no longer a 'native' and Colchester oysters are not grown in Colchester. Chris Leftwich of Fishmongers' Hall considers the best natives now might be Mersea or South Coast. There are a number of farmed oysters available in this country, all of them Gigas-Pacific with a deeply frilled shell. The Portuguese, which has a slightly elongated stone-like shell, is now hardly if ever

found. Increasingly available are the farmed Pacific oysters from the west coasts of Ireland and Scotland where they are reared in Atlantic waters. I have sold and tasted them, and they are extremely good.

There are a number of ways to cook oysters: Rockefeller; wrapped in bacon and grilled; breaded and spiced. The southern regions of the United States have been particularly creative in their dealings with oysters: fried; stuffed; pan broiled; scalloped; or pickled. Diamond Jim Brady would have a mid-morning snack of two or three dozen oysters and clams, then more at lunch (an hour later) and start dinner with at least another two dozen—large Lynnhaven—oysters. Given what else he could consume, he lived to quite a ripe age—61.

If you like oysters, particularly the natives (or *fines clairs*), the best way to eat them is raw, from the shell, with a squeeze of lemon. Some like a dash of Tabasco. The French seem to like finely chopped shallots in wine vinegar. The Pacific oysters, however, tend to be large and 'meaty' and cook very well. This recipe from Kampuchea, based on one in *Asia: The Beautiful Cookbook* is absolutely delicious. Allow 4–6 oysters per person. The sauce should be enough for 4–6 people):

Pacific oysters
2 tablespoons vegetable oil
2 cloves garlic, finely chopped or crushed
1 stalk lemon grass, finely chopped or minced
1 large red chilli, finely chopped or minced
Piece of preferably young ginger, about 2.5cm/1in, finely chopped or minced

1 tablespoon finely chopped mint
2 tablespoons lime or lemon juice
2 tablespoons fish sauce
1 teaspoon sugar
Sprigs of fresh fennel, coriander or parsley to garnish

Open the oysters over a dish to catch the liquor. Loosen the oysters from the bottom shell and discard the top shell.

In a small frying pan, heat the oil; add the garlic, lemon grass, chilli and ginger; fry gently until the aromas start to tickle the nostrils; add the chopped mint, stir, and set aside. In a small saucepan, heat together the lime juice, fish sauce and sugar, adjusting to taste, and stir until the sugar has dissolved. Drop the oysters in with their reserved liquor, and cook gently just long enough to heat through. Remove the oysters from the cooking liquid and put them back into their bottom shells and arrange them on a platter or individual plates. Spoon the sauce over the oysters,

191

sprinkle the fried herb mixture over, and garnish with fresh fennel, coriander or parsley.

Frozen oyster meat (usually from Japan), after defrosting and rinsed, can be dipped in batter and deep fried. Serve with a side dish of soy sauce, rice vinegar, a little slivered ginger and/or a little chopped chilli pepper. Oyster meat can also be added to a steak and kidney pie to recreate a Dickensian favourite (it was probably added to stretch the meat, which would have been much more expensive than oysters).

Periwinkle (Winkle)

French: *Bigorneau*
German: *Strandschneche*
Spanish: *Bigaro, Mincha*

Category: Shellfish, single shell.
Waters: Home waters.
Shape and colour: A small spiral shell, dark green to black, the little creature within closes a little door to keep itself cosy.
Price: Very low.
Market size: Up to 2.5cm/1in.
Sold as: Whole and cooked, by the weight or measure.
Market availability: Very good.
Seasonal availability: Year round.
Remarks: An essential part of a seafood platter. Traditionally, the meat is extracted with a pin. Eat as is, or dip in salt and/or spiced vinegar.

Prawn (Northern, Deepwater or Greenland Prawn)

French: *Crevette Nordique*
German: *Tiefseegarnele*
Spanish: *Gamba*

Category: Shellfish, crustacean.
Waters: North Atlantic.
Shape and colour: This prawn is usually cooked at sea and frozen, thus rarely seen fresh. The flesh is pinkish white and very sweet.
Price: Low to high (see below).
Market size: 2.5–10cm/1–4in.
Sold as: Fresh: whole, peeled; frozen: whole, peeled and packed with glaze.

Market availability: Very good.
Seasonal availability: Year round.
Remarks: Most of the prawns sold in the United Kingdom are northern prawns and prices depend on size and, when peeled and frozen, the amount of glaze used. Local species seem rarely to be exploited, and when they are to be found they are overpriced. It is said that a glaze on peeled prawns is necessary to protect them from dehydration and freezer burn and is simply a layer of frozen water which can vary from between 6% (the minimum necessary) and 40% of total weight. So, if you have to buy frozen peeled prawns, choose those with the least glaze, even though they cost more, otherwise you are paying for prawns and water. Legislation is soon to be introduced which will require clear indication of the net weight of prawn. Also, look on the package to see where they are from. A lot of the prawns from South-East Asia are cheap, but have very little flavour and are really only good for strong-flavoured recipes such as curries.

PRAWNS IN GARLIC BUTTER (SEAFISH in conjunction with *Woman's Realm*)

This is a microwave recipe, but you can easily prepare it on a conventional hob. It will serve two, or just me.

2 cloves garlic, crushed
60g/1oz butter
Pinch of paprika or cayenne
1 tablespoon lemon juice

1 teaspoon fresh thyme
 or ½ teaspoon dried
250g/8oz prawns in shell

Put the garlic and butter in a bowl, cover and microwave until the butter has melted, about 1½ minutes. Stir in the paprika or cayenne, lemon juice and thyme; add the prawns and toss them around to coat. Microwave uncovered for 1 minute to heat through, and garnish with a sprig of fresh thyme.

Tiger Prawns

Category: Shellfish, crustacean.
Waters: Indian Ocean, Gulf waters, waters of South-East Asia.
Shape and colour: Dark greenish-brown with darker rings in the raw state. Shell turns rosy red and the flesh pale pinkish-white when cooked.
Price: Very high.

Market size: 12–30cm/5–12in.
Sold as: Whole; tails only; fresh or frozen.
Market availability: Fair to good, fresh; good, frozen.
Seasonal availability: Year round (imports).
Remarks: Imports are increasing with demand throughout the country.

To see 2 or 3 large tiger prawns on a plate is a special pleasure. I particularly like them fried with a little garlic, paprika, a spoonful of tomato purée, and a dash of brandy. Six prawns would be a feast for two, best eaten by candlelight.

Each summer I invite a number of friends to join the family in a fish feast. It means quite a lot of preparation, but it's a marvellous day starting from noon and going until whenever. If the weather is good we set tables in the garden, and the great platters of seafood, which of course include tiger prawns, are augmented by barbecued sardines, snappers and whatever looks good at the time.

The Thai chef, Vatcharin Bhumichitr, includes in *The Taste of Thailand* a very good recipe for prawn curry:

2 tablespoons vegetable oil
1 large garlic clove, finely chopped
1 tablespoon red curry paste (available pre-prepared—use Thai paste or substitute an Indian paste)
250ml/8fl.oz coconut milk*
2 tablespoons fish sauce
1 teaspoon sugar
12 large raw prawns (about 7.5cm/3in long, beheaded, peeled, deveined, but with the small tail shell left on)

2 lime leaves, finely sliced (or substitute 1 stalk of lemon grass, finely chopped)
1 small red chilli, finely sliced lengthwise
A few leaves of 'holy' (Asian) basil, or substitute sweet basil

In a wok or frying pan, heat the oil, add the chopped garlic and fry until golden brown. Add the curry paste, stir to mix, and cook briefly. Add half

* Coconut milk is now available in cans in major supermarkets and Oriental stores. The milk can also be made by pouring boiling water over unsweetened dessicated coconut (about 250ml/8fl.oz water to 120g/4oz coconut). Stir, and let the mixture stand for about 10 minutes. Line a sieve with muslin and, over a bowl, pour the coconut liquid through the sieve. Gather the corners of the muslin together and squeeze as much coconut milk out as possible. Alternatively, use a packet of dried coconut milk powder and follow directions on the packet.

194

the coconut milk, the fish sauce and the sugar, and stir to blend—the mixture should thicken slightly.

Add the prawns and cook until they start to become opaque. Add the remaining half of the coconut milk, the lime leaves or lemon grass, and the chilli. Continue to cook, turning the prawns in the sauce until they are cooked through.

With a perforated spoon, remove the prawns and arrange them in a serving dish. Add the basil leaves to the sauce, stir, simmer for a few seconds, then pour the sauce over the prawns and serve with boiled rice. If you want to add a vegetable, a few string beans cut in 5cm/2in pieces could be added after the curry paste—they should still be crunchy when the dish is finished.

Scallop (Escallop)

French: *Coquille St Jacques*
German: *Kamm-Muschel, Pilger-Muschel*
Spanish: *Vieira*

Category: Shellfish, bivalve.
Waters: Home waters.
Shape and colour: Fan-shaped ribbed shell. The upper shell tends to be flatter and a reddish-brown, the lower is bowl-shaped and pale. The edible meat inside comprises the white muscle and orange and white male and female roes (the scallop is an hermaphrodite). They will usually be ready cleaned.
Price: High to very high.
Market size: 10–15cm/4–6in.
Sold as: Intact, whole (on shell); meat only, fresh or frozen.
Market availability: Fair for fresh; good for frozen.
Seasonal availability: Year round, but best from December to March.
Remarks: It's the only bivalve that can be sold with the shell gaping open. Sweet creamy flesh with an excellent flavour and texture. Can be eaten raw; and should not be overcooked. The bright orange roe is a particular delicacy. On holiday in Florida recently, I was amazed to see that this was thrown away.

Unless baking or grilling the scallops on the shell, the roe should be separated from the white meat and cooked a minute or so after as it is very delicate and cooks very quickly.

A word of warning on buying frozen scallops: because fish processors often soak scallops in water to plump them before glazing and freezing, you can find that after defrosting you have a scallop half the size you bought sitting in a pool of water. The best thing is to cook them *immediately* they are defrosted. It is not the fault of the fishmonger—he can only sell what he can buy from the wholesaler. Advice? Buy only fresh, on the shell, though you can sometimes find fresh scallop meat sold by weight which is a good buy.

The scallop, or rather, its shell, has for centuries been the symbol of Santiago de Compostela in Galicia, the western Spanish province on the Atlantic coastline. Medieval Christian pilgrims flocked there to worship at the tomb of St James and, on arrival, each would buy and eat a scallop and fix the shell to his hat or cloak to attest that he had made the journey to the holy place. *Coquilles St Jacques*, beloved as a starter in many French restaurants, means simply 'St James's scallops'.

The following recipe is a Spanish way of cooking scallops combining them with ham. As you have seen throughout, fish and bacon (or ham) make a good pair.

SPICED SCALLOPS WITH HAM

500g/1lb scallop meat (queenies cut the cost slightly), large ones should be chopped into 2 or 3 pieces

2 shallots or 1 medium onion, finely chopped

125g/4oz good smoked ham, finely chopped or minced

90ml/3fl.oz good olive oil

Few sprigs of parsley, finely chopped

½ teaspoon dried thyme

½ teaspoon dried chilli flakes

Sea salt and freshly ground white pepper to taste

Approximately 3 tablespoons dry white wine

Dash good white wine vinegar or lemon juice

Approximately 8 tablespoons coarsely ground dry breadcrumbs

1 teaspoon paprika

Lemon juice

Rinse the scallops and thoroughly pat dry. If you have bought scallops in the shell, reserve and thoroughly clean six shells to serve, and lightly oil them.

In a bowl mix together the scallops, onion, ham, a third of the olive oil, half the chopped parsley, thyme, chilli flakes, salt and pepper. Add enough white wine to moisten the mixture without making it at all sloppy, and add the dash of vinegar or lemon juice.

Either divide the mixture between the oiled scallop shells, or put it in an oiled or buttered medium-sized baking dish (to fill it within 1cm/½in of the top). Mix together the breadcrumbs, the remaining oil and parsley, and the paprika, season with pepper and a squeeze of lemon juice. Spread the breadcrumbs mixture over the scallops. Bake in a preheated oven (200°C/400°F) for 15–20 minutes. Serves 6.

I lecture on fish to the students at the Leith School of Food and Wine in London once or twice a year. Prue Leith and Caroline Waldegrave have recently produced *Leith's Cookery Bible* and the following recipe is given here with their blessing.

FRIED SCALLOPS WITH BACON

---

12 fresh scallops	Salt and freshly ground black
4 rashers of back bacon	pepper
1 tablespoon chopped parsley	

If you have bought scallops on the shell, clean the scallops, pulling away the hard muscle (opposite the coral) and discarding. Cut the white core in half horizontally.

Cut the bacon into slivers and fry until it begins to brown. Reduce the heat and add the scallops. Fry gently for about a minute on each side. Add the parsley, season and serve immediately. Particularly delicious served on fried bread.

A special dish for a special occasion for your microwave from SEAFISH. It would serve 4 as a starter or 2 as a main dish with, perhaps, rice and a crispy green salad.

SCALLOPS AND PRAWNS IN BRANDY CREAM

120g/4oz scallop meats, sliced	240g/8oz cooked peeled prawns
1 tablespoon brandy	2 tablespoons double cream
60g/2oz button mushrooms, sliced	salt and pepper
	chopped chives, to garnish

Put the scallops in a microwave-proof dish and spoon over the brandy. Cover and cook on HIGH for 2–2.5 minutes, stirring once during cooking.

Stir in the mushrooms and prawns and cook for a further 2 minutes on HIGH. Stir in the cream and cook on HIGH for 30 seconds–1 minute or until piping hot.

Season to taste and sprinkle with chives.

You could vary this by replacing the mushrooms with small florets of broccoli or chopped green beans; or by replacing the cream with yoghurt or *crème fraîche*; or add a little cayenne.

Queen Scallop (Queenie, Scallop)

French: *Vanneau*
German: *Kamm-Muschel*
Spanish: *Volandeira*

Category: Shellfish, bivalve.
Waters: Home waters.
Shape and colour: Smaller than the king scallop, and both half shells are bowl-shaped and pink-coloured. The roe is proportionately smaller than the scallop.
Price: Very low, in shell; moderate, out of shell.
Market size: Width of shell 5–8cm/2–3in.
Sold as: By weight, fresh intact, or just meat; fresh or frozen.
Market availability: Fair. A high percentage of the United Kingdom catch is exported owing to lack of demand here.
Seasonal availability: Year round.
Remarks: The queen scallop is similar to the larger scallop (king) in flavour and is much cheaper, especially in the shell. If you want scallops to cut or chop rather than serve whole, queenies will do very nicely. Queenies sautéed in garlic butter are another favourite of mine.

Scampi See Dublin Bay Prawn.

Shrimp (Pink Shrimp and Brown Shrimp)

French: *Crevette*
German: *Garnele, Krabbe*
Spanish: *Quisquilla, Camaron*

Category: Shellfish, crustacean.
Waters: Home waters.
Shape and colour: In life almost colourless, the pink shrimp is like a small

prawn and grows larger than the brown and has a pointed snout. On cooking the flesh becomes white.

Price: Low.

Market size: 2–4cm/1–1½in.

Sold as: Whole, cooked, by the pint or kg/lb.

Market availability: Good fresh and frozen.

Seasonal availability: Better in summer months.

Remarks: Can be eaten whole, or just the tail or tail meat, though they are so small to be hardly worth shelling. The shells are very tender and add to the flavour. Most people find the brown shrimp sweeter, but they are becoming quite rare since, once again, most are exported to France. Morecambe Bay shrimp have some reputation.

The traditional 'shrimp tea', while a simple affair, was a great Sunday treat associated mainly with the East End of London—a heap of pink and/ or brown shrimp, perhaps a squeeze of lemon juice and a shake of ground white pepper, eaten with slices of brown bread and butter. It was splendid.

The potted shrimp, a curiously English dish, is really nothing more than cleaned shrimp covered in seasoned clarified butter. It is worth making your own rather than buying the commercial product.

Personally, I prefer to eat them without any dressing, and they always form part of a good platter of *fruits de mer*.

Squid

French: *Calmar, Encornet*
German: *Kalmar*
Spanish: *Calamar*

Category: Mollusc, cephalopod.

Waters: Home waters.

Shape and colour: Basically boneless creature, comprising a long body sac from which protrude the head and tentacles, eight short and two long. It has two swimming fins on each side of the sac towards the rear. Has a thin pinkish-brown mottled skin easily removed to expose the translucent white of the body.

Price: Low–moderate.

Market size: 15–50cm/6–20in.

Sold as: Whole, fresh; whole or cleaned body sacs, frozen.

Market availability: Very good.

Seasonal availability: Year round, but best in winter months.

Remarks: Until recently squid was mainly eaten in the Mediterranean and the Far East, but travel has broadened the mind and the appetite of the British and more squid is being consumed in this country. However, a large proportion of the United Kingdom catch is exported to France.

Squid, particularly the smaller ones, tend to 'shoot' their ink on capture (as do octopus), but if you want to use it to colour a dish or make 'black' pasta it can be bought separately in sachets.

SQUID WITH PARSLEY

This is best made with small squid, and you could use pre-cleaned squid.

1kg/2lb cleaned squid	Sea salt and freshly ground
3 tablespoons good olive oil	pepper
2 garlic cloves, finely	Small bunch of parsley,
chopped or crushed	preferably flat-leaved,
Grated nutmeg	finely chopped

If you are cleaning the squid yourself, use tentacles as well as the body sacs; pre-cleaned squid comprises body sacs only. Slice into wide rings, rinse and pat dry.

In a large frying or sauté pan, heat 1 tablespoon oil over high heat. Add the squid and cook over moderate heat, turning constantly, until they start to take a little colour, and grate a little nutmeg over (up to half a nut according to taste). Add salt and pepper, and the parsley. Over the heat, quickly stir to blend, and serve. Serves 4.

The squid was born to be stuffed, and there are some excellent recommendations around, and you may have your own ideas. A stuffing using ham is very popular. If you are cleaning the squid yourself, include the chopped tentacles and side wings in the stuffing. Michelle Berriedale-Johnson's *Cook for Hire*, which has some excellent ideas if you have to cater for large numbers, suggests the following, which can be served hot or cold:

STUFFED SQUID

12–18 small squid, cleaned
and rinsed
360g/12oz smoked ham,
finely sliced
2 large handfuls parsley,
finely chopped
200ml/7fl.oz olive oil
2 medium onions, peeled and
finely chopped

Salt and pepper
2–3 eggs
3 tablespoons tomato purée
150ml/5fl.oz dry white wine
360ml/12fl.oz water
Dash of Tabasco to taste

If you have cleaned the squid yourself, mix the finely chopped tentacles and wings with the ham and parsley. In a frying or sauté pan heat 3 tablespoons oil and gently cook the onions until they are soft. Add the ham mixture, and cook together for 2–3 minutes. Remove from the heat, season well, and allow to cool a little. Mix in 2 eggs; if you feel the mixture to be too stiff, add another one. Stuff the cleaned squid sacs with the mixture and close the top with a cocktail stick. Heat the remaining oil with the tomato purée, wine and water in a pan, lower in the squid and poach them gently for 25–30 minutes. Season the liquid to taste with salt, pepper and Tabasco.

If hot, they can be served in the sauce and will serve 6. If cold, they should be removed from the sauce, allowed to cool, refrigerated for a little, then sliced (the sauce can be used as the base for a soup). They are said to cater for 25 as a cocktail snack. We have seen them demolished by half that number.

Whelk

French: *Buccin*
German: *Wellhornschnecke*
Spanish: *Bocina*

Category: Shellfish, single shell.
Waters: Home waters.
Shape and colour: Single spiral shell, pale sandy brown. The whole animal can be eaten.
Price: Low to moderate.
Market size: 5–10cm/2–4in (in shell)

201

Sold as: Cooked in shell, cooked and picked out of shell. Fresh and raw.

Market availability: Very good.

Seasonal availability: Year round, best in summer.

Remarks: Very popular. I remember eating whelks in the south of France. They had been simply boiled in sea water with *herbes de Provence* and were wonderfully tender.

A friend tells me that whelks are supposed to be an aphrodisiac. He adds that if that is true they must be marvellous value for money—you can chew for more than a little on a hefty whelk.

Those who live in or visit coastal towns will be familiar with whelks on the numerous shellfish stands. Like cockles, they are served on little paper plates with a bottle of malt vinegar and a jar of ground white pepper to shake over them. Not truly to my taste.

SMOKED AND PRESERVED FISH AND SHELLFISH AND OTHER DELICACIES

'Our breakfasts are a disgrace to England . . . Your ladyship must really acknowledge the prodigious advantage the Scotch possess over us in that respect . . . In Aberdeenshire you have the Finnan haddo' with a flavour all its own, vastly relishing—just salt enough to be piquant, without parching you up with thirst. In Perthshire, there is the Tay salmon, kippered, crisp and juicy—a very magnificent morsel—a leetle heavy, but that's easy counteracted by a teaspoonful of the Athole whisky.'

Susan Ferrier
1782–1854

Smoke curing was an ancient method of preserving fish, necessary when fresh supplies were doubtful, and, before refrigeration, necessary to keep fish in good condition during transportation between port and inland market. For the same reason fish was often salted, wind dried or pickled.

In fact, the preservative effect of smoking is shortlived. Now we smoke fish for the distinctive flavour. Any fish can be smoked, as can most shellfish, but in this country we have been sadly conservative in our tastes and other than the occasional pack of smoked oysters or mussels have left the many possibilities to the rest of Europe.

Things are changing. At the 1991 International Food Exhibition I was delighted to see British producers offering not only the usual smoked fish but also monkfish and scallops, barracuda, tuna and black-banded bream from the Persian Gulf, red snapper from the Caribbean, parrot fish from the Seychelles, Emperor fish and Tiger Bay prawns from the South China seas, and even alligator. If your fishmonger has his own smoker, or an amenable supplier, ask for whatever you would like to be smoked. Or you could invest in your own smoker, or even build one, in which case I would recommend the chapter on smoked fish in Jocasta Innes' *Country Kitchen*.

The process involves four stages: (1) splitting (e.g. finnan haddock), filleting (e.g. mackerel), or just washing (e.g. bloaters); (2) dry salting or brining—this is the point at which dyes might be used; (3) dripping, to remove all surplus moisture; (4) smoking, either hot or cold. Cold smoking does not exceed 33°C/85°F and the fish is still essentially raw; hot smoking temperature is rather higher and cooks the fish.

We have all become much more concerned about additives and their possible effects. Dyes used in smoked fish simply give a more attractive colour. They don't help to preserve, don't add to nutritive value, and don't add flavour. I find that more and more of my customers do not want that bright yellow piece of fish; they want a natural product, so I usually stock only undyed smoked fish.

So how do you know if a smoked fish is fresh and good to eat? Again, use your eyes and nose. It should have a bright glossy surface and a pleasant smoky smell; and it should be firm to the touch. If it is soggy then the raw fish used may have been either of poor quality or frozen. And the older it gets, the stickier it gets.

Ways of preserving fish are endless. Wind drying is not often seen here now, and dried fish has largely been replaced by smoked fish, except perhaps for salt fish. Most people assume that the fish used for salting is cod, but I have seen the cheaper coley or ling salted and sold as cod.

Prices of smoked fish vary dramatically, dependent on the species. As everyone knows, you don't get smoked salmon for the price of a kipper.

Anchovy
Canned, of course, Also filleted and preserved in oil; stuffed with an olive and canned or preserved in oil.

Cod
Occasionally seen is 'smoked fillet' or 'gold cutlets'. The retailer should be precise about what fish is on offer, so ask what it is, as it is *not* generally cod. It could be coley, haddock or whiting.

Cod's roe, dyed or undyed (also ling roe), is sometimes used to make *taramasalata*, though this popular dip should more properly be made from the roe of the grey mullet. Smoked cod's roe, sliced, sprinkled with a little cayenne or paprika, served with watercress and a piece of lemon to squeeze as you eat makes an excellent start to a meal or a light lunch in itself. Also good on toast; and can be mixed with butter to dot onto a poached steak or fillet.

Salt cod is used throughout the world. The two dishes that come immediately to mind are the Jamaican salt cod and *ackee*, and the Portuguese *bacalau*, almost a national dish.

Eel
Hot smoked: gutted whole fish or skinned fillets. Another good start to a meal or part of a smoked fish platter. Jellied eels are not preserved, but cooked in their own juices and allowed to set.

Haddock

Finnan haddock (cold smoked) is a whole fish, beheaded, gutted and split (also known as Findon haddock, from the Scottish village where the name derives, or Finnan haddie); fillets (cold smoked); Arbroath smokies (hot smoked) are small fish, beheaded and gutted, traditionally tied in pairs with string to hang in the kiln and, according to a number of my friends, the most delicious of all smoked fish; golden cutlets (cold smoked) are small haddock or whiting.

Halibut

Filleted and sliced (cold smoked). Becoming quite popular, though that packaged in vacuum packs is usually Greenland or mock halibut. I have halibut smoked for me, and it is quite delicious. It makes a wonderful start to a meal with a little lime or lemon juice or as part of a smoked fish platter for a light lunch.

Herring

A Scandinavian friend has estimated there might be as many as forty different varieties of preserved herring. In this country we know best the kipper (cold smoked) gutted and split, or filleted, dyed or undyed. We are also lucky enough to have available Loch Fyne, Craster and Manx, all full of flavour and worth looking for. Let us hope, as Michael Bateman has pleaded in the *Independent*, that the men in Brussels will not legislate them out of existence with unrealistic directives.

The bloater is a washed ungutted herring, cold smoked; a buckling is ungutted but with the head off, hot smoked; a red herring (and I'm not trying to confuse you here) is whole, ungutted, cured in dry salt for seven days, then cold smoked for three or four periods of twelve hours, depending on the type of kiln used (also called hard smoked herring). The bloater came into favour in the 17th century and largely replaced the red herring. It could keep for so long, could be transported inland and, importantly, was available throughout the meatless period of Lent.

And of course there are *matjes* herring, rollmops, soused herring, herrings pickled in dill, in spices, with onions, without onions, in wine, almost any way you can think of.

Mackerel

Gutted whole fish or fillets (hot smoked). Smoked mackerel pâté appears to have gone out of fashion, but there are several kinds of smoked mackerel fillets appearing on the market: peppered; spiced; garlic-flavoured and dill-flavoured. I have eaten some cold-smoked mackerel in Israel and it was delicious. I had some smoked for me here and at first customers were wary, but some have become converts and it is starting to sell.

Pilchards

Not smoked, but canned, often in tomato sauce. If you must . . .

Salmon

King of the smoked fish. Whole fillets are cold smoked and known as 'sides'. Scottish or Irish? Not an argument I would care to enter. If you ever become bored with having thin slices of smoked salmon carefully cut from a prime side, laid on a large plate with a slice of lemon or lime to squeeze upon it, a little horseradish, a little cayenne or paprika, or perhaps a little dill sauce, there are other ways to eat it. A few scraps added to scrambled eggs with a little cream is rather good; or wrap it around a fish mousse; or make a salad with strips of smoked salmon, watercress, chopped baby courgettes, tossed in a light dressing of oil, lime juice and fresh dill. The only use for canned salmon, so far as I can see is to make a quick sandwich, and you have to season it with dill, lemon juice and pepper. I would much rather use fresh.

Salmon Trout

Cheaper than smoked salmon, but I find it just as good. I see that some of the larger supermarkets are starting to sell it pre-packaged. Good for them.

Sardines

Arguably the most popular of the canned fish. Head removed, and closely packed in oil or tomato sauce, the process softens the bones so you can eat them whole. They are a good standby if there is absolutely no way you can get a piece of fresh fish. Canned sardines (in oil) mashed up with lemon juice, cayenne, a dash of mushroom ketchup, a little dried tarragon or dill, lightly grilled on toast, will at least keep you from starving.

Sprats

Brined and only lightly hot smoked so they still look bright and silvery.

Trout

Gutted whole fish or skinned fillets, hot smoked. I prefer the whole fish smoked, then skinned and eaten with a little horseradish.

Tuna (as well as Marlin, Swordfish, Sturgeon and other game fish)

Smoked fish won't be found very often, but you can ask your fishmonger to supply it; you won't be disappointed. Then there is the ever-present canned tuna in brine, olive or soya oil. Again, it is better than nothing if you are desperate.

Smoked shellfish are all hot-smoked and ready to eat.

Clams

In or out of the shell, they are usually vacuum-packed, so if you see them, grab them as they will store in the refrigerator (watch the 'use by' date). All smoked clams are good, and I'm particularly fond of razorshells. You don't need to do anything to them except perhaps add a drop of lemon or lime juice. You could incorporate them into a green salad.

Mussels

The same goes for mussels.

Oysters

Smoked oysters sometimes come in cans. I would rather have them straight from the smokery or vacuum-packed.

Prawns

Not something you see a lot, but when you do, try them. The large king or the tiger prawn are usually used, and they are smoked in the shell. So just peel and eat.

ARNOLD BENNETT OMELETTE

While writing his book *Imperial Palace*, Arnold Bennett stayed at the Savoy and this omelette was invented for him. Apparently thereafter he demanded it wherever he travelled. It is extremely rich, as you will see. The recipe is taken from *The Savoy Food and Drink Book*.

For 4;

300g/10oz smoked Finnan
   haddock fillets
300ml/½ pint milk
12 eggs
Salt and freshly milled
   pepper
40g/1½oz unsalted butter

300ml/½ pint bechamel sauce
15ml/3fl.oz hollandaise sauce
60ml/2fl.oz double cream,
   whipped
20g/¾oz Parmesan cheese,
   grated

Poach the haddock in the milk for about 3 minutes. Remove from the pan and flake the fish. Whisk the eggs, add salt and pepper and half the haddock. Heat an omelette pan, add a quarter of the butter, swirl around the pan. Add a quarter of the egg mixture and cook very quickly, stirring constantly until the mixture is lightly set. Slide the omelette onto a plate.

Mix together quickly the bechamel and hollandaise sauce. Add the remaining flaked haddock and carefully fold in the whipped cream. Cover the omelette completely with a quarter of the sauce. Sprinkle with a quarter of the Parmesan and glaze under a hot grill.

Repeat with the remaining mixture to make three more omelettes.

There are simpler recipes where, for example, you can make one large omelette and divide it, but this is the original. Finnan haddock is usually sold on the bone, and it can be cooked whole, then bones and skin removed.

POACHED FINNAN HADDOCK

A whole Finnan haddock on the bone is best served in the simplest possible way: poached in water with a few black peppercorns, a few juniper berries and a couple of bayleaves. And it doesn't take long, about 5 minutes. And to gild the lily, poach an egg or two in the cooking liquid and pop it on top of the cooked fish with a knob of butter.

PHIL'S KEDGEREE

There are an amazing number of recipes for kedgeree, brought back to England from the Raj. Some include a little curry powder or other spicing; some cook the rice in the cooking liquid from the fish, and some add raisins or sultanas.

For 4:

500g/1lb smoked haddock	3 tablespoons single cream
fillets	3 large eggs, lightly beaten
60g/2oz butter	Salt and freshly ground black
120g/4oz long grain rice,	pepper to taste
cooked	Parsley, finely chopped

Poach the haddock in water for about 10 minutes. Lift away the skin and flake the flesh. In a large saucepan over a low heat, melt the butter, add the cooked rice and the fish and gently mix. Raise the heat, add the cream and the beaten eggs. Stir gently until the eggs set. Season to taste and garnish.

JIMMIE MCNAB'S KEDGEREE

The following recipe for kedgeree is from Jimmie McNab, a cook at the Creggans Inn, Loch Fyne, who gave up some of his secrets to Elisabeth Luard of *Country Living*.

250g/8oz long grain rice	300ml/10fl.oz single cream
250g/8oz smoked haddock,	Salt and pepper
poached in a little milk	60–90g/2–3oz butter
4 eggs	Chopped parsley, about
2–3 spring onions, chopped	1 tablespoon

Boil the rice until tender, dry and fluffy. Drain the haddock, skin, debone and flake it. Boil the eggs until just hard, about 5–6 minutes, cool in cold water and shell. Reserve two yolks for garnish and finely chop the rest.

Toss the flaked fish with the rice and chopped eggs, mix in the spring onions and cream, and season. Spread the mixture in a very lightly buttered baking dish, dot with knobs of butter, cover with foil and bake in a preheated oven (180°C/350°F) for 20–30 minutes. Garnish with the two reserved yolks, chopped, and the parsley.

I enjoy Sophie Grigson's food column in the *Evening Standard*. Not long ago she gave a delicious recipe for salt cod cakes which she had been given by the chef of the Swallow Hotel in Birmingham, though she exchanged lobster for much cheaper fish, a move of which I thoroughly approve.

SALT COD AND CORIANDER FISH CAKES

180g/6oz salt cod that has been soaked for at least 24 hours, water changed at least once, drained, rinsed and dried
360g/12oz whiting or cod fillet
3 shallots, finely chopped
2 cloves garlic, finely chopped
2 tablespoons chopped coriander

1.5cm/½in piece ginger, finely chopped
1 teaspoon sugar
1 tablespoons light soy sauce
Juice of ½ lime
Pepper to taste
60g/2oz finely chopped fennel bulb
Flour
Oil
Lime or lemon wedges

Skin and bone the salt cod and cut into small chunks. Skin and bone the fillet, and roughly chop. Mix the fish thoroughly with all the seasonings—shallots, garlic, coriander, ginger, sugar, soy, lime juice and pepper. Leave for half an hour, then use a food processor to whizz the mixture to a paste. Turn the mixture into a bowl, add the chopped fennel, mix to blend.

Divide the mixture into 12 portions, roll each portion into a ball and then flatten to a thickness of about 1cm/½in. Coat lightly with flour. In a frying or sauté pan , pour oil to a depth of about 1cm/½in and heat. Fry the fish cakes over a medium heat until golden brown on each side. Serve with lime wedges. Serves 6.

You can easily adapt this recipe to your own taste by adding some chopped chilli, celery instead of fennel, lemon instead of lime, cayenne instead of pepper, and importantly any other fish, such as coley, conger or hake.

SMOKED MACKEREL PÂTÉ

One of the simplest ways to make this is to use a food-processor. Also use smoked mackerel fillets (so you only have to remove the skin—simple), and you could use any of the spiced or flavoured mackerel fillets. Whatever you choose, you need:

500g/1lb smoked mackerel	Paprika
250g/8oz cream cheese	1 tablespoon snipped fresh
Lemon juice	dill or 1 teaspoon dried
Sea salt	Approximately 2 tablespoons
Freshly ground black pepper	double cream

In the food processor combine the mackerel and the cream cheese. Add a little lemon juice, salt, pepper and paprika, add the dill, add some cream, and readjust seasoning to taste.

A spoonful on some hot toast makes a very good light snack.

Caviar and Other Delicacies

'Champagne and caviar' has long been the phrase to epitomise a life of luxury, and both can be outlandishly expensive.

Caviar is the eggs of the sturgeon, but not just any old sturgeon. It comes in various colours and sizes and is named after the particular fish. The most expensive—imported from Iran and the Black Sea area—is Beluga. It also has the largest grains which are silvery grey. It is packed in tins of various sizes. There is also the slightly cheaper pasteurised, and the pressed which is made from damaged eggs, slightly salted and pressed together. Osetra is rather smaller-grained and comes in a variety of colours. The Sevruga is much smaller grained, greenish-black, and can also be found pressed.

Caviar can be eaten with a spoon, from a bowl set over ice, and washed down with vodka or aquavit that has been kept in the freezer, and possibly a slice of good brown or rye bread. Side dishes of chopped egg yolk, chopped egg white, finely chopped or sliced shallot or onion, sour cream, and slices of lemon are better used with lumpfish roe.

The most popular caviar substitute, and there is a great deal of difference between the two, is lumpfish roe, black and orange coloured. A spoonful or two on top of scrambled eggs makes breakfast rather festive, or use it to garnish smoked fish or canapes. Available in jars.

The very large-grained salmon roe can be eaten and used in the same way.

Bombay duck is a sun-dried fish from the Indian Ocean and if you have ever come across it you know that it is crushed and sprinkled over curried dishes, and adds texture and a slightly salty tang. The fresh fish is occasionally available.

Shark's fin, the dried cartilage of the fin and best known in the Chinese

211

dish, shark's fin soup, is another delicacy. *China The Beautiful Cookbook* has two recipes for the preparation of this highly esteemed delicacy other than in soup, both of which are quite complicated, one including chicken, duck, ham and dried scallops.

There are many other dried fish available in Oriental and special stores: anchovy, scallops and, widely used in South-East Asia, shrimp or prawns, sometimes ground and used sprinkled over a finished dish to add texture and a rather salty flavour. The dried shrimp 'cake' *blachan* is often used in curries and other dishes of South-East Asia, first baked a little to release the flavour.

Seaweeds

All seaweeds are very high in vitamins, particularly A, B1 and B2, and in the minerals calcium, phosphorus and iron and various trace elements.

Carrageen, a seaweed found on the coasts of both sides of the North Atlantic, can be eaten as a vegetable and is similar to spinach. When bleached and dried, it is sometimes known as Irish moss. It is high in vitamins and is used as a gelatine. Theodora Fitzgibbon in *A Taste of Ireland* gives a simple recipe for Ocean Swell Jelly using dried carrageen.

Laver is another seaweed, popular in Wales, turned into a purée called laverbread (available ready prepared) which is then made into sauces, patties or soups. In *A Taste of Wales*, Ms Fitzgibbon says that it is 'an acquired taste like caviar, olives, or oysters, but once acquired it can become a passion'.

Dulse is another dried seaweed that can be cooked like spinach, as can kelp, used as a food and medicine since time immemorial.

The Japanese probably make the most use of seaweeds: *kombu*, processed and dried kelp, is used with dried bonito flakes to make the soup stock *dashi*, used so extensively in Japanese cuisine; *hijiki*, a brown algae seaweed; *nori*, a kind of laver, usually dried in sheets and what you will find wrapped around the vinegared rice and fish speciality, *sushi*; *mekabu*, a lobe-leafed weed also used in soups; the kale-like *wakame*, sold dried and, after soaking and softening, eaten like a vegetable.

Samphire is Britain's own marsh-grown herb, harvested in the summer in East Anglia, but sometimes imported from northern France. It is often called 'sea asparagus' and looks like a small skinny bright green cactus without the spines. Late in the season it needs to be picked over to get rid of the woody end and any odd bits and pieces, and should be very thoroughly washed and rinsed. After that, it can be eaten raw; or, if you prefer, blanched and drained, served with a splash of good quality vinegar

212

(seaweed flavoured is good); or lightly steamed for a few minutes and served hot with a spoonful of butter and some ground pepper. The samphire season is something to look forward to each year. If you can't find it, ask your fishmonger to try to supply it.

If you ever get to the Dutch coast in April or May, try the locally picked *lamsoor*, with leaves that look remarkably like lambs' ears. Sauté chopped shallots or onions in oil or butter, add the *lamsoor*, cook together until the leaves are slightly limp. You won't need salt as it already tastes of the sea, but you might like a little pepper. It makes a marvellous accompaniment to a piece of simply cooked fish.

GENERAL RECIPES FOR FISH AND SHELLFISH

FISH CAKES, FISH PIES AND MISCELLANEOUS DISHES

FISH CAKES

Essentially cooked fish mixed with an equal or lesser amount of mashed potato, seasoned, shaped into small flat cakes, dressed in egg and bread-crumbs or floured and shallow or deep fried or baked. The following is a list of suggested ingredients from which to choose.

- Any white fish, brill, cod, coley, haddock, hake, huss, ling, grey mullet, plaice, sole, whiting or leftovers of the more expensive halibut or turbot or any other left-over white fish. If fresh, cook by poaching or grilling and remove skin and bones. A little smoked fish or smoked cod's roe gives a particularly luxurious flavour if it is mashed into the sauce. You could also add peeled shrimp, cockles, chopped mussels, crab meat, chopped scallops or even oyster meat.
- Mix the fish with a roughly equal amount of: mashed potato; potato and celeriac; celeriac and swede; with or without an egg.
- Add chopped and sautéed celery, fennel (bulb), onion or shallot, green or red peppers; spring onion (scallion); chopped chilli; preferably fresh coriander; dill; fennel; mint; parsley or tarragon.
- Additional spices: ground coriander; cardamom; cumin; fenugreek; five-spice powder; lemon or lime (a little juice and/or grated zest).
- Dip in flour; or egg and breadcrumbs; or oatmeal (*not* oatflakes); or cornmeal.
- Deep fry or shallow fry, or bake, or fry and bake;
- Serve with sauce: cheese; spiced tomato; *salsa verde*; mustard; dill; coriander; parsley or red pesto.

FISH CROQUETTES

A variation on fish cakes. To cold boned fish, add a thick white sauce, some soft breadcrumbs, season as you wish, and mix thoroughly. Form into blunt-ended rolls, dip in egg and dry breadcrumbs, and fry until golden brown.

217

FISH PIES

Usually cooked fish, seasoned, mixed with a quantity of white sauce—flavoured if liked—thick enough to bind, but thin enough not to lose too much liquid in the cooking and thus form a pudding and topped with mashed potato, dotted with butter and baked in the oven.

This is a list of suggested alternatives.

- Fillets of brill, cod, coley, conger, haddock, hake, whiting, witch, sole, plaice or any left-over white fish.
- Poach fish, if using fresh, in water with or without a little white wine or vermouth, or semi-skinned milk, with a bayleaf; black or white peppercorns; 1 small onion (studded with 2/3 cloves if you wish); 5–6 juniper berries; and use the poaching liquid to make the sauce.
- Possible additions to mix: smoked haddock (cooked), fresh cockles, mussels, oysters or chopped scallops, crab meat (don't forget that crab is quite rich, particularly the brown meat). Remember that oily fish is *not* very good in pies.
- Sauce. Make a roux with 30g/1oz butter and 30g/1oz flour (or more if you are making a big pie); use the poaching liquid and add fish stock, milk, cream, water, dash of vermouth or white wine to make up the volume if necessary.
- Add to sauce: chopped fresh herbs like coriander, dill, fennel, mint, parsley or tarragon; or ground spices such as coriander, cardamom, cayenne, chilli, curry powder, fenugreek, paprika; or a little chopped and sautéed celery or fennel, or onion, shallot or green or red pepper.
- Add to sauce or layer on top of fish: hard-boiled egg; cooked spinach; sliced tomatoes.
- Top with: mashed/creamed potato; potato mixed with celeriac, carrot, or swede (or all mashed together); puff pastry; filo pastry (good with a layer of chopped spinach between two layers of fish mixture).

FISH PUDDING

This is another old-fashioned dish with recipes to be found in Eliza Acton, Mrs Beeton and Constance Spry, as well as many others of that ilk, but it's another way to deal with left-over fish and can make a satisfying and filling meal, particularly if served with an interesting sauce.

The principle is quite simple: cooked fish, soft breadcrumbs, seasoned, bound with eggs and enriched with cream, turned into a pudding basin and baked in the oven in a *bain-marie*.

218

So, for 500g/1lb cooked, boneless fish, mashed with a fork, (and mixed with a few peeled prawns or a little crab meat), 250g/8oz soft bread-crumbs, 4 eggs, 120ml/4fl.oz cream, 1 teaspoon anchovy essence, ground white or black pepper to taste, dash of paprika/cayenne/Worcestershire sauce/Tabasco (or combination), ½ teaspoon dried tarragon (or 1 tea-spoon finely chopped fresh tarragon/coriander/parsley), all thoroughly mixed together.

Oil or butter a pudding basin or mould, fill with the fish mixture pressing well down, brush the top with oil or melted butter, bake in a preheated oven (180°C/375°F) in a *bain-marie* (half-fill a baking tin with water and set the pudding basin in it) for about 1 hour or until the top springs a little when pressed with a fork.

Turn out onto a plate and serve with a well-seasoned sauce: spicy tomato, *salsa verde*, or something of the sort; and a green salad. Should serve 4–6.

FISH JELLY

According to Michelle Berriedale-Johnson, a 'jellie of fyshe' was a spe-ciality of the medieval cook. It involves poaching a selection of white fish with onions, wine, vinegar and spices, and adding some shellfish. The cooking liquid is strained thoroughly and mixed with gelatine. The jelly is then slowly built up in a mould with layers of jelly and the fish decoratively arranged within. Unmould and decorate as you will. Something for a special occasion perhaps.

FRITTO MISTO (MIXED FRIED FISH)

You can't have been to Italy and not found this dish on offer. Usually sliced squid and prawn, it can include pieces of any firm-fleshed fish like cod, huss, monkfish, salmon or whole pin hake. All dipped in a light batter, deep fried, and sprinkled with sea salt. No need for anything else but slices of lemon and some freshly ground pepper.

OMELETTES AND PANCAKES

A smoked salmon omelette made with a little cream and seasoned with snipped fresh dill has become a classic dish. You can also make a 'filled' omelette using a mixture of left-over poached or grilled salmon or trout, or good quality white fish, seasoned and flavoured. Pancakes, too, can be

219

filled with a mixture of fish and/or seafood, seasoned, and bound with a stiffish white sauce or velouté. Very good covered with a thinner white sauce or a seasoned tomato sauce, and baked briefly.

PAELLA

The best-known dish of Spain and apparently originally cooked over open fires outdoors. You get a different recipe from every Spanish person you talk to, and it can be quite simple or very complex. Some of the best are mixtures of shellfish and meat.

Ideally you need a paella pan, but you can also use a wok. The principle is simple: long-grained rice slowly cooked in a well-seasoned broth with vegetables, meats (often pre-cooked) and fish, all adding their flavours to the whole dish. The essentials are olive oil, rice and saffron. The vegetables might be beans, peas, tomatoes, garlic, onions, red and green peppers; meats can be chicken, duck, rabbit, *chorizo* (the highly-spiced Spanish sausage); fish might include any one or combination of clams, mussels, prawns, crab, lobster, squid.

PIZZA

Using your favourite pizza base and tomato sauce with or without a little cheese, try a topping of mixed shellfish, a combination selected from shrimp or prawn, cockles, mussels, roundels of squid, strips of tuna, a little crab meat and anchovy. Best to toss the fish quickly in oil with some chopped herbs like coriander, dill, fennel, parsley or tarragon.

RISOTTO

The Italian answer to paella, and the principle is much the same: rice (the Italian Arborio) cooked in a well-flavoured broth with saffron, and with cheese usually added at the end. Risottos using seafood are usually shellfish, but there is no reason why firm-fleshed white fish can't be added. Plus, of course, any vegetable additions that seem appropriate and are available.

In your large pan heat butter or oil (or a mixture), add a chopped shallot or two, fry until starting to brown, add rice (roughly 120g/4oz per person) and stir until the grains are coated with oil. The stock you will start to add should be really well-flavoured. If you are using a mixture of shellfish, heads and shells should have been included as well as any white fish bones and trimmings to hand, and thoroughly strained to extract all flavour. You can also add a generous glassful or so of white wine. Add the liquid, which should be warm, a cupful at a time, stirring after each addition. Let the risotto cook over moderate heat, adding more stock as it becomes absorbed (for 500g/1lb rice you will need about 1 litre/2 pints or more of liquid—top up with hot water if necessary). Keep a check on the rice which should be cooked through at the end of about 30 minutes. If you use saffron, this is the moment to add it (dissolved in a little stock or water), plus your fish which has been lightly sautéed in butter. Lightly mix to combine, then add 30–60g/1–2oz each of softened butter and of grated Parmesan cheese, toss together and there you are.

SALADS

In his *Shilling Cooker for the People* (1854), Alexis Soyer gives the following instruction for a fish salad (he uses lobster, but says that the same method can be applied to crab and all kinds of cold fish—cod, sole, halibut, brill, turbot, sturgeon or plaice):

> 'Have the bowl half filled with any kind of salad herb you like, either endive or lettuce, &c. Then break a lobster in two, open the tail, extract the meat in one piece, break the claws, cut the meat of both in small slices, about a quarter of an inch thick, arrange these tastefully on the salad, take out all the soft part from the belly, mix it in a basin with a teaspoonful of salt, half of pepper, four of vinegar, four of oil; stir it well together, and pour on the salad; then cover it with two hard eggs, cut in slices, a few slices of cucumber, and, to vary, a few capers and some fillets of anchovy; stir lightly, and serve.'

Not too far from *Salade Niçoise* which most frequently uses tuna and anchovies, and adds olives and tomatoes, hard-boiled eggs, on a mixed green base, with an olive oil dressing. Soyer's recommendation to use cold cooked fish is one we shouldn't ignore; it is very good, and sometimes the flavour is better than when served hot.

Cold seafood salads—crab, prawn, lobster, mussels, squid—can be wonderful when made with fresh ingredients, but absolutely dreary when the seafood is from a poorly drained can. But over the past few years *warm* salads have become very popular. They can be very successful made with fish and seafood. And there are endless possibilities: grilled fillets of red mullet; smoked salmon; tuna; chunks of any firm-fleshed fish that, after sautéeing or grilling, can stand a light tossing in a dressing with some green leaves (such salads have been popular vehicles for the use of nut oils and flavoured vinegars, such as balsam, raspberry or sherry).

SASHIMI

Japanese restaurants are becoming very popular and young working people who have limited time for lunch find them useful for a fast nourishing meal. The Japanese make the greatest use of fish of any nation and consume five times as much fish as the British. Michael Crawford and David Marsh in *The Driving Force* say that if the Japanese were to grow enough food on land to replace the amount of fish they eat, they would need seven times the amount of land they have. Hardly any wonder that the Japanese restaurant is the place to go for imaginative and beautifully prepared fish dishes. They demand the best and the freshest. A recent article on sushi in *Esquire* quoted Oscar Gizelt of Delmonico's in New York: 'A fish should smell like the tide. Once they [sic.] smell like fish, it's too late.' *Sashimi* is a presentation of raw fish, carefully and skilfully sliced into bite-sized pieces, and served with simple but mouth-tingling sauces. And it can be prepared at home.

First, the fish, and it has to be the freshest you can buy: use at least three varieties and provide 90–125g/3–4oz per person (you can use even less if you prefer since *sashimi* is most often served as a first course). Choose from: sea bass, sea bream, bonito, cuttlefish, haddock, mackerel, prawns, large red mullet, salmon, sole, squid, trout, tuna. The fish should be filleted and skinned, the prawns shelled and deveined (though you can leave the tail on), the cuttlefish or squid thoroughly cleaned. All should be patted as dry as possible. You need a very sharp knife to cut the fish into fine slices *across* the fillet; tuna can be cut into strips, then into chunks. The Japanese have special names for particular cuts. The slices of each fish are then fanned out or placed decoratively on a large platter or tray.

The simplest accompaniments are: a small dish of soy sauce (which can be mixed with a little rice vinegar and you can also add a few fine slivers of fresh ginger); a small amount of *wasabi* (Japanese green horseradish with a wonderfully clean and pungent flavour) which can be bought in a tube pre-prepared or in a small tin of powder (mix with a little water to make a paste); these two are really essential to *sashimi*. Other possible accompaniments are sliced pickled ginger, if you can find it (or make your own by peeling and finely slicing a piece of ginger and soaking the slices in rice vinegar and/or dry sherry overnight), or just a mound of very finely slivered or shredded ginger; very finely shredded white radish (*mooli* or *daikon*). Another way to serve this is to make holes with a skewer in a peeled *daikon*, insert small red chillis, then grate the whole thing—the result is interesting; finely chopped green onion, cucumber, carrot; and some plain boiled rice.

To eat, take a piece of fish, dip into the *wasabi*, the soy sauce, then straight into the mouth. The combination can be quite spicy and the rice is used to cool the mouth. The other bits of vegetable can be nibbled on as you are inclined or mixed with the *wasabi* and soy before dipping the fish.

SEVICHE (CEVICHE)

Unlike *escabeche*, this dish, originating in Spanish America, uses raw fish (firm-fleshed white fish, sliced squid, octopus, prawn) to marinate in an acid dressing, usually lemon or lime juice with a chilli or two, and slices of onion. The acid 'cooks' the fish which becomes opaque, and the process takes a minimum of three hours. If you like dishes with a bit of a spark, this is for you.

SOUFFLES

A particularly good way to use left-over cooked salmon or other fish. All ingredients should be at room temperature. Preheat the oven to 180°C/375°F and remember that soufflés need bottom heat. Prepare a soufflé dish: butter the inside and dust with flour. Flake the fish (250–310g/8–10oz), mix in juice of half a lemon or lime, ground black or white pepper, and any chopped herb you might like. Set aside. Make a thick roux with 3 tablespoons butter, 3 tablespoons flour, and bring to a sauce with 250ml/8fl.oz liquid (fish stock/milk). Stir in the fish mixture. Separate five eggs, lightly beat four of the yolks (save the remaining yolk to use in some other way), beat the five whites until firm, but not stiff. Mix the beaten egg yolks into the fish mixture, then fold in the beaten egg whites. Pour into the prepared soufflé dish and put it immediately into the oven. Bake for about 30 minutes, and remove when golden brown and fully risen. Serve and eat immediately. Serves 4.

SOUPS AND STEWS

BISQUES

These are cream soups based on shellfish. You can often buy them in cans or jars, crab and lobster being the most common, but you can make a bisque from any shellfish—clams, mussels, oysters, shrimp or prawn, crab or lobster. You need a good fish stock which will have included chopped onion, carrot, celery, and bay leaf, parsley and thyme, preferably with some white wine. Cook your shellfish in the stock (if you use bivalves make sure you have cleaned them thoroughly since you are going to use the broth—discard the shells after cooking). Crush the shells of the cooked crustacea and return to the cooking liquid and continue to cook to extract all their flavour. Finely dice, mince or pound the flesh (using a food-processor if you prefer), reserving a little cut in slices (or whole, in the case of small clams, mussels or prawns) to garnish.

Then you have a choice: *Method 1*. Make a roux with 2 tablespoons butter and 2 tablespoons flour, add the strained cooking liquid to make a thinnish soup, add the minced flesh, add if you like a tablespoon sherry or flamed brandy, 150ml/¼ pint cream, adjust seasoning using cayenne if you like.

Method 2. Use egg yolks to thicken your soup: beat 2 egg yolks, add a little of the stock to blend, return to the stock and then continue as in *Method 1*, making sure the soup never boils once the eggs have been blended.

BOUILLABAISSE

Originating in Marseilles and the French Mediterranean coast, bouilla-baisse has to be the most well-known fish soup. Like paella, recipes abound. Olive oil, onions or leeks, garlic and tomatoes form the base plus saffron and other seasonings. It can combine any kind of fish and shellfish you have available, though there is a view that an authentic bouillabaisse cannot be made without *rascasse*. It may be cheating a bit, but many of my customers buy a jar or two of ready made fish soup (various kinds are available—crab, lobster or sea-urchin) and add a mixture of fresh fish and shellfish, such as bream, gurnard, John Dory, *rascasse*, red mullet, snapper, crawfish, prawns (cleaned, head on/off, cut into serving pieces).

224

I recommend that they add some of my own fish stock. Add as well a bayleaf or two, additional fresh herbs if liked (parsley, fennel), season with sea salt, pepper and/or a little paprika or cayenne. Then all you need is a spoonful of *rouille*, the wonderful garlic and saffron-flavoured mayonnaise, some good crusty bread, and good company.

> *This Bouillabaisse a noble dish is—*
> *A sort of soup, or broth, or brew,*
> *Or hotchpotch of all sorts of fishes,*
> *That Greenwich never could out do:*
> *Green herbs, red peppers, mussels, saffron*
> *Soles, onions, garlic, roach and dace;*
> *All these you eat at Terre's tavern*
> *In that one dish of Bouillabaise*
>
> W. M. Thackeray

That's an indication of one recipe, but like paella or risotto you will get a different one from everyone you ask. Alan Davidson in *Mediterranean Seafood* has some worthwhile observations which are worth repeating:

'The following points seem to be common ground:

(1) Marseilles is top city for bouillabaisse.
(2) A wide variety of fish should be used, among which there must be a *rascasse*, several fish with firm flesh and some with delicate flesh.
(3) The liquid used consists of olive oil and water which must be boiled fast to ensure their amalgamation.
(4) Onions, garlic, tomatoes, parsley, saffron are always used.
(5) The fish is served separately from the broth. The broth is poured over pieces of toast or served with croutons. The whole dish is accompanied by *rouille*.

Points in dispute include whether you eat all the fish or let the delicate ones disintegrate in the cooking; whether any crustaceans or molluscs are essential, and if so which; whether white wine should be substituted for some of the water; whether the water must be brought to the boil before it is added; and questions about ingredients such as whether it is permissible to include potatoes, compulsory to put in a piece of orange peel, desirable to add fennel or a bayleaf, and so on.'

Whatever you own feelings are on such matters, we give below a version of Mr Davidson's own instructions for a straightforward bouillabaisse.

2kg/4½lb mixed fish
including 1 or 2 *rascasse*,
some firm-fleshed fish (e.g.
conger, gurnard,
monkfish), some delicate
fish (e.g. whiting) or
flatfish (e.g. dab, plaice,
small sole), crustacea or
molluscs (e.g. a few
prawns or mussels)
300ml/10fl.oz olive oil
1 large onion, finely sliced
2 cloves garlic, crushed or
chopped

500g/1lb tomatoes, peeled
and chopped (or substitute
a large can of tomatoes)
About 3 litres/6 pints boiling
water*
Pinch of saffron
1–2 bayleaves
Sprig of thyme or 1 teaspoon
dried
Handful of chopped parsley
Piece of orange peel
(optional)
Salt and pepper to taste

Gut and scale the fish, cut in pieces as necessary, rinse all the fish and drain. Set the delicate fish apart.

In a large pot, heat half the oil and lightly brown the onion and garlic. Add the tomatoes, stir, add the boiling water, stir, then add all the fish, except the delicate fish. Add the remaining ingredients, stir, add the remaining oil. Bring to and keep at a boil for about 15 to 20 minutes, stirring occasionally, adding the delicate fish in the last 5 minutes so they just cook through.

Lift out the whole pieces of fish and lay on a platter. Pour the broth (strained if you prefer) over pieces of toast rubbed with garlic in soup plates. Serve with *rouille* on the side. Some purists say a bouillabaisse cannot be improved upon and frown upon the addition of *rouille*.

* An even richer result will be obtained if you use fish stock.

CHOWDER

When made with clams, this is the soup most often associated with the United States, and then you must choose whether you go for Manhattan (tomato-based) or 'New England' (cream or milk-based). Herman Melville in *Moby Dick* waxed lyrical: *'But when that smoking chowder came in, the mystery was delightfully explained. Oh! sweet friends, harken to me. It was made of small juicy clams, scarcely bigger than hazel nuts, mixed with pounded ship biscuits and salted pork cut up into little flakes! the whole enriched with butter, and plentifully seasoned with pepper and salt . . . we despatched it with great expedition.'*

MATELOTES

Fish stews made with freshwater fish. Like all such dishes, cook the firmer-fleshed fish first, then add the more delicate to ensure they will all be cooked through at the same time. Cleaned and prepared fish, cut into suitable pieces, are laid on a bed of chopped or sliced shallots or onions, as much crushed garlic as you normally like, a few fresh herbs or a *bouquet garni*, salt, a few peppercorns and whatever other flavouring you like. The fish is then covered with liquid—white or red wine, stock made with the fish trimmings—or a mixture. When all the fish is cooked through transfer it to a serving dish, strain the cooking liquid, reduce and thicken it with either a velouté made with fish stock or a *beurre manie* and pour over the fish. Garnish with fried croûtons and some chopped parsley, chervil or coriander. You could also add some lightly sautéed sliced mushrooms.

WATER SOUCHET/SOUCHY

An old-fashioned dish I haven't seen served in a long time. Eliza Acton gives a rather loving description of what she calls the 'Greenwich receipt'. It is essentially a fish stew cooked in water (as the name suggests), the main seasoning being parsley. Best made by making first a *court-bouillon* with water, a little white wine, *bouquet garni*, a stalk or two of celery (chopped), a good handful of parsley, washed and chopped. When that has simmered for about half an hour, add pieces of white fish fillet or use slices of small fish such as dabs or slip soles (freshwater fish, including eel, is often used); bring to the boil, skim, simmer for about ten minutes until the fish is cooked through. Adjust seasoning, adding more chopped parsley if you like.

227

Lady Sysonby's Cook Book was written in 1935 and the revised edition was published in 1948. The painter and designer Oliver Messel illustrated it and Osbert Sitwell wrote the introduction: '. . . Lady Sysonby's selection is beyond criticism. Varied, historic, traditional, and not intended for the rich man's table alone.' She gives a good simple recipe for a fish chowder, but you do need a heavy bottomed pan, and watch the heat.

LADY SYSONBY'S FISH CHOWDER

Any fish will do, boned and filleted. In a deep iron pan place a layer of thin bacon (the fatter the better). On top of that place a layer of the fish, then a layer of thinly sliced raw potatoes, a layer of thinly sliced raw onion, and lastly a layer of water biscuits. Dot with butter, salt and pepper. Add water half-way up the pan, cover and simmer slowly until fish, onions and potatoes are tender. The liquid must cook entirely away so that the bottom layer of bacon and fish is well browned. Then add cream to cover, heat to boiling and serve immediately.

FLOATING FISH SOUP (SEAFISH in conjunction with *Woman's Realm*)

A starter for 4, delicate and elegant, using the microwave.

250g/8oz skinned white fish fillets (look at your fishmonger's slab and see what looks good—could be cod, haddock, whiting, gurnard)	1 tablespoon finely chopped parsley
	1 onion, thinly sliced
	250g/8oz carrots, cut into strips
	3 sticks of celery, sliced
30g/1oz peeled prawns	Scant 1 litre/2 pints hot fish stock
Salt and black pepper	

Finely chop or process together the fish and prawns. Season with salt and pepper, mix in the parsley, and shape into small balls. Chill. Put the onion, carrot, celery and stock in a bowl and microwave for 5 minutes. Add the fish balls and microwave for a further minute. Leave the soup to stand for another minute, covered.

You could add a drop or two of soy sauce and perhaps garnish with a few leaves of chervil or coriander.

The BBC magazine *Good Food* is an extremely useful publication and gives fish a fair airing. This dish of mixed fish from Anthony Worrall

Thompson suggested cod as a first choice for white fillet, while mentioning the alternatives of haddock, pollack, ling or monkfish. We could add coley, conger, gurnard, hake or whiting to that list. Shellfish can be a mixture of anything that catches your eye on the fishmonger's slab— prawns, squid, a few clams or mussels. The basic recipe can be embellished with herbs and flavourings of your choice.

The following two recipes come from the shop and restaurant of Loch Fyne Oysters Limited at Elton, near Peterborough. On journeys up and down the A1 it's a charming place to stop for a meal or snack—perhaps a plate of oysters, a platter of smoked fish, or one of their splendid soups.

FISH CREOLE

1kg/2lb mixed fish and shellfish, half of which might be a piece of white fish fillet cut in 4 pieces
2 tablespoons olive oil
1 onion, finely chopped
1 clove garlic, finely chopped or crushed
400g/14oz can chopped tomatoes
Grated rind and juice of 1 lemon
Seasoning
Can or jar artichoke hearts, drained and cut in half (300g/11oz)
To garnish—flat-leaf parsley or coriander

Clean and prepare all the fish and shellfish ready for cooking. Heat the oil in a shallow flameproof casserole and fry the onion until softened, about 5 minutes. Stir in the garlic, tomatoes, rind and lemon juice, season. This would be the point to add any additional flavourings. Add the white fish fillet then scatter the pieces of the remaining fish and shellfish, and the artichoke hearts on top. Cover and simmer for 10–15 minutes until the white fish can be flaked with a knife. Spoon onto warmed plates, garnish and serve with rice or garlic bread.

This will serve 4 people generously, and the recipe can easily be increased.

CULLEN SKINK

A very popular fish soup which, although it appears to have originated at the fishing village of Cullen on the Banffshire coast, is typical of fisher food in the whole area. The best flavoured 'skink' (an old Scots word for 'broth') is made with the whole unboned Finnan haddock.

2 small or 1 large Finnan haddock	cooked mashed potato to thicken
1 large onion, finely chopped	salt and pepper to taste
2 litres/4 pints water	cream and chopped parsley to garnish
750ml/1½ pints milk	
60g/2oz butter	

In a pan, place the fish and onion in water and bring to the boil. Simmer gently until the fish is cooked. Lift the fish from the liquid, remove all the skin and bones and return them to the stock, set the flesh aside. Simmer the broth for another 20 minutes. Flake the fish. Strain the stock and return the strained liquid to the pan. Add the milk, fish, butter, and enough mashed potato to thicken. Heat through and serve with some cream and chopped parsley. You could use Arbroath Smokies instead of the Finnan haddock.

MUSSEL CHOWDER

Mussels	125ml/¼ pint stock
1 onion, chopped	1 large potato, chopped
4 slices streaky bacon, chopped	½ teaspoon curry powder
30g/1oz butter	4 tablespoons cream
425g/14oz chopped tomatoes	seasoning to taste
½ teaspoon sugar	additional cream, paprika and parsley to garnish

Cook the mussels and remove from shells. Fry the chopped onion and streaky bacon in butter. Add the tomatoes, sugar, stock, potato and curry powder, and the mussels. bring to the boil, simmer until the potato is cooked through. Stir in the cream, season, and heat gently. Garnish with cream, paprika and parsley.

Patrick Anthony's East Coast Chowder is from Anglia Television's 'Food Guide' programme using ingredients from Lowestoft Fish Market. This will certainly serve 6. The list of ingredients looks rather long, but it's not a complicated recipe. We might be tempted to reduce the amount of potato and increase the amount of shellfish, but then, we would, wouldn't we? In the United States this would be called a New England chowder.

PATRICK ANTHONY'S EAST COAST CHOWDER

1 tablespoon oil or butter
120g/4oz salt belly of pork or streaky bacon, diced
250g/8oz onions or shallots, chopped
1 heaped tablespoon flour
1 teaspoon curry powder
450ml/15fl.oz fish stock
450ml/15fl.oz milk
1 *bouquet garni*
1 bayleaf
6 medium potatoes, diced
Pinch grated nutmeg
Pinch cayenne
750g/1½lb firm white fish, cubed
150ml/5fl.oz cream
120g/4oz shelled mussels, cockles, scallops or prawns
½ sweet red pepper, seeded and diced (optional)
120g/4oz sweetcorn (optional)
Seasoning
Chopped fresh parsley, to garnish

Heat the oil or butter, and brown the pork or bacon with the chopped onions or shallots. Stir in the flour and curry powder, and cook for 2–3 minutes. Gradually add the stock, stirring constantly, then the milk. Add the *bouquet garni*, bayleaf and diced potatoes. Season, add the nutmeg and cayenne. Bring gently to the boil, cover and simmer.

When the potatoes are nearly cooked through, add the white fish, Cook for a further 4–5 minutes, then stir in cream, shellfish and the optional red pepper and sweetcorn. Bring to the boil, then remove from the heat. Check the seasoning and sprinkle with parsley. Serves 6.

BHOPALI FISH WITH GREEN SEASONINGS

Madhur Jaffrey's television series and her books have been enormously popular. This recipe, taken from *A Taste of India*, is quite spicy and very delicious.

750g/1½lb steaks or thick fillets of firm white fish, such as cod, coley, haddock, halibut	90g/3oz fresh coriander leaf
	6 green chillies (or fewer)
	4–6 cloves garlic, peeled
	180ml/6fl.oz yoghurt
Sea salt	Enough oil to shallow or deep
2 tablespoons lemon juice	fry

The fillets should be cut into pieces roughly 6–7cm/2.5–3in long and 5cm/2in wide. Spread the pieces in a single layer, sprinkle with a little salt and 1 tablespoon lemon juice. Turn the pieces over and repeat. Set the plate at a tilt (you can rest one end of the plate on a small upturned bowl or something similar). As liquid accumulates at the lower end, discard it.

Using a food processor or blender, whizz together the coriander, chillies, garlic, ¼ teaspoon salt, and 2 tablespoons water until they form a paste. Scrape the paste into a shallow bowl or dish; pour the yoghurt into a similar dish, adding a pinch of salt and mixing.

Pour oil into a frying pan or wok. When a very light haze appears, dip 2 or 3 pieces of fish at a time first in the yoghurt, then in the chilli paste to cover completely, and drop them in the oil. Fry for about 5 minutes, turning the pieces once. When all the fish is cooked, serve at once. Serves 3–4.

Serve with rice and a salad.

SIMPLE FRIED FISH

Clean, scale and trim a whole fish (red mullet, snapper or sea bream). Rinse and thoroughly dry, inside and out. Salt and pepper the cavity.

Finely slice two or three onions, spread the slices (separating the layers) over a serving dish, sprinkle a good handful of parsley, finely chopped, over the onion, and the juice of half a lemon over the whole.

Dip the fish in seasoned flour, shallow or deep fry in hot olive oil. Drain on kitchen paper, then lay the cooked fish on the prepared serving dish and serve with a sauce of your choice or just slices of lemon and sea salt.

MEDITERRANEAN BAKED FISH (SEAFISH)

This is a *very* simple way to cook any thick fillet of white fish and if you use a prepared sauce you can take your pick of the jars on the shelf.

500–750g/1–1½lb skinned thick white fillet, or use steaks	1 tablespoon lemon juice
	1 small jar tomato pasta sauce

Divide the fish into four portions and put in a lightly oiled ovenproof dish. Sprinkle with lemon juice and pour the sauce over the fish. Cover and bake for 25–30 minutes.

What could be simpler? And the variations can be endless: if you have some of your own very good tomato sauce, use that; add a few slices of black olive; use a jar of pesto sauce mixed with yoghurt or *crème fraîche*.

Seafood seems always to be cooked in the simplest ways in South-East Asia. It was a great enjoyment when I visited Malaysia to sample the delicious sauces that make all the difference to their dishes, and they're often just served on the side to dip into.

While squid is specified here, the sauces could equally well be used for other simply grilled fish and seafood.

SQUID AND ITS SAUCES

There is little point in giving quantities for the squid, or whatever else you are going to use, because it will depend on how many people are going to enjoy it and whether it is the whole or only part of a meal. But let's say 500g/1lb of cleaned squid will serve at least 2–3. You have a choice: cut it into rings or into wedges. Brush with oil and grill until opaque, turning as necessary, not more than 2 or 3 minutes. Turn onto a serving plate and present with one or more of the following dipping sauces:
Mix together:

1. 2 tablespoons light soy sauce
   2 tablespoons rice vinegar
   2 cloves garlic, finely chopped or crushed
   2 red or green chillies, finely chopped (deseeded if you prefer)
   1 teaspoon sugar
   Juice of 1 lime or lemon
   1 tablespoon finely chopped coriander

2. 2 tablespoons light oil (peanut, safflower, sunflower, grape)
- 2 tablespoons fish sauce (*nam pla*, optional, but increase soy if not used)
1 tablespoon dark soy sauce
1 small piece ginger, finely chopped
1 clove garlic, finely chopped
½ teaspoon sugar

3. 2 tablespoons tomato sauce
1 tablespoon oyster sauce
1 tablespoon light soy sauce
1 red or green chilli, finely chopped
Few coriander leaves, coarsely chopped

This simple but rather rich recipe comes from *The French Seafood Cook Book* published in Australia. Cod was used in the original, but any good white fish can be used.

COD WITH WHITE WINE AND TARRAGON SAUCE

Use white fish steaks or cutlets—cod, conger, coley, halibut, turbot—one per person.

Arrange your steaks or cutlets in a large frying pan, dot with small pieces of butter (about 30g/1oz in all), sprinkle with approximately 1 tablespoon fresh tarragon leaves or 1 teaspoon dried, season with salt and pepper and pour over 120ml/4fl.oz white wine.

Cover the pan and simmer over a medium heat until the fish is cooked through, about 10 minutes, depending on the thickness of the fish. Use a spatula or fish slice to transfer the fish to a heated serving dish and keep warm. Bring the liquid to a boil and reduce for 3–5 minutes. In a bowl combine 120ml/4fl.oz cream with 3 egg yolks. Carefully add to the pan liquid, having reduced the heat, blend and stir constantly until the sauce is thickened without allowing it to boil. Pour the sauce over the fish and serve, garnished with sprigs of fresh herbs.

In *The Cook's Companion* Josceline Dimbleby has a very good section on fish and shellfish. We were intrigued by her recipe called the Emperor's Fan. It was designed for skate, hence the name, and the lovely aromatic sauce can be used with any good firm white fish. Try it with fillets of snapper, mahi-mahi, haddock, halibut or whatever else appeals to you.

FISH WITH SPICED ORANGE AND MUSHROOM SAUCE

1 orange
550ml/1 pint good fish or
  chicken stock
Juice of 1 lemon or lime
  (approximately
  4 tablespoons)
2.5cm/1in piece of ginger,
  peeled and slivered
4–6 snapper, or other, fillets
  180–250g/6–8oz each
2 teaspoons arrowroot

Salt and cayenne pepper or
  Tabasco to taste (optional)
120g/4oz button mushrooms,
  sliced (optional)
Large handful of fresh
  coriander, roughly
  chopped
Additional orange rind and
  wedges and sprigs of
  coriander to garnish
  (optional)

Take a few strips of zest from the orange, and squeeze the juice. In a deep frying pan, pour in the stock, the orange and lemon or lime juice, the ginger and the orange zest. Heat through and add half the fillets. Cover and simmer until the fish is just cooked, about 5–6 minutes. Use a fish slice to transfer the fish to a heated serving plate, cover and keep warm. Poach the rest of the fish and transfer to the serving plate.

Boil the liquid in the pan for about 5 minutes to reduce slightly, strain into a saucepan. Mix the arrowroot with a little water or cooking liquid until smooth, then stir into the saucepan until thoroughly blended. Cook, stirring, for 2 or 3 minutes, season with salt and cayenne or Tabasco to your taste, add the optional mushrooms and cook for a minute or two, then stir in the coriander. Pour over the fish and serve, garnished if you wish.

You could increase the spiciness if you like by using a small chopped red or green chilli which also makes the sauce even prettier. Serves 4–6.

BIBLIOGRAPHY

Algar, Ayla Esen: *The Complete Book of Turkish Cooking* (Routledge & Kegan Paul, London, 1985)

Anthony, Patrick: *Simply Special – Recipes for Family and Friends* (Hodder & Stoughton, London, 1991)

BBC *Good Food* Magazine, London

Bentley, James: *Life and Food in the Dordogne* (Weidenfeld and Nicolson, London 1986)

Berriedale-Johnson, Michelle: *The British Museum Cookbook* (British Museum Publications Ltd., London, 1987)

Berriedale-Johnson, Michelle: *Cook For Hire* (Macdonald & Co. Ltd., London, 1987)

Bhumichitr, Vatcharin: *The Taste of Thailand* (Pavilion Books, London, 1988)

Bonomo, Giuliana: *The Great Book of Seafood Cooking* (International Culinary Society, New York, 1990)

Boxer, Arabella and Traeger, Tessa: *A Visual Feast: The Year in Food* (Random Century Ltd., London, 1991)

Boyd, Lizzie (ed.): *British Cookery* (Croom Helm Ltd., London, 1977)

Country Living Magazine, London

Cracknell, H. L. and Kaufmann, R. J. (trans.): *ESCOFFIER: The Complete Guide to the Art of Modern Cookery* (William Heinemann, London, 1986)

Crawford, Michael and Marsh, David: *The Driving Force* (Heinemann, London, 1989)

David, Elizabeth: *French Country Cooking* (Penguin Books, London, 1966)

David, Elizabeth: *French Provincial Cooking* (Penguin Books, London 1970)

David, Elizabeth: *Italian Food* (Penguin Books, London 1969)

David, Elizabeth: *Summer Cooking* (Penguin Books, London 1965)

Davidson, Alan: *North Atlantic Seafood* (Penguin Books, London, 1980)

Davidson, Alan: *Mediterranean Seafood* (Penguin Books, London, 1989)

Del Conte, Anna: *Secrets from an Italian Kitchen* (Bantam Press Ltd., London, 1989)

Dimbleby, Josceline: *Sainsbury's The Cook's Companion* (Websters International Publishers for J. Sainsbury plc, London, 1991)

Edwards, John (trans.): *The Roman Cookery of Apicius* (Random Century, London, 1988)

Fitzgibbon, Theodora: *A Taste of Ireland* (Pan Books, London, 1970)

Fitzgibbon, Theodora: *A Taste of Wales* (Pan Books, London, 1973)

Floyd, Keith: *Floyd on Fish* (BBC, London, 1985)

Goodman, Cheryl and Bacon, Vo: *The Fresh Seafood Cook Book* (Regency, New South Wales, 1990)

The Good Wife's Cook Book (Pettigrew & Stephens, Glasgow, c.1900)

Green, Henrietta and Moine, Marie-Pierre: *Ten-Minute Cuisine* (Conran Octopus, London, 1991)

Grigson, Jane: *Fish Cookery* (Penguin Books, London, 1975)

Grigson, Sophie: from her *Evening Standard* column

Hicks, Susan: *The Fish Course* (BBC Books, London, 1987)

Hicks, Susan: *The Seafish Cookbook* (Hamlyn Publishing, Twickenham, 1986)

Innes, Jocasta: *Jocasta Innes' Country Kitchen* (Frances Lincoln Publishers Ltd., London, 1987)

Jaffrey, Madhur: *A Taste of India* (Pavilion Books, London, 1985)

Kafka, Barbara: *Microwave Gourmet* (Barrie & Jenkins, London, 1989)

Lassalle, George: *The Adventurous Fish Cook* (Macmillan, London, 1976)

BIBLIOGRAPHY

Leach, Alison (ed.) *The Savoy Food and Drink Book* (Pyramid, London, 1986)
Leith, Prue and Waldegrave, Caroline: *Leith's Cookery Bible* (Bloomsbury Publishing Ltd., London, 1991)
McAndrew, Ian: *A Feast of Fish* (Macdonald & Co., London, 1987)
McGee, Harold: *On Food and Cooking* (George Allen & Unwin, London, 1986)
Marsh, Chandra and David: *The Great Nutritional Detective Story* (forthcoming)
Morris, Nicki and Borton, Paula (eds.) *The Great Fish Book* (Absolute Press, Bath, 1988)
Mosimann, Anton: *Anton Mosimann's Fish Cuisine* (Macmillan London Ltd., London, 1988)
Passmore, Jacki: *Asia: The Beautiful Cookbook* (Merehurst Press, London, 1987)
Peel, Mrs C. S.: *Ten Shillings a Head Per Week* (4th edition, 1902)
Pinney, Richard: *Smoked Salmon and Oysters* (The Butley-Orford Oysterage, Orford, Suffolk, 1984)
Prunier, Madame: *Fish Cookery Book*
Quaglino: *The Complete Hostess* (Hamish Hamilton, London, 1936)
Richardson, W. *The Practical Fishmonger and Fruiterer* (Virtue, London, 1914?)
Roden, Claudia: *The Food of Italy* (Chatto & Windus, London, 1989)
Rombauer, Irma S. and Becker, Marion Rombauer: *The Joy of Cooking* (Signet, New York, 1973)
Seeber, Liz and Gerd: *Simple Food: A Menu Book for All Seasons* (Dorling Kindersley Ltd., London, 1987)
Smith, Delia: *Complete Cookery Course* (BBC Books Ltd., London, 1982)
So, Yan Kit: *Classic Chinese Cookbook* (Dorling Kindersley, London, 1984)
Spurling, Hilary: *Elinor Fettiplace's Receipt Book* (Penguin Books, Harmondsworth, 1987)
Stanley, Fortune: *English Country House Cooking* (Pall Mall Press, London, 1972)
Stein, Richard: *English Seafood Cookery* (Penguin Books, London, 1988)
Strang, Jeanne: *Goose Fat and Garlic* (Kyle Cathie Limited, London, 1991)
The Cooking of Scandinavia (Time-Life, 1970)
Sysonby, Ria: *Lady Sysonby's Cook Book* (Putnam, London, 1935)
Walton, Izaak: *The Compleat Angler*
Willan, Anne: *Great Cooks and their Recipes from Taillevant to Escoffier* (Pavilion, London, 1991)
Willock, Colin: *The Angler's Encyclopaedia* (Odhams Books Ltd., London, 1960)

RECIPE INDEX

This list includes whole recipes and notes towards recipes.

INDEX

Italics indicate foreign names of fish and book titles. Page numbers in **bold** indicate main text entries.

241

INDEX

246